The 21 Stages of Meditation

Gurucharan Singh Khalsa, PhD

Kundalini Yoga as taught by Yogi Bhajan®

Kundalini Research Institute
Training • Publishing • Research • Resources

© 2012 Kundalini Research Institute
Published by the Kundalini Research Institute
Training • Publishing • Research • Resources
PO Box 1819
Santa Cruz, NM 87532
www.kundaliniresearchinstitute.org

ISBN 978-1-934532-77-5

Editor: Sat Purkh Kaur Khalsa
Consulting Editor: Gurucharan Kaur Khalsa
KRI Review: Siri Neel Kaur Khalsa
Design and Layout: Prana Projects (Ditta Khalsa, Biljana Spasovska)

Cover Illustration: Yogi Bhajan
Photography: Ravitej Singh Khalsa
Models: Mandeep Singh, Harjeet Kaur, Jai Satya Kaur, Hari Krishan Kaur, Manvir Singh, Jagbir Kaur, Emiliano Garcia-Held, Bobby Romanski, Mahan Deep Kaur, Gurunam Kaur, Narayan Jot Kaur

The diet, exercise and lifestyle suggestions in this book come from ancient yogic traditions. Nothing in this book should be construed as medical advice. Any recipes mentioned herein may contain potent herbs, botanicals and naturally occurring ingredients which have traditionally been used to support the structure and function of the human body. Always check with your personal physician or licensed health care practitioner before making any significant modification in your diet or lifestyle, to insure that the ingredients or lifestyle changes are appropriate for your personal health condition and consistent with any medication you may be taking. For more information about Kundalini Yoga as taught by Yogi Bhajan® please see www.yogibhajan.org and www.kundaliniresearchinstitute.org.

© 2012 Kundalini Research Institute. All teachings, yoga sets, techniques, kriyas and meditations courtesy of The Teachings of Yogi Bhajan. Reprinted with permission. Unauthorized duplication is a violation of applicable laws. ALL RIGHTS RESERVED. No part of these Teachings may be reproduced or transmitted in any form by any means, electronic or mechanical, including photocopying and recording, or by any information storage and retrieval system, except as may be expressly permitted in writing by the The Teachings of Yogi Bhajan. To request permission, please write to KRI at PO Box 1819, Santa Cruz, NM 87567 or see www.kundaliniresearchinstitute.org.

This publication has received the KRI Seal of Approval. This Seal is only given to products that have been reviewed for accuracy and integrity of the sections containing 3HO lifestyle teachings and Kundalini Yoga as taught by Yogi Bhajan®.

*Dedicated to the legacy of Yogi Bhajan
as embodied in The Yogi Bhajan Library of Teachings
and preserved by the Kundalini Research Institute,
and to the global network of teachers
who share the experience of these techniques with All.*

About Yogi Bhajan

Yogi Bhajan was declared a Master of Kundalini Yoga at the age of 16. He came to the United States in 1969 and openly taught this transformative technology for the next 35 years.

In the turbulent, drug culture of the 70s, Yogi Bhajan first reached out to the youth. He recognized that their experimentation with drugs and "altered states of consciousness" expressed a desire to experience themselves and a longing for family, for connection to their own soul and to their community. In response to this innate longing, he created a family, known as 3HO (Healthy, Happy, Holy Organization) and soon 3HO ashrams began springing up across the United States and throughout the world.

He sparked a movement whose tendrils have woven their way into numerous aspects of our culture. Yoga and meditation have gained widespread acceptance in the West, as well as, the holistic health movement he introduced through diet, herbs and lifestyle technologies. Born Harbhajan Singh in what is now Pakistan to a family of healers and community leaders, Yogi Bhajan studied comparative religion and Vedic philosophy in his undergraduate years, and went on to receive his Masters in Economics with honors from Punjab University. Years later, he earned his Ph.D. in communications psychology from the University of Humanistic Studies in San Francisco.

He emerged as a religious, community and business leader with a distinguished reputation as a man of peace, world vision, wisdom, and compassion. He founded several foods companies that manufacture and distribute natural products based on these teachings. He fostered economic development in communities around the world and authored several books on yoga philosophy as well as business and communication during his lifetime.

The Kundalini Research Institute continues his legacy through The Yogi Bhajan Library of Teachings, International Teacher Training in Kundalini Yoga as taught by Yogi Bhajan®, and continuing to publish collections of lectures and kriyas to serve the community of teachers, students and practitioners around the world. See www.yogibhajan.org and www.kundaliniresearchinstitute.org to learn how you can help keep the legacy alive!

Table of Contents

Preface	12
Foreword	14
Note to the Reader	17
Before You Begin	19
The Stages of Meditation	25

FIRST JOURNEY:

The Crystallized Self	41
Stage One: Upset	43
Meditation to Conquer Upset	53
Stage Two: Boredom	57
See Your Horizon	66
Stage Three: Irritation	73
Eyeglass Traatik	84
Stage Four: Frustration	87
Self-Hypnosis to Dissolve Frustration	94
Stage Five: Focus	99
Praan Naadi Shabad Guni Kriya	106
Stage Six: Absorption	109
For Absorption in the Crystal Being	116
Stage Seven: Experience and Crystallize the Self	123
Becoming the Sound Current	134
Open Lotus Heart Meditation	136
Traatik Dhyan to See the Unseen	138
Meditation of the Two Teachers to Balance Karma	140
Heart Seal Meditation	142
Deep Relaxation	143

SECOND JOURNEY:

The Expressive Self	145
Stage Eight: Rasa	147
Invoking a Meditative State	154
Stimulate the Chakras	156
Haumei Bandhana Kriya	158
Stage Nine: Delight	163
Meditation for Delight, Destiny and Creative Flow in Life	172
Stage Ten: Politeness	175
Sat Kriya Variation to Merge with the Sense of the Infinite	182
Stage Eleven:	185
Bowing Before the Infinite	194
Speaking Humbly before the Creative Infinity	196
Bowing for Humility to Transfer Praana	198
Stage Twelve: Elevation	201
Meditation for Elevation	210
Meditation for Rasas and the Inner Eye	120
Meditation for Elevation	215
Stage Thirteen: Graceful Enlightenment	217
Meditation for Graceful Enlightenment and Strength of Heart	226
Stage Fourteen: Express and Be Your Self	231
Laya Yoga Meditation Series	240
To Clear the Channels and Raise the Kundalini	240
Meditation on the Laya Yoga Kundalini Mantra	244
Sankh Mudra Kriya: A Naadi Sodhana Laya Kundalini Kriya	245
Laya Meditation to Beam and Create	247
Sukh Saadhana: Peaceful Creative Projection with the Heart Center	248
Meditation to Express Your Real Self and Develop the Subtle Body	250

Third Journey:

The Transcendent Self	253
Stage Fifteen: Presence Like a Beacon	255
Tattva Siddhi Meditation for Presence like a Beacon	264
Stage Sixteen: Radiance Everywhere	267
Polishing the Radiant Body	276
Stage Seventeen: Prayerful Stillness	283
Deeksha Patra for Prayerful Stillness	292
Stage Eighteen: Preacher	295
Chautay Padma Nirgun Mantra	302
Stage Nineteen: Teacher	307
Enchantment of the Infinite: Traatik to See Love Within	320
Stage Twenty: Sage	325
Sarab Gyan Kriya	340
Stage Twenty One: Infinite Pulse	345
Sodarshan Chakra Kriya	352
Realization	357
Appendices	365
The Nature of Meditation	367
Laya Yoga Mantras	375
The Laya Yoga Kundalini Mantra	384
Skill Enhancement Meditations	387
The Adi Shakti Mantra	389
Long Ek Ong Kaar	398
Witness Your Consciousness from within Yourself	402
Developing the Beaming Faculty and the Self as a Witness	404
Healing, Mental Beaming and Delight	407
Breath of Fire	415
End Notes	419
Glossary	423
Resources	431
About the Author	433

Preface

"What should I teach at yoga class this week?" This question is silently asked by countless teachers every day. To find the answer, one sunny Spring day in 1998, Gurucharan Singh went to his bookcase and pulled out Women in Training XII, 1987, Crossing the Crossroads of Crisis. He fanned through the book of Yogi Bhajan transcripts and stopped at the title "The Process of Jappa." In the first paragraph it says, "I'm just telling you what you go through. First you become upset." Yogi Bhajan went on to list twenty stages that we experience when we meditate and then he challenged the class, "Now you understand all that? Who volunteers to write the best article on this?"

Gurucharan Singh acted like he had uncovered a hidden jewel; one that had been overlooked and allowed to grow dusty and dull. I remember how excited he was when he explained to me the significance of this understanding for students trying meditation for the first time as well as long-time practitioners. Gurucharan Singh started to increase his personal awareness, learning to sense and recognize the distinct stages during his meditations. If he was going to fulfill the idea of writing an article, even though it was nine years later, he wanted to be sure it would be accurate and complete. He practiced specific meditations under the guidance and instruction of Yogi Bhajan so that he could write descriptions of each stage by first putting himself inside the state.

Then in June, we brought the descriptions of the twenty stages of meditation to Española during Summer Solstice. Yogi Bhajan graciously gave a time for us to meet at his home and Nam Kaur Khalsa, then the CEO of KRI, joined us. We four sat together in the living room. Gurucharan read aloud the name of the stage with its description. Yogi Bhajan listened very carefully; occasionally commenting, adding and adjusting, correcting, sometimes just smiling, and even exclaiming "I said that!" After hearing each stage, he drew a sketch to illustrate his experience of the stage and explained the meaning of the drawing. This sequence was repeated twenty times. I thought we were done. That was all the stages mentioned in the 1987 class. We were all quiet, and a bit tired from the focused concentration.

Gurucharan Singh said, "But, Sir, there must be twenty-one stages? What is the name of the twenty-first stage?" I think I had an expression of shock and embarrassment as I turned my head to look in his direction. I was thinking something like, "Why is he asking such an outrageous question?" Yogi Bhajan became very still and then he started laughing. "Yes, there is a twenty-first stage." He called it Infinite Pulse. He began describing the experience of the stage and made a sketch just as he had for all the previous stages. I got the feeling it was a stage that he wished he could dwell in for longer periods himself.

That afternoon we all went up to Guru Ram Das Puri after White Tantric Yoga. Yogi Bhajan asked Gurucharan Singh and Nam Kaur to talk about the project and relay what they had learned. Nam Kaur explained, "In that stage (Stage 21—Infinite Pulse) you don't feel God, you don't have an experience of God, you have the experience that you are God."

Yogi Bhajan said, "Now we are entering the Age of Aquarius and we have to have the science of mind totally brought into a geometry so that you can understand this is depression, this is expression; this is what you are doing and this is what you have to do. So for that reason, we are trying to create all this work for you."

Yogi Bhajan and Gurucharan Singh continued to work together with the intention of creating a book. They refined outlines, and experimented with meditations to develop a systematic approach to the 21 Stages of Meditation that could be easily conveyed and experienced by everyone.

Every living thing has its own time to grow from a seed to its innate maturity. Twenty-five years. Maybe we simply needed to wait until the Age of Aquarius was here? The teachings presented in this book have been developed with love and care and genuine reverence. That is the beauty of the Kundalini Research Institute and the devoted Kundalini Yoga teachers who are leaders of its academy. We trust the institutions Yogi Bhajan established and the people who work within them to patiently hold the integrity of the teachings and continue to nourish projects that make them available to the world.

I am grateful to have witnessed this entire process from the seed of Yogi Bhajan's lecture to the publication of this book. May it provide a foundation for elevation and enlightenment to all who love meditation.

Gurucharan Kaur Khalsa
February 2012

Foreword

You have probably already begun the journey into meditation that this book describes. As you discover how to live a creative, meaningful human life, you may find that some lessons are pleasurable, some are painful, and some take long roundabout detours. As you read this book, realize that you are entering a special moment in your life, a rare chance to learn the very lessons you've been looking for all along, for here you have an opportunity to benefit directly from wisdom that has accumulated over thousands of years.

Recent studies show that meditators have a 47% less chance of having a heart attack, and yet to many people meditation can seem intimidating. How does one begin? In truth, meditation can be as simple as stopping to sit and notice a flower. It is nothing more than our natural capacity to focus, direct the mind and be present to everything. Human beings have always meditated. Our ancestors observed nature closely for important information on how to not only survive but thrive. They contemplated the stars for knowledge of their place in the vast cosmos. They observed the cycles of nature and intuited their own place within it. Mothers listened deeply to the regular breath of their infants, alert to every sound in the vicinity.

In the past hundred years life has changed dramatically. Today we meditate in front of the television or computer screen. Many of us spend hours in the enormous flow of information on the internet instead of meditatively walking, weaving, or plowing. Yet even as we sense that so much of the natural rhythm of life has been lost, collectively we are waking to an experience of our connectedness. We have intense feedback and input from all over our planet. The human mind and the human psyche are facing an unprecedented flow of information. For this reason, in 2012, we all need to meditate.

Throughout history yogis, saints and sages have realized that we are all one, a sensation we are all now beginning to feel. These great ones—Guru Nanak, the Buddha, Saint Teresa—were not so different from you. They were human. They lived intensely and showed how best to be human. Like you, they had animal bodies and instincts, along with subtle angelic qualities and human hearts. All exceptional men and women have left a legacy of wisdom for us to follow. They discovered how to make their minds their friends and not their masters. They learned how to see the divine in themselves and in everything. Even though they understood that human life entails suffering, they were relaxed and happy. Discoveries like theirs remain alive in the ancient technology of Kundalini Yoga as taught by Yogi Bhajan® presented in these pages.

This book offers a systematic approach to realization and self-healing through meditation. Meditation is a continuous process—not a skill you learn at once, but a practice you apply yourself to again and again. The practices in this book are so rich and profound that you will never feel that you've outgrown them. They are down to earth and yet touch the heavens within. They deal with any frustration, boredom, or upsets you may have and offer skillful ways to work with all of your feelings and emotions. They will help you become intuitive, stable, compassionate and free.

According to our tradition, spiritual practice benefits seven generations before and seven generations after. So know that you do this practice not only for yourself but for your ancestors and those who follow. You do it in this spirit because we are one world community waking up together.

You may have years or decades of experience with meditation or, on the other hand, your formal practice may be just beginning. After practicing the meditations in the book, I experienced firsthand that they are solid in their timing, exquisite in their use of mantra and mudra and praanayam. They will benefit both beginners and seasoned meditators alike.

Gurucharan Singh taught in my Kundalini Teacher Training course in the early 1980s, and I am grateful to have studied and collaborated with him ever since. I recognized something magical flowing through him when he taught. It was the legacy of Kundalini Yoga awakened within him, flavored by his humor, profound intelligence and big, warm heart. A great yoga teacher doesn't focus on himself but leads you beyond, to a master or an infinite source within yourself. Gurucharan always pointed me toward his teacher, who in turn led me to the wisdom and depth inside my Self. In this book Gurucharan shares what he has learned through a lifetime of practice and teaching, but even more importantly, he offers us the wisdom of his teacher, the great yogi and spiritual teacher, Yogi Bhajan, whose life was dedicated to providing the tools to find the infinite within our Self.

Hari Kirin Kaur Khalsa
March 2, 2012
www.artandyoga.com

Note to the Reader

This book and the course that accompanies it are available and open to everyone from every contemplative tradition. This text was created in concert with The Aquarian Teacher Training Program and, as such, the write-ups and meditations assume a certain fluency in Kundalini Yoga as taught by Yogi Bhajan®. If you are new to Kundalini Yoga and Meditation, please review the material found in *Before You Begin*; this information will ground you in everything you need to know to have a successful experience. In addition, we recommend that you seek out and study with a certified Kundalini Yoga Instructor (see the Resources page for more information) as well as read and review our classic beginner's text, *Kundalini Yoga Sadhana Guidelines*, 2nd Ed.

One clarification that we offer to practitioners of all levels regards the syntax found within the book; in particular the use of the words "part" and "series." Within an individual meditation, the word "part" indicates one exercise within a sequence of exercises that make up that particular meditation. Within this tradition, this sequence of exercises is known as *kriya*; and all parts within a particular kriya or meditation must be done in order and within one practice period in order to complete the kriya. Within a "meditation series," there are multiple meditations or kriyas which have been sequenced for a particular process. Each meditation or kriya within a "series" stands alone as a technique you may practice in Kundalini Yoga; they are included in specific series in order to create a particular experience and refine each stage of meditation.

In addition, please see the Appendix to orient yourself to the skill enhancement exercises required between certain stages.

Before You Begin

Beginning Your Practice – Tuning-In

The practice of Kundalini Yoga as taught by Yogi Bhajan® always begins by tuning-in. This simple practice of chanting the Adi Mantra 3-5 times aligns your mind, your spirit and your body to become alert and assert your will so that your practice will fulfill its intention. It's a simple bowing to your Higher Self and an alignment with the teacher within. The mantra may be simple but it links you to a Golden Chain of teachers, an entire body of consciousness that guides and protects your practice: *Ong Namo Guroo Dayv Namo,* **which means, I bow to the Infinite, I bow to the Teacher within.**

How to End

Another tradition within Kundalini Yoga as taught by Yogi Bhajan® is a simple blessing known as *The Long Time Sun Shine* song. Sung or simply recited at the end of your practice, it allows you to dedicate your practice to all those who've preserved and delivered these teachings so that you might have the experience of your Self. It is a simple prayer to bless yourself and others. It completes the practice and allows your entire discipline to become a prayer, in service to the good of all.

> *May the long time sun shine upon you*
> *All love surround you*
> *And the pure light within you*
> *Guide your way on.*
> *Sat Nam.*

Other Tips for a Successful Experience

Prepare for your practice by lining up all the elements that will elevate your experience: natural fiber clothing and head covering (cotton or linen), preferably white to increase your auric body; natural fiber mat, either cotton or wool; traditionally a sheep skin or other animal skin is used. If you have to use a rubber or petroleum-based mat, cover the surface with a cotton or wool blanket to protect and support your electromagnetic field. Clean air and fresh water also helps support your practice.

Practice in Community

Studying the science of Kundalini Yoga with a KRI certified teacher will enhance your experience and deepen your understanding of kriya, mantra, breath and posture. Find a teacher in your area at http://www.3HO.org/ikyta/. If there isn't a teacher in your area, consider becoming a teacher yourself. There are Aquarian Teacher Trainings all over the world. Go to www.kundaliniresearchinstitute.org for more information.

Breath & Bandhas[†]

Kundalini Yoga incorporates profound praanayams throughout its practice. Understanding and mastering the breath is an important part of successfully practicing any Kundalini Yoga kriya. We have provided the descriptions of three of the most basic praanayams in the practice of Kundalini Yoga but as you work through the meditations and kriyas in the *21 Stages of Meditation*, please read the instructions for the breath carefully.

Long Deep Breath

To take a full yogic breath, inhale by first relaxing the abdomen and allow it to expand. Next expand the chest and finally the collarbones. As you exhale, let the collar bones and chest relax first, then pull the abdomen in completely.

The diaphragm drops down to expand the lungs on the inhale and contracts up to expel the air on the exhale.

As you inhale feel the back area of the lower ribs relax and expand. On the exhale be sure to keep the spine erect and steady.

Breath of Fire

This breath is used consistently throughout Kundalini Yoga kriyas. It is very important that Breath of Fire be practiced and mastered. In Breath of Fire, the focus of the energy is at the solar plexus and navel point. The breath is fairly rapid (approximately 2 breaths per second), continuous and powerful with no pause between the inhale and exhale. This is a very balanced breath with no emphasis on either the exhale or the inhale, but rather equal power given to both.

Breath of Fire is a cleansing breath, renewing the blood and releasing old toxins from the lungs, mucous lining, blood vessels, and cells. It is a powerful way to adjust your autonomic nervous system and get rid of stress. Regular practice expands the lungs quickly. See the Appendix for more complete directions on this powerful praanayam.

[†] Adapted from Kundalini Yoga Sadhana Guidelines, 2nd Edition.

Cannon Breath

Cannon Breath is a powerful continuous and equal inhalation and exhalation through the mouth, similar to Breath of Fire, but through rounded lips instead of through the nose. Very cleansing, this breath is invigorating, energizing and rejuvenating.

To consolidate the energy at the end of a kriya, many will call for a Cannon Fire exhale, which means we suspend the breath on the inhale and then use a single strong exhale through the mouth like a Cannon.

Bandhas

Bandhas or locks are used frequently in Kundalini Yoga. Combinations of muscle contractions, each lock has the function of changing blood circulation, nerve pressure, and the flow of cerebral spinal fluid. They also direct the flow of psychic energy, *praana*, into the main energy channels that relate to raising the Kundalini energy. They concentrate the body's energy for use in consciousness and self-healing. There are three important locks: *jalandhar bandh, uddiyana bandh*, and *mulbandh*. When all three locks are applied simultaneously, it is called maahaabandh, the Great Lock.

Jalandhar Bandh or Neck Lock

The most basic lock used in Kundalini Yoga is *jalandhar bandh*, the neck lock. This lock is practiced by gently stretching the back of the neck straight and pulling the chin toward the back of the neck. Lift the chest and sternum and keep the muscles of the neck and throat and face relaxed.

Uddiyana Bandh or Diaphragm Lock

Applied by lifting the diaphragm up high into the thorax and pulling the upper abdominal muscles back toward the spine, *uddiyana bandh* gently massages the intestines and the heart muscle. The spine should be straight and it is most often applied on the exhale.

Applied forcefully on the inhale, it can create pressure in the eyes and the heart.

Mulbandh or Root Lock

The Root Lock is the most commonly applied lock but also the most complex. It coordinates and combines the energy of the rectum, sex organs, and navel point.

Mul is the root, base, or source. The first part of the *mulbandh* is to contract the anal sphincter and draw it in and up. Then draw up the sex organ so the urethral tract is contracted. Finally, pull in the navel point by drawing back the lower abdomen towards the spine so the rectum and sex organs are drawn up toward the navel point.

Pronunciation Guide

This simple guide to the vowel sounds in transliteration is for your convenience. Gurbani is a very sophisticated sound system, and there are many other guidelines regarding consonant sounds and other rules of the language that are best conveyed through a direct student-teacher relationship. Further guidelines regarding pronunciation are available at www.kundaliniresearchinstitute.org.

a	hut
aa	mom
u	put, soot
oo	pool
i	fin
ee	feet
ai	let
ay	hay, rain
r	flick tongue on upper palate

The Stages of Meditation

When we meditate we begin where we are as we are. Then we steadily sharpen our consciousness, clear our mind and strengthen our body; this happens in stages. It doesn't happen all at once nor can it be forced. Realization is when the You within you works—and you relax. Even though Kundalini Yoga and Meditation is the fastest path we know of, it still takes time and requires moving through the stages of development, continuously refining and perfecting the contemplative skills of each stage.

Yogi Bhajan divided the meditative path toward realization into 21 stages. These 21 stages are composed of three journeys. Each journey has seven stages which represent the mastery of a particular meditative skill as well as the development of a particular dimension of the Self. Each stage has its own beauty, challenges and qualities. Yogi Bhajan named each stage to reflect its qualities and challenges and described the journey that leads to happiness, and ultimately, realization:

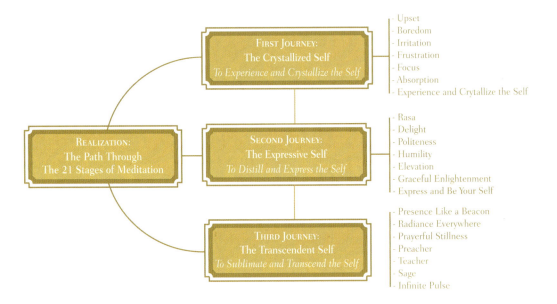

As we progress through the stages of meditation, we acquire the resources to live more fully and successfully, we steadily refine our ability to experience happiness in our lives—a fulfillment of our birthright.

The term *happiness* is used in many ways. To understand what it means within the stages of meditation, think of these three qualities: joy, happiness and bliss. Joy is what we normally think of as happy; it's that positive state we get when we enjoy something, feel pleasure in an activity, or leave behind our burdens and stress. Joy increases throughout the first journey as the emotional, reactive and unconscious blocks clear from our mind. Happiness includes joy but adds an aspect of the Self; so it's not just the pleasure of what we do but how we do it—the level of excellence, commitment and fulfillment we bring to it. Happiness begins when we have a sense of Self. As we complete the skills of the first journey and begin the second, our experience of happiness expands and is refined and stabilized in every part of our life.

Bliss is the fruit of the third journey. The word bliss comes from the Sanskrit word, *ananda*; it includes joy and happiness but adds a deep sense of fulfillment and clarity that only comes as we transcend the finite Self and the burdens of the ego. In the state of bliss, we become the flow of wisdom, infinite innocence at play, a presence that observes and yet participates in all things with spontaneity and grace. *Ananda*, or bliss, comes from within the Self and magnifies in direct relationship to the ego—less ego, more bliss.

Joy is transitory, happiness enduring, and bliss always and ever abiding. Joy often comes from outside of us, material things and other people; happiness often comes in comparison to others and our Self; bliss is found from within our Self by becoming consciously conscious in every moment and savoring the infinite variety found in all things. When we are happy, in this deep blissful manner, we radiate. We become a magnet; whatever we need to express our particular gifts and contributions comes to us; we become a creative consciousness. When we find our innocence and awaken our intuitive Self, the entire universe comes to support us.

Yogi Bhajan often recounted the classical stages of meditation as referred to in the writings of Pantajali and others. He explained the four basic states of waking, dreaming, deep sleep and awakened mind.

> *"Understand what meditation is. In simple yogic terminology we call it dhyan; it means when you gaze toward something, when your mind's mental eye focuses. People call it the third eye, the eye of the mind, through which you daydream, think, imagine and hallucinate. When you concentrate on any problem, between a subject and an object, you are supposed to be meditating through this mental eye.*
>
> *"Your mind has four basic stages. The awake stage, which you all are in; but mentally you may be daydreaming. Sixty percent of people day dream. Sixty percent! Then there is a dream stage, when you want to sleep and rest but you have such a good dream that you are actually doing the whole thing for real. Then there comes a stage of deep sleep in which you are so solid and helplessly asleep that you forget about everything around you and have no dreams either. The final stage is the state of* turiya *in which you sleep, rest, relax, live, talk and eat; you do everything but the pros and cons do not disturb you, and you always maintain your equilibrium and balance. It is a stage of ultra-consciousness, super-consciousness.*

They have a lot of names for it and create a big mess about it; but there is nothing serious in it. It's a very simple, ordinary stage in which a person can know the pros and cons and his own neutral position in that. You can act quickly, neutrally and objectively within your Self.

"According to all the sciences of meditation known to humans so far, there are thousands and thousands of ways of meditation, and there are hundreds of thousands of mantras, and people practice them variedly for varied reasons." [1]

What was missing was a detailed guide to the stages of meditation, which touched on the fundamentals of the process of change in meditation, and was based less on philosophy and more on experience. Yogi Bhajan laid the foundation for such a guide in his many years of teaching about the mind and its projections and facets. He described the effects of the meditation process through metaphors: a raw stone becoming a jewel was one particular favorite of his. We start as rough stones covered in dirt and debris. Then we are cleaned up, the first stage in becoming a gem. Then we are cut, with all facets perfectly capturing the light and reflecting our true nature. Finally, through full realization, we can become a "museum quality gem"—unique, clear and priceless.

In the same way, we all begin as a mixed substance. Our minds are impure and filled with commotion, imprints, ego, subconscious memories and more. When we apply the heat of discipline, tapas, we experience and crystallize the Self. Then we continue the energetic refinement as we distill the purity and authenticity of the Self from its diversions and entanglement in the maya of life. Finally we complete the refinement by sublimation into the infinite Self; we transcend the finite Self and merge into our unlimited Self. We become *saibhang*, self-illumined, realized human beings. With each consecutive chapter, we will explore these stages and detail the meditative processes we will use to sensitize our experiences and master the quality and expression of each stage. The progression through the stages is systematic but our individual accomplishment within each of them will vary. Some of us will be more accomplished in one stage or another. We may be better at some meditative skills than others; and better at some stages of self-refinement than others. We may all begin with different capacities and skills, but the entire path to realization— no matter our starting point—is covered in these three journeys.

"We have our own capacity to do what we are going to do. Among us, there are scattered minds; there are minds that are trying to become one pointed; there are minds that have fears; there are minds that are sex oriented; there are minds that have come just for curiosity; there are minds that do not understand why they are

here; there are minds that are very happy and happy to be here. There are all types of minds.

"This total concentration of all types of minds presents to us all the facets of mind in different stages of development and consciousness. At this moment, I do not know how much garbage each mind has, and neither is there a reason to know. But there is a reason to act. Start with a call to your higher mind and go from the top down to the toe. Do a very purifying, self-cleansing, self-meditation. Feel that just as you are, just as you were, you are here. The very fact that you are here is enough. You have an intention, which is enough; the very fact that you have an intention to cleanse yourself and make your soul bright is enough reason for your mind to concentrate. The very fact that you can concentrate gives you the power to meditate, and the power of a meditative attitude is samaadhi in action! Man always has the same basic faculties. It takes the same energy to become a man of God as it takes to become a demon. It takes the same mind to become sick as it takes to become healthy. Mind does a lot of jobs; the activity of mind is unlimited." [2]

"We begin with different capacities, different problems, different hopes and different qualities of the mind. But through steady discipline, progress is made. People sometimes do not understand what discipline is. Discipline is the self-experience of self-consciousness, where a person feels that he or she exists. That is the greatest experience." [3]

These three journeys represent three developmental processes, which mature the full range, potential and relationship to the Self. Each journey cultivates disciplines and practices appropriate to each stage on the path. If we think of each journey as a mountain climb, each step, every effort, elevates us. Gradually we see things we would never have seen at a lower altitude. The trees, plants and animals change; the quality of the air changes. The exercise and discipline of the climb make us feel more alive; we have a sense of accomplishment and self-satisfaction. We begin to get a measure of our self as we take the measure of the mountain.

At the beginning of any climb we have to arrange our affairs and gather what we need to make the ascent. If we anticipate various challenges, plan well and execute that plan (and the weather cooperates) we make it up the mountain to form a base camp. This is our touchstone, our initial experience of Self, that we can always return to and rest in. Here is where we prepare for the final ascent to the peak. The final journey is qualitatively different from the first. The air is rarer. The demands on the body increase and we must walk and eat with greater mindfulness and precision. As we ascend our entire perspective changes; the heavens and the earth form a seamless panorama both familiar and completely new. We cannot put it into words, only our radiance and our projection will tell the tale.

When attempting that final ascent, we may take several practice runs at first. As we approach the peak the path narrows. The effort required takes a quantum leap. At this stage even a single thought can misdirect our steps with devastating consequences. As we apply our Self time goes away. We attune to the mountain and the turns and twists of the path become a flow, no longer separate from us. We merge with the journey as the journey merges with us. The peak is the *bindu*, the *shuniya*, a point of absolute stillness. We hear everything. See everything. And in that vastness, recognize our Self, awakened, with greater scope and depth. The next step is ours and ours alone; the forces of gravity and the unseen hand are with us; and we descend confident and ready to embrace life with an open, full heart.

Each of the three journeys takes us through seven of the 21 Stages of Meditation; and each journey is like that mountain climb. The first four stages within each journey form our base camp. As we begin, we have to face our actual condition, gather appropriate resources and get rid of any blocks, fears or ignorance. Once we make it to the higher plateau, our base camp is established for the final ascent, the last three stages of each journey. These stages take us to a new level and require the most effort. They consolidate the basic skills and sense of Self for that journey. Every mountain has its own characteristics: height, incline, trails, history and surprises; and every time we climb a particular mountain we become more skilled. But those who climb regularly know that one experience is a preparation for the next; yet even still, the same mountain seems different each time we climb it. We are in fact different, more developed, and time and space have changed the trail.

So, too, the three journeys on the path to realization are meant to be experienced again and again and again. We climb our own mountain with regularity and the disciplines on the path toward self-realization flower into a joy that only expands as we experience, express and transcend our sense of Self.

FIRST JOURNEY
The Crystallized Self

The focus of the first journey is to recognize, experience and crystallize the Self. The blocks are encountered in the first four stages: upset, boredom, irritation and frustration. These reactions to our thoughts and emotions often lead to a loss of our center; we lose touch with our basic sense of Self. We become negative, fearful and allow our thoughts to lead us away from our own consciousness and will.

Here's an example of how these commotions and emotions rob us of our sense of Self:

> *"What is a God? God is a point, a source from which everything springs. So when we go into the realm of consciousness, we need a nucleus. Suppose you have jealousy. You have a state of jealousy, state of frustration, state of slander, state of deceit, write that down. All right, what is jealousy? Jealousy is when the Self is not known. It is when you find yourself in somebody else. It's a total betrayal of the Self, total and complete. At that time you are worse than zero. There is nothing left in the being. That's the weakest state because you have lost the Self totally. Instead you have started to see your Self in something else. It means your total value is gone, total being is gone, total radiance is gone, total Self is lost; and such losses are very, very irreparable. Do you follow the situation?"* [4]

The primary skill at this stage is to become a witness to all the thoughts and feelings. Many, but not all, are from our own subconscious. We begin to separate our Self from our feelings; we quit identifying with them. Instead, we let them flow through us without resistance. We simply release them instead of reacting or attaching. The emotions in these first four stages make us dense, dull and gross. When we work to clear them, the energies associated with them can be transformed. As we become more alert and focused, our attention must shift from pure awareness to experience, from observer to participant, passive to active, from outside to inside.

When we first shift our attention to a more subtle sense of Self, our minds resist by dumping old thoughts, wrapping the mind in fantasy or inducing sleep. Hold steady to the discipline and stay present; be kind. The sounds and breath patterns of the meditation will carry us across these obstacles.

The first ascent starts where these initial four stages left off. We have a sense of our Self, separate from all the commotions, emotions and sensory impulses; we begin to focus and recognize a still point, a nucleus within, which is the Self. It is this crystallized sense of Self that is needed in order for consciousness to work. This nucleus of Self allows us to be fully open to the world and yet still present as our Self; we only grow more subtle as we begin to drop the identification with our impulses and emotions. Compassion and self-compassion arise.

The final stage in this first journey is a 2 ½ hour meditation that opens the heart center. Here, the crystallized sense of Self becomes stable and we can feel all our emotions and sensations without getting lost in them. They become our friends. We are light and free to find kindness and compassion in any situation.

The Stages of Meditation

SECOND JOURNEY
The Expressive Self

Once we recognize the Self, the question becomes: How do we express that Self creatively, authentically and effectively through our actions? In this second journey, the initial challenge is to develop a sensitivity to the Self, especially as we engage in relationships and partipate in life and all its commitments.

To be successful, we need to cultivate the manners and mannerisms that support and express our maturing character. We must develop the skill to distill our authentic sense of Self from the many personas, projections and roles we adopt. In the first journey we had to learn to recognize the differences between our Self and our thoughts and feelings. In this second journey we learn to discern our Self among the many identities we hold and the various roles we play.

When we take the seed of our Self and our identity and project it into the world, it expands. As we express our potential and our creativity, we create relationships and roles that reflect how we understand our Self. In this second journey, we cultivate the meditative skill to merge with our projection yet still be able to distill our Self from the outcomes and circumstances of that projection. Normally, we create what Yogi Bhajan called an "identical identity" made up of the various roles we engage in throughout our lives: father, son, mother, daughter, husband, wife, teacher, student, doctor, writer, gardener, cook, you name it. In the early stages of this second journey, we develop the skill to maintain a sensitivity and relationship to our real identity, rather than becoming identified with the identical identities created as a result of those roles.

> *"You are basically alone. You are basically supposed to decide everything for yourself within your Self. But you are also a social animal; therefore you will relate to the creativity and corresponding relationships of the surrounding world, which creates your individual 'identical identity' or position in relationship to everybody else. If you lose your identity, then you are just like sheep regimented into a group—that's not human. You must maintain your identity; you must maintain your individuality. Maintain your consciousness, but be harmonious, with total understanding in your projection through all surroundings and all the pressures of the surroundings. You are harmonious within your Self, then your corresponding relationship with the surroundings has to have a neutral mind with the pros and cons, cause and effect,*

action and reaction. Then you can find your individual security in the 'identical identity' and at the same time you should be you, even then." [5]

In meditation, we need the ability to observe the Self observing the Self. We cultivate a sensitivity to our own sensitivity, which we call savoring. We savor the sensation of our own Self. In this way the first four stages of this second journey prepare us to maintain our integrity in action. Why is this such an essential skill? Because it helps us be in relationship without losing our sense of Self. We are able to help people without imposing our will on them. These stages develop our ability to step back from our own involvement and personality and act from consciousness. We learn to live lightly and brightly. Other essential skills are cultivated as well, such as the skill to beam the mind, and the skill to take a thought and mature it through any and all conditions of life. These skills prepare us to heal through awareness and *praana*, the life force.

In this journey we deepen our sensitivity and understanding that we are involved in creating each and every moment of our lives. The four stages that form our base camp for this second journey are rasa, delight, politeness and humility. Each one deepens our self-trust and creativity and prepares us for the next ascent in which we elevate the Self in action. We must engage in life and its games, but we want to engage them consciously and successfully, with effectiveness, elegance and elevation. In these stages we prepare to project and beam our expressive Self like a North Star. We become steady as we commit to following the truth of our identity; and we never lose our orientation because the North Star lies within.

In the final three stages of this second journey we use these enhanced sensitivities to expand our projection and creativity beyond the play of life's polarities—good and bad, claim and blame, joy and sorrow. This requires shuniya, zero; we learn to create from stillness. We elevate and free the energy of the Self by learning to project through intention not just direct action. Again, the final stage of this second journey is a 2 ½ hour meditation into the heart of the the Laya Yoga Kundalini Mantra. In its essence, Laya Yoga teaches us to expand the sense of Self within the vastness of the sound current. We beam our Self not just toward a goal but toward the creativity and flow of our infinite Self. We express our Self, we create and we mature our vision without being diverted by ego or circumstances. We expand and in that expansiveness our creativity, our capacity to heal and our prosperity realizes itself in practical and mundane but also sublime ways, each and every day.

This second journey stabilizes our sense of Self while in relationship to others. It heals relationships; and in that healing, gives you the capacity, in consciousness, to heal anything in the universe. We become a graceful, enlightened presence that creates, heals and uplifts everything we touch.

> *"The light within and the light without are the two phenomena of our life. If there is a light outside and there is no light inside, man is still in darkness. If there is a light inside but it will only shine outside in a close up view, he is still in darkness. Both states of mind are not right. Therefore, man has to relate within and without at the same level of consciousness, which is known as totality. In this totality we can express reality, which is known as the truth; they call it 'Sat Naam,' the path of truth. The path of truth is not a miracle; the path of truth is the same reality on which the totality of the Self is based."* [6]

THIRD JOURNEY
The Transcendent Self

The focus of the third journey through the 21 stages is merger and the transcendent Self. In the first journey we mastered the differences between our Self and our emotions. In the second journey we mastered being and expressing our Self within the game of polarities. In this final journey, we sublimate our sense of Self. We recognize all that we are as the formless presence of the infinite Self. We open the dimension of our transcendent Self. This journey requires us to go beyond differences and similarities into reality and unity.

By forging an elevated identity with our infinite Self within our finite self, we become spontaneous, creative and flexible. We excel in this infinite game of the soul. Love, compassion and kindness become the core of our experience. Supported by clarity, courage and character, these qualities are no longer goals, but the natural consequence of the meditative mind.

The stages which form the base camp for this third journey mature and stabilize two basic meditative skills: the ability to project and expand our inner light, our consciousness, beyond any boundary set by time and space, or our own minds; and the ability to become absolutely still, zero. During this journey we learn to be everywhere and create from anywhere by being exactly where we are. We locate the still point of infinity within the Self and from the eternal present, we create, expand and influence our environments.

> *"Become enlightened like a lighthouse. Just by being you project that enlightenment to all around you. You are everywhere and you are felt everywhere. Become prayerful. Next you'll become a preacher and then you can talk about God and everything."* [7]

For the final ascent we will need all the qualities developed in these four stages: presence like a beacon, everywhere radiance, prayerful stillness, and the preacher. Instead of manipulation and cleverness, prayer becomes a touchstone of power within our Self. Instead of seeking out the things we think we need, our radiance attracts whatever we need. Instead of accumulating wisdom and holding it in secret we share it freely and uplift others. We stop using prayer to ask for things, and we become our own living prayer, we become our own answer. This is a major shift in perspective.

The final ascent takes us beyond any finite concept of Self as we merge into a continuous meditative flow with the infinite. This is *simran*, deep continuous meditation. We shift perspective in consciousness once again. We go from radiance and presence everywhere to the pulse of the sacred Self, which flows through us and all things. The Self becomes the teacher, the sage and finally, nothing at all, except the infinite pulse of God and the fullness of the Self—realization.

Words do not capture this stage, not because it is abstract or esoteric; but because our behavior, upon reaching this stage, becomes spontaneous, unique and is at once both unclassifiable and standard. The steadiness of our character is unlimited, and the flexibility of our consciousness turns every plus and minus of our personality into service of what is valuable and real. All scriptures say that this stage cannot be captured by any list of qualities for it is the quality that generates all other qualities. This is the ascent to the highest peak, in which a deep intuitive consciousness joins with our applied intelligence to open new pathways in life. It activates what Yogi Bhajan called the diagonal energy of the kundalini, which always finds a way to flow between the polarities. As a filament in a light bulb uses the positive and negative electrical charges to make light so the diagonal energy of the kundalini uses the positive mind and the negative mind to light up our consciousness and alert the neutral mind to see beyond the polarity.

We begin to see the subtlety of the world and make practical choices within it. We understand the distinctions in meditative states in the same way climbers know that Mt. Everest is the highest mountain, Mauna Kea is the tallest (from base to top) and that Chimborazo is the peak furthest from the center of the earth. All the subtle distinctions of life become clear, and we walk through life lightly and brightly as fully realized human beings, co-creating with the Creator, whose presence resonates throughout this entire universe.

But before we begin this final ascent, we must make a big change; we must put aside the ego. It is simply too heavy to take to the top. It is very useful in the valley, and even entertaining up to base camp. But it is a burden too heavy for the final climb, which is both narrow and sublime. At the peak of this journey we become the nothing within the center of all that is. At this point mystery is now mastery. The sacred space opens up to intuitive presence, which serves innocence, savors life, blesses all, and praises the Infinite, the all within All.

You become you, nothing more, nothing less. In this final journey, we become realized human beings. We can love and know that love is all. We are one with God in that love: "God and me, me and God, are one." [8] Yogi Bhajan often joked that we have three possible ends: to be a human bag, full of the garbage we start out with in the first journey; to be a human balloon, full of our ego's inflations and expansive claims; or to be a human being, who loves and is nothing but a living God, the Infinite seen through the finite.

> *"How many people know this word L-O-V-E? What is it? Let me understand what love means. Don't you have any experience of it? Didn't someone tell you, 'I love you,' and then bang you on the head? What happened? You fell in love or you love somebody? You feel so expanded, and you feel very good and it gives you so much joy?*

> *"That is the tragedy. Once the heart opens up in love, it never closes. One thing about love, in experience, is that once you love you cannot come out of it. Love is an experience of one's own Self. Love is an experience of one's own selflessness within the Self. Follow?*

> *"Once you become selfless and experience your own selflessness you can never come out. We fake love and we make love. But we never just experience love. Because love is God and God is infinite; therefore love has to be infinite. It cannot be defined, it cannot be stopped. It is one-way traffic, and meditation as a science teaches you to expand from the finite to the Infinity so that you can become a living love.*

> *"I have to fight with time and space because the human mind is beyond time and space. Human body is subject to time and space. But the human mind is always beyond time and space. The problem is when it is interlocked with neurosis, and then you become a pattern of action instead of consciousness. Anybody who becomes just a pattern of action cannot live happily, because once you are interlocked in your neurosis, you have to break the pattern. When you are asked to break the pattern, you cannot break the pattern, and then you get back into that ditch again and again and again.*

> *"The only way is to get out of it all the way—and meditation helps to break through. What else does meditation do? It makes you intuitive. If you start the sequence, you must end up with the consequences. And if you start obeying your consciousness you never stop; otherwise don't start. What is the use of reaching the consequences and then saying, 'I never started the sequence.' If you never started the sequence how did you reach the consequences?*

"As human bags we lie to ourselves all the time. We always remember to blame the others. We have two things: blame the other and claim for yourself. You know that it cannot work in the long range; and what cannot work in the long range can only work in the short range. And what works only in the short range cannot carry you through. That's why our relationships are a mess, our friendships are a mess, our marriages are a mess, and our social relations are a mess. This whole mess is because we cannot make it through. We can do it for a while. But what you can do for a while will serve you only for a while. What you can do for infinity can serve you up to infinity." [9]

As we continue through the stages of the three journeys, we shift our identification of the Self from gross forms and experiences toward a formless sense of Self that is both immanent and embodied—transcendent. This sense of our transcendent Self is reached through practice; the journey toward realization is gradual.

FIRST JOURNEY
The Crystallized Self

STAGE ONE
Upset

Upset

Jappa begins.
You recite the mantra
Beautiful words but somehow
not your own.
Long forgotten thoughts and feelings are
no longer supported.
Your mind reacts.
You become upset.
Your mind wants control.
Your ego wants to speak.
Instead you speak.
Instead you control.
Consciously you return awareness to the
rhythmical mantra.
With jappa you hold the mind to the task.

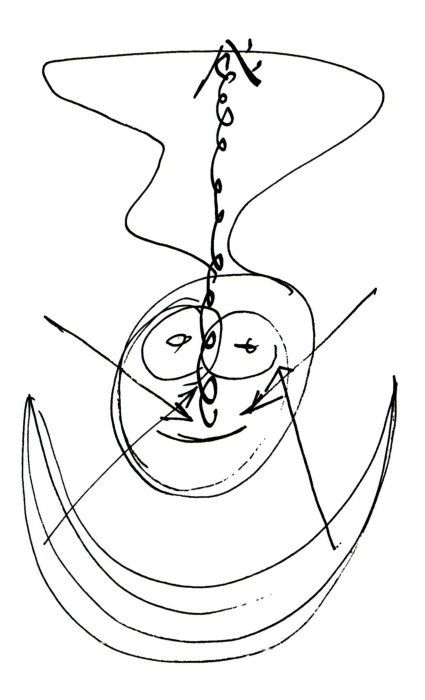

Negative thoughts come at you like arrows. Your strong positive arcline in the aura absorbs the energy of the thought and moves it spiraling up through the central channel of the spine to create more awareness above. The jappa of the mantra cuts each thought so its form changes from negative to positive and it can be passed on to the central channel. In this way you are still, happy and master the upset that comes from the defensive thoughts.

When we think about meditation, upset is the last thing on our minds. We want to be peaceful, tranquil, meditative! Why sit if it's just going to make things worse? But the truth is, we often never get better without getting a little worse—first. So we must start at the beginning, even when it makes us uncomfortable. And the truth is, we are often upset; and even if we are not aware of our own upset, others are. They sense our frustration and generally respond negatively to our projections. Therefore, how we act and connect with other people often starts with our assessment of the emotional and energetic state of the other person: What is their emotional state, their projection, their intention? In addition, our own conscious and unconscious upset is a powerful contributor to our capacity to successfully communicate, connect and create.

Stage One: Upset

Upset becomes apparent when we first sit to meditate. We sit and meet our mind. We still the body. We gather our attention as we focus on the breath or on a repeated sound, a mantra, and in that instant we notice and then amplify the swirl of thoughts in our mind. Some thoughts are immediate reports about our experience, our position, our comfort or more likely discomfort; others are ruminations on our daily concerns, our intentions, or echoes of what we have heard, said or done throughout the day or yesterday. Some are from distant associations propelled by feelings, impressions and the processes of the subconscious. And some are from our tendency to constantly and immediately react and comment upon our feelings.

Yogis describe this as a powerful artesian spring, from which our thoughts flow—a thousand per blink of the eye! Many are from the old brain and the brain stem. They are automatic, instinctual, and often without context. A mix of desires, memories, fears and anticipation, they are not the whole story but they often become more apparent the longer we sit. Our normal activities and distractions of daily life push them into the background. In stillness they come to the forefront and demand our attention. They are the beginnings of a thousand story lines, presenting themselves to be sorted, directed, accepted or rejected. In the flood of all these thoughts, it's easy to lose sight of, or perhaps never even recognize, the story line of our authentic Self. When we begin this journey to crystallize the Self we must deal with all these thoughts and with the upset that often accompanies them.

In *The Mind*, by Yogi Bhajan, the three primary functional minds were characterized as negative, positive and neutral. In most people the Negative Mind is the strongest, fastest and most insistent. It sends negative thoughts like arrows—swift and pointed. The Negative Mind uses our emotions, along with the amygdala and older structures of the brain, in order to avoid danger; it alerts us when something is wrong, whether it be a threat, a challenge or a loss.

The task for the meditator is not to avoid these natural thoughts but to guide them, and embrace them with our greater Self. Absorb their impact and add to them the resources of our Neutral and Positive Minds; we take the instincts that would bind us to the earth alone and add the intuition of the heavens to create intelligence and subtlety in our actions. In this way, we can use them to increase awareness and move us toward our center, our truest sense of Self. We continue to be alert to real dangers and challenges; but we are able to release them and transform them. Yogi Bhajan described the stage of upset this way:

> *"Negative thoughts come at you like arrows. Your strong positive arcline of the aura absorbs the energy of the thought and spirals it up through the central channel of the spine to create more awareness above. The jappa—repetition—of a mantra can cut that thought so its form changes and you can be still and happy as you master the upset that can come from negative thoughts and your reactions to them."* [10]

What is the real source of upset? Yes we are flooded by these thoughts, and certainly the Negative Mind tries to alert and protect us from them. But why do we get upset? The simplest answer lies in our basic human instincts. First, our ego wants to control and dominate. We want what we want when we want it. Second, we are unaware of our own mind. We do not know the state or nature of our mind before we engage it, either in communication with ourselves or with others. Third, we do not use our sensitivity to understand the impact of our thoughts or feelings on others. We see the beginning of a sequence but we do not look to the end result, nor are we aware of the unexpected results that come from the situations we weren't focused on. So, we are upset. We doubt that our way will prevail. We become insecure. We have positions but not strategies. We find ourselves doing things that do not get us the results we want. We lose track of what is important and real to us as we struggle for control. We chase thoughts or intense feelings that arise instead of acting in consciousness. In other words, we've lost the plot.

All of this is normal, especially when we don't have the appropriate training. A thought comes and we feel some necessity to keep pushing, spinning and following that thought. The thought becomes more real than the Self. We have not practiced the art of stopping, focusing on the sensations of the Self and then giving our self a chance to just be and express from an authentic space. Our ego—our attachments and instincts—becomes defensive because our focus is on what we think we want, not on what is.

Once we get reactive and defensive we become upset, then angry and then ugly. The entire range of emotional defensiveness arises instead of the spontaneous, flexible and creative presence in action. We shout and pout; we become paranoid instead of alert; we become tricky instead of straight; we trust no one and in so doing, become untrustworthy ourselves. Our natural divine nature, the clarity of the Self, becomes clouded. Meditation is a balm; it is a simple process that transforms our thoughts and brings us into the present moment so that we can embrace and direct the thoughts and feelings that are congruent with the Self. The practice of meditation brings an alertness and attention to each thought. We sense each thought, and its arc is apparent. We begin to anticipate our mind, and get to know its tendencies.

Stage One: Upset

Ideally, the mind is our servant not our master. So, we must practice the art of anticipating the mind. We live within this mind; it is the framework in which we shape and shade all our actions and beliefs. Meditation reshapes the tendencies of the mind, and opens a field of awareness that allows us to channel the upset and create with confidence, courage and love. As our kundalini rises we come to a basic realization that it is we who must select, plant and nurture each thought to fulfillment. Each moment is an opportunity to align our thought, word and action with our hearts and with the cosmos. We become very attractive to the cosmos. And life becomes real. There are no more excuses. As we start to take control of our life through the practice of sitting and confronting the Self, this first stage of meditation gives us the capacity to transform the upset that naturally arises. We face two problems: We always want what we want and, in relation to that, we always forget that we are part of something more. We go against the basic law of nature: the Self is not isolated; it exists in a rich context and interplay of environments, conditions and even mystery. We are given a mind; and whether we see it as a gift of God or the pinnacle of nature, it is ours and we are responsible for it and to it. In addition, we have a process in which we adapt, act and shape our lives and our identity, uniquely. But most of us suffer because we hold this one thought, "My mind should control your mind." We feel entitled; we believe that what we want is what everyone must want. We are essentially egocentric and self-centered. And thus begins the whole history of pain and trouble.

Instead, consider this guideline from Yogi Bhajan:

> *"Then what should I wish? One, I should wish my mind should help your mind to recognize that you have a mind. Second, your mind must serve you, as my mind serves me. Third, your mind should become your friend and your assistant and not your master as my mind is my servant and my assistant. What will that give me? That will give me a deep satisfaction that there is another individual alive, alike and beautiful, and that's a very, very beautiful satisfaction, and it can go on and on, today, tomorrow, all the time."* [11]

We forget that we are part of a much greater whole. The core mantra within this practice is the Adi Shakti Mantra: Ek Ong Kaar Sat Naam Siree Whaa-hay Guroo. The very first phrase (Ek Ong Kaar: there is one creative energy in all things) contains the rub. We do not recognize that we are part of all; and we certainly don't want to admit that not only are we not running the show, but that we are on God's leash! Yes, we can create; but our ego wants to be the king. We imagine we have control when in fact we don't. We inflate our control by ignoring all the times we were misdirected, or failed or had our desires go unfulfilled.

A regular discipline of meditation helps us become conscious, neutral, alert, and present in all circumstances. We will not lose our Self in nonsense and commotion, but instead, with the sensitivity of meditation, we can realize the interconnection that does in fact exist, helping us act on the abundant and constant flow of opportunities that surround us, opportunities we're normally blind to.

Thoughts set us up to be upset; we lose our center, the Self, and our energy is used up in the drama of the thoughts. Effective meditation makes us the kind of person who has a setup to not be upset. We still have the full range of emotions and feelings, but the Self that reflects and projects our consciousness will never be upset. This is the state of true relaxation.

> *"What is the difference between an ordinary man and a man of God? An ordinary man can be upset by ordinary things; a man of a God doesn't get upset even for the heaviest things because he feels everything comes from Him. Why should he be upset? If God is going to save him, He is going to save him. If not it is His head, His headache, what is it to him? You call it fate. It is not fate. It is a reality in which you live. We have come from that reality. We are a part of that reality. We have to merge in that reality. Therefore, why be upset? What for? And that is the secret of every happiness."* [12]

> *"I went into my deeper Self to understand what the most powerful thing was. And the most powerful thing in the behavior of a man is when he is totally relaxed. Nothing can upset that man, not even with minute observations can you find any kind of vibration coming out of that man that shows he is upset. The capacity of such a person is to sit down calmly and watch very respectfully, undisturbed, undaunted, uninvolved in the whole game—that is the greatest power.*

> *"I am not saying you should not have emotions. Emotions are there to lead us as waves are there to carry you across an ocean. But if you want to sail smoothly you have to learn to sail smoothly across those waves. Smooth sailing is smooth sailing. Exactly as the big ship sails on the surface of the great ocean, they have a definite longitude and latitude and they have a definite aim and destination to reach. If we on our journey do not know the art of relaxation then we get involved, reactive and entangled. We even get so involved that on one side we go and on the other side try to remain safe. We get torn apart between the two poles. Right man and wrong man, man of sacrifice and man of ego, like waves, they pull each other. Who should win? Should the rib cage just tear apart in the center? And the man*

Stage One: Upset

of ego takes his part, and the man of sacrifice takes his part and the man himself cannot exist?"[13]

"This worrying yourself and making yourself uptight, it is just like sitting on a pyre. When they put the dead body on the wood to do the last rites, at least that rapidly does it. But this is a slow fire on which you get burnt slowly. Actually, life is not meant to be like that; life is meant to be relaxed under all circumstances. Your own aura—the shield, or the circumvent force of your magnetic-field psyche—is your life protector.

"Monday is a hard day. Tuesday is going to be a very good day. Wednesday may be a much better day. Thursday may come as the worst day of your life. Friday you may be promoted to an unexpected height, which you cannot even understand. So each day has a message for you, and each message has either a promotion or a demotion. This is how the life moves, and if you are living, you have got to move as well. Then why are you upset? Why live under a fear complex?

"There is a difference between a carefree man and a careless man. Don't be careless. Careless is your deficiency. It is because of your laziness, you don't put in the proper effort to be conscientious. To be carefree is your higher mind. You do your best and feel good. One who feels good against the odds is really a good man.

"Everything can provoke you but you must understand, Are you going to get provoked by it? If anything and everything can provoke you where is your balance? You have to always understand, Are you a human being or a yoyo? Just question yourself before acting. Who am I? What am I going to do? Am I an individual slave to be played on the strings of environment, commotions, emotions and circumstances, or am I an individual who has to make a way? This is the basis on which you can shape your life.

"Some people say, 'There is only one way to live.' This is very confusing. Some people say, 'Well there are many teachers and many paths and many this and that.' No, no, no, that doesn't work. Whether you are Christian, you are a Jew, you are something, anything or nothing, it doesn't make any difference! As long as you are a human being you have to understand one thing: either you are to play in the hand of circumstances or you have to make the circumstances play in your hand. You have to decide either way.

"There is one human quality: to practice one-pointedness of mind. And that is righteousness. So often life is called a battle; don't call it a battle. Life is a voyage, *a journey. It's got to be done. It travels on the waves of time, which are up and down, good and bad, harmony and disharmony. That will always continue anyway. Healthy, unhealthy, happy, unhappy, holy, unholy, everything has two polarities. But you keep on going, because your life is not a mystery. Understand it clearly! It is yours. And you are a created creature, a part of all existence, and life and death are not in your control. So why are you upset?"* [14]

"Everything which happens, creation to creation and destruction to destruction, is all God. And I will tell you something, God also has to cleanse Himself of Himself, which nobody teaches. Every religion is silent about it; and that is the biggest hypocrisy of religions. No religion is complete. I have studied them all.

"What is a neutral force, please? A neutral force is spring and fall. Positive is summer, negative is winter. Everything that grows and everything that dies or is gone away is part of that cycle. That is the creativity of God. So is your day, so is your breath of life, so is your thought, so is your wealth, so is your relationship. Everything you are going to create, you are going to destroy. I know you don't accept it and you get upset, and I am not going to waste my time trying to convince you. You are the one who creates your youth. You are the one who becomes old. That is the science of yoga." [15]

To experience and master this stage we will practice the *Meditation to Conquer Upset*. It is a most effective and beautiful experience, which can take us deeply into the stillness in the center of the storm. It not only conquers the mental tendency for upset, it creates a powerful projection in our words and in our presence.

It strengthens the arcline and the aura and uses the power of the Fifth Chakra, which represents our ability to bind our word and our consciousness into action. It gives the power to create and to penetrate. That penetrating power must accompany any idea, thought, or intention in order to reach the hearts of others or to create an alignment between the Self and the cosmos.

The meditation uses a mudra, a hand position, in which the palms face the throat with the arms balanced, parallel to the ground. The interlocking fingers represent discipline and the energy of life. The mudra combines patient wisdom with the powerful urge to act and create. The thumbs are extended up like antennae, open to the full experience of life and thought. The position of the hands works with the sound of the mantra to manifest your actions and projections at an astounding level. Practicing this meditation will center and focus you, fortifying you with confidence and radiance.

Stage One: Upset

Meditation to Conquer Upset

March 16, 1978

POSTURE: Sit in Easy Pose, with a straight spine, and apply Neck Lock.

MUDRA: With the palms facing the body, interlace the fingers so that they are on the inside of the palms. Bend the Saturn (middle) and Sun (ring) fingers toward the throat. The pads of these two fingers touch the pads of the corresponding fingers and they press against each other with mild to moderate force. The Jupiter (index) and Mercury (pinkie) fingers are straight. They cross over each other in line with the forearms and perpendicular to the middle and ring fingers. The thumbs point straight up. The arms are parallel to the ground and the forearms create a straight line with the mudra at the level of the throat.

EYES: Focus at the tip of the nose.

MANTRA: Ong Kaar

Inhale deeply and then chant the mantra five times on one breath: Ong Kaar, Ong Kaar, Ong Kaar, Ong Kaar, Ong Kaar. Pace: 8-10 seconds per recitation. Inhale deeply and continue.

As you chant keep a steady pressure, 10-15 lbs., on the interlocked fingers, Saturn and Sun. Keep the shoulders balanced. For the last 5 minutes, increase the pressure to 25-50 lbs. (Note: If you pull very hard, say 50 lbs., then limit the practice to 11 minutes.) As you chant feel the central channel of the spine. As the navel pulses and the sound of Ong strikes the Brow Point like a mallet strikes a gong, sense the flow of thoughts and feel the flow of energy spiral up the spine. With each inhale feel the breath go all the way to the navel. Stay present and centered in your body as the energy from the chant increases, transforming thoughts and feelings.

TIME: 31 minutes

TO END: Inhale deeply, suspend the breath, and focus the eyes upward at the Brow Point. Exhale. Repeat twice more. Then inhale and stretch the arms up. Move; shake the fingers and hands. Recuperate the muscles and relax.

Hints for Practice and Mastery

Think of the spine as a spiral along which flow all the thoughts that might normally distract you or make you upset. As you chant each of the five cycles of the mantra, allow yourself to sense the gradual refinement of energy from the chant. Imagine the sound forming a space in which you sit in the center. At the end of each cycle of the chant become aware of a sensation, an impression left in the quiet and stillness of that space. That echo of sound sculpts the space as winds sculpt the air. As you inhale smoothly and deeply allow that sensation to stay present and the next cycle to build naturally upon it.

The sound creates no pressure in the throat. The "Ong" sound is like a gong strike at the Brow Point; it is powered from the Navel Point pulsing inward with "Ong" and relaxing with "Kaar." The sound "Kaar" releases from the throat. As you sense the shape of the sound, it is as if you can hear the ongoing drone of a gong reverberating in the silence as you inhale. Though you look at the tip of the nose to control the thoughts your actual attention is on the sound and the flow of sensations that undulate with the sounds.

In a group, the sounds will form a greater envelope as everyone pulses the beat together. Your own sound and space will be the dominant sensation, but the larger group sound and space will add to your experience; at times you may feel vastly expanded. When you inhale in such moments, sense your embodied center and the larger expanded space simultaneously. Merge the expanded group space with the personal center you are cultivating.

With each inhale bring yourself consciously to the body. Be present and viscerally connect the energy of the breath to every cell. Keep the shoulders relaxed. The arms are held up but instead of feeling the shoulders bunched up, sense the elbows extending to the sides as you pull on the finger lock so the shoulders are relaxed and stretched. At the conclusion of the meditation either relax or give yourself a few minutes to reconnect with your surroundings and other people. You will notice many immediate changes in your perception. The upsets and subconscious conflicts that are cleared by this meditation open up new connections to yourself and to others.

STAGE TWO
Boredom

Boredom

Used to feeling your impulses and emotions
You are at ease with your reactions to life.
Not used to feeling just you
You are uncomfortable with life itself.
Unaccustomed to being present the mind wanders.
You become bored.
Awkward is the sense of your own awareness,
reality and purity.
Gather the scattered parts of your mind
in the present.
Dare to experience you with new clarity,
and the boredom will end.

Your mind, like a boat, crosses the ocean. It is vast and threatening. It rains from above. Holes can appear at any time in the boat. You think nothing can change and you lay down as if doing nothing will make it go away. You have to get up and grasp the rudder. Hold it steady. Progress is being made.

The second stage of the meditative process is when we confront our innate, natural tendency to drift into boredom. As we continue to confront the upsets provoked by taking charge of our mental flow and learning to focus, boredom arises; it happens spontaneously. We can be pulled by boredom even in the midst of intense activity or during otherwise meaningful pursuits and relationships. Like small gusts before the hurricane, mild persistent boredom can build to an all-encompassing malaise, a kind of depressive disengagement from life, as if all meaning and purpose had been drained out of it.

Stage Two: Boredom

Boredom that we observe and confront as part of our normal meditative process can be a source of great insight. It can alert and realign us to our purpose. It can signal us to fixed egocentric perspectives that are drawing us toward isolation. It can tell us when we have spiraled into self-centered fantasy or memory; it can let us know when we need to clear our own projections so that we can be more present and centered in our true Self.

Boredom, when embraced and confronted, reveals how much our world begins and ends with our own projection and attitude. In this way, boredom can serve as a catalyst, calling on our deeper values, purpose and character. When we believe things are hopeless, repetitive or that our efforts are in vain, we encapsulate our Self and insulate our senses; essentially we shut ourselves off from the moment; we give up and boredom takes over. We lose our sense of awareness and witnessing and become entangled in fitful and dispiriting efforts to seek solutions outside our Self. We run to sources of stimulation rather than becoming the source of ongoing engagement, curiosity and commitment within ourselves.

We must become experts in handling the wave of boredom that arises because it as often as not accompanies achievement and focus. As part of our contemplative journey we must recognize that boredom and achievement are inextricably linked.

> *"There is one law which cannot be denied: In human energy, we are achievers. And every achievement—remember that—with every achievement comes equal boredom. That's the law. You know how to achieve, but you cannot continue to achieve because you do not know the other side of the coin, which is boredom. You do not know what to do with it, or how to master it. Instead you destroy things because you're bored. Actually, achievement is boredom; it is not separate. Only the name is different. Don't misunderstand that. It is a basic reality. That is the nature of polarity and maya. That is the maya. If you want to see beyond this maya understand this connection. When you achieve something it's achieved, it's over; beyond that achievement, that target, there is nothing. When there is nothing, nothing becomes boredom. In nothing there is no movement; it means boredom. No life, no expression, you can't move. You become unmovable in shuniya. Human energy reaches its end by being zero; but then you do not know how to get out of it.*
>
> *"There is a simple key to getting out of it and it applies to prosperity as well—widen the horizon. You shall never lose prosperity or be trapped by boredom if you decide to act with dedication. When we dedicate our Self to something, to the Guru, to our purpose, we go beyond our Self. There cannot be boredom because*

> *our dedication and commitment will not let things come to a limit. Infinity means when you cannot measure time and space. There is no boredom in unlimitedness. There is no boredom in the experience of infinity. Boredom shall hit you when things are too defined, when your focus is too finite or too known. To defeat boredom, every achievement should continue, should be extended. That is the principle to avoid boredom, defeat, poverty and destruction."* [16]

Mastering boredom is part of the meditative journey. The key is to neither run from it nor to wallow in it. Recognize it, sense it, clear the reactions, re-energize, expand and transform. We embrace boredom as *our* boredom; we don't reject it as something external to us. When we become present, we find that boredom is at its core an invitation to exert ourself. We see past the immediate reaction to the unseen and keep going, staying in touch with our dedication, grace and purpose. We command our breath, mind and heart to express our purpose; we own and engage in the moment. We stop reacting.

As we continue to meditate and clear the things that upset us, we repeatedly align the mind to our purpose. We can become lost for a moment or for an entire life. We feel nothing can change. We try to create change by pouting, shouting, withdrawing, running, disengaging, hiding, demanding, turning toward addiction; all our efforts seem insufficient. Unexpected things occur no matter what our intention or discipline. We slip back into distraction and habit. Ultimately we give in to boredom itself, as if it were a property of life, as though it were real; but it's not. In fact, this state of boredom actually has no force in itself. It is not permanent. Nor is there anything to fear. It is one of many polarities the mind confronts us with. Boredom can even be useful if we're able to recognize it, embrace it and rise beyond it; it can be the gateway to a new stage in your meditative Self.

> *"You get bored by everything. You are bored by your life, and so you are bores. Life is a bore to you. You are bored, your wife is bored, your children are bored, home is bored, sofa is bored, and your car is bored. Boredom haunts you like a devil. You are depressed, bored, insensitive, why? Because you were not ground and chiseled in the basic lofty values, you don't have any experience with what is beautiful, or that beautiful is beautiful in you."* [17]

Part of the problem is that we look to things outside of our Self to solve boredom instead of developing the richness and beauty of the Self within.

> *"What is Kundalini Yoga? It's a technology of the mind through which the finite can experience infinity. We are teaching you how to control the mind and live*

happily. Because we have a mission to accomplish and that is our mission. Still, among us, the desire to live in truth is not dead. Still, among us, the desire to find out who we are is not dead. And that is what everybody basically has to understand. You may have the wealth, and you may have whatever conveniences and luxuries the jet-set age provides you. But it doesn't mean a thing. To have wealth is a good idea, but to have a rich mind is equally good. To have a rich mind and rich living is very comfortable. To have a poor mind and rich living is terrible; it's boredom. It is so boring you can't even believe it." [18]

From the beginning he told us that we needed an ability to sense our own sensitivity in order to enjoy life. Without a practice to support that sensitivity and inner complexity, we become bored and disconnected no matter what. If the environment or society overwhelms us with information, turbulence and luxuries, boredom can slip gradually into a deeper, and more pervasive cold depression. We avoid and transform boredom through our meditation, through *pratyahar*, which synchronizes our sense of Self with the experience of the world. It broadens our horizon even as it deepens our own relationship to our inner world; pratyahar matures the creative relationship between the Self and the world.

"Let me tell you something very funny. Human beings by nature and in virtue are very happy and creative. But the only enemy man has is his own boredom. Boredom comes from insecurity and insecurity comes from boredom, so it is a catch-22. It can be very difficult to handle boredom. People who think that they can find happiness outside of themselves always end up with boredom; there is no way out. Basically you have to learn to go inside to find peace in your heart and head. Going inside is called pratyahar. Pratyahar means synchronize, meditate, go inside you. One who does not know the science of pratyahar becomes a misrepresented, misunderstood, misplaced human being who is not very happy." [19]

This stage of meditation may be very easy for some to master, while for others it will be an enduring challenge that must be re-mastered repeatedly over the course of one's meditative journey. A little boredom is easy. A profound acute boredom triggered by disappointment is more challenging. And at times we might confront the full depth of boredom, which wells up from the Self longing to connect but seemingly unable to.

When we master boredom and clear it, we see life as it is. We tear away the projected veil which separates us from the turbulent, relentless flow of life. There is very little in our life that we actually control; and it's much less than our ego wants to admit. And it's far less than our own stories and beliefs would convince us of otherwise. Yogi Bhajan estimated that after instinct and circumstance we have a maximum margin of choice of around 15%. But we think it's 75%!

Boredom whether small or large is the catalyst for creativity; it is a moment when we experience a disconnection from our purpose and we are called upon to create anew! Yogi Bhajan echoed this same theme in describing the creativity which is hidden in the heart of boredom. To open the potential inside our boredom, we must find the Self, crystallize the Self and add the Self into the mix of our life and thought.

> *"Everybody wants to be in samaadhi. They see this as the ultimate, perfect stage of the perfect One. But do you know the truth of that state? It is a complete living infinite boredom. I do not understand what these people are doing. What is samaadhi? That is an absolute stage of boredom in which Almighty God was, which is why He created the earth and all this creation.*
>
> *"Why then do we want to go there? Why go into that state where even He was upset! Something which could upset the Almighty, wonderful Lord, Creator of the whole Universe! If in that absoluteness, in that samaadhi, even God couldn't exist, why are you asking for it? May I know? What's wrong with you? You don't trust your deep character, your innate nature. You are a light of God; God created the Universe out of boredom. He couldn't remain bored. So how, when the One Whole cannot be bored, can His unit of creation—you—possibly be bored?*
>
> *"Boredom, depression and unhappiness is not your way of life. You lack self-trust, and you create your own nonsense and lies. You want to live anti-God, anti your nature. You don't have the will to trust your truth within you; therefore you do things which ruin your own tomorrow. You create an imagery, a non-reality. And you count within that imagery, that non-reality, your imagined gains and losses. Do you ever stop and consult your soul instead? Do you ever ask your Neutral Mind and Positive Mind and Negative Mind what is what? Did you ever sit with these four? The three minds and the soul within you and just talk to them? Have you befriended them? When they have an understanding with you, and you have an understanding with them, you can befriend the whole world and banish boredom."* [20]

What is the opposite of boredom? A sense of flow. It is when we connect and are fully engaged; it is when we're not trapped by our own self-concerns. Instead we trust our Self, open our senses and engage in committed action freely, without self-judgment. In meditation we gradually take the mind, one thought at a time, beyond its attachments and fears. As we open the mind up to all that is, especially to all of our own thoughts,

Stage Two: Boredom

there is a tendency to stop attending to what is, to deny reality. We enter into a state of self-imposed boredom that only sees the same things happening over and over again. We lull ourselves into a state of boredom. We lose the capacity to attend. We want to sleep, to be taken away, to escape. We want to lie down and simply pretend there is nothing to do.

This stage of the meditative experience is a place to practice attentiveness. The quality of our attention, how well we stay in the present, how elegantly we embrace our own life determines how boredom serves us, or not. Whether we can allow it to become a catalyst, bringing with it new creativity and flow, or whether we allow it to become an unending malaise, when we experience boredom in meditation, it's time to clear our emotional impulses and grasp the rudder of the boat. We use the breath as the keel to keep us steady and to give us energy.

As common as boredom is in modernity, it was not always known or at least it remained unnamed in the past. Sadness was known. Melancholy and states of not caring, such as *acedia*, similar to apathy, were written about by the ancient Greeks, but not boredom. As we enter the modern age, we have far more choices, far more distributed wealth, and a far greater range of expectations and entitlements. Paradoxically, with the increased options has come the advent of boredom. More options give rise to greater expectations, but not necessarily greater willingness to commit; so when our expectations are not met, we generate a form of boredom within our self as a result of these higher expectations. We begin to seek the interesting rather than the valued. We begin to seek distraction outside our self rather than going within to see our path of action.

Yogi Bhajan asks us to cultivate the courage to engage. To put aside doubts and to apply willingness and commitment and effort toward those things that are important and valued, those things that are true to our goals and purpose. Our mind is meant to be our partner in action; but it can all too often be our folly, taking us into fantasy and distraction. A central contemplative capacity that we cultivate in this first journey is to open the sensitivity to the experience of the Self and to separate that from the reflexive flow of thoughts and emotions; in this way, we build our ability to stay present and open to experiences, both positive and negative, as we simultaneously experience and observe our experience. The meditation for this stage will engage us in our own lives and put us in touch with our purpose. It will build our capacity for relaxation while remaining ever alert.

See Your Horizon

May 18, 1990

Note: According to Yogi Bhajan, one should eat as much cantelope as possible prior to practicing this kriya.

PART ONE

POSTURE: Sit in Easy Pose, with a straight spine, and apply Neck Lock.

MUDRA: Place the elbows along the sides touching the ribcage. Lift the forearms up to a 45 degree angle and rotate them outward to 45 degrees. Turn the palms to face upward with fingers relaxed and slightly cupped. [Note: The mudra in the photo shows the hands wider than originally demonstrated. The fingers should be pointing forward.]

EYES: 1/10th open and looking down toward the tip of the nose.

BREATH: Breathe very slowly, consciously and steadily. Breathe in through the left nostril and out through the right nostril. Do not use the fingers to change the nostrils. Use your meditative mind to direct the flow of the breath. Meditate on the sensations of the flow of your breath. If you are not used to directing your breath mentally, you can train yourself by slightly tensing the nostril that you wish to breathe through. Initiate the breath with this sensation, and your body will open the tensed side after a few seconds. To continue it, just focus on the sensation of flow, temperature and pressure. You can switch nostrils by shifting that tension and attention. It becomes very smooth and automatic with minimal practice.

MANTRA: The subtle sound of the breath is your mantra. Nirinjan Kaur's Say Saraswati was originally played in the background for grace, protection, contentment and calm.

Stage Two: Boredom

Feel that the arms are like antennae, which sense every ripple in the flow of life. Be aware of each side with equal intensity as you breathe. You may have many sensations in the fingers and palms. Stay centered and alert; don't allow the distraction. Focus on the nostrils and direct your breath.

TIME: 31 minutes.

TO END: Inhale deeply and close the eyes. Suspend the breath and squeeze the muscles from the pelvis to the spine to the rib cage. Hold for 15-20 seconds. Then exhale powerfully. Repeat this breath three times. Rest your arms and relax all tension either sitting or lying down for 5 minutes.

PART TWO

A) Sitting in Easy Pose, return the focus to the tip of the nose. Bring the hands up in front of the face at the level of the mouth, and press the fingertips of both hands together but keep the palms separated. The fingers are slightly spread. The elbows are up, parallel to the ground, in line with the shoulders.

Begin to flap the elbows up and down like wings; the movement is six inches, maximum. Keep the fingertips pressed and the hands fixed in position as the elbows move rapidly.

Use Derek Ireland's Snake Music to create a rapid pace and to work through the *tattvas*. (Nirinjan Kaur's Rakhe Rakhanhaar was used in the original class.) Continue for 5 minutes.

The pace is very fast and it will move the ribcage and shake the body from the force of the movement. Be rhythmic, steady and strong. The hands and fingertips act as the still point to the energetic movement.

B) Still in Easy Pose with the fingertips together, reverse the focus of the movement. The elbows remain steady and the hands move up and down, extending the fingers and pressing the fingertips together as the hands move up and rounding the fingers as the hands move down toward the solar plexus. Move quickly, in rapid bursts of movement. Continue listening to Derek Ireland's Snake Music. 5 Minutes.

TO END: Inhale deeply. Press the fingertips together firmly in front of the face. Squeeze the spine and the entire body. Suspend the breath. Exhale powerfully through the mouth. Repeat this final breath a total of three times, each time suspending the breath a bit longer: 10 seconds, then 15 seconds, and finally 30 seconds.

The movements in Part Two are polarities of each other as well as the energetic polarity to Part One.

TRANSITION TO STAGE THREE

Still in Easy Pose, sit absolutely still. Arms are relaxed at the sides touching the earth. Feel alert and fully present. Sense your Self. Sense the field of sensations throughout your aura. Allow the richness of the moment. Become aware that you are aware. Observe and fully engage in this moment. 5 minutes.

RELAXATION: Move smoothly onto your back. Relax on your back for 10-15 minutes. Let the sounds of a gently played gong penetrate every cell. Let your mind project to infinity. Let go completely. Expand your sense of space, time and Self; become unlimited and aware.

This is called beam guidance, where your totality flows through you with continuous purpose. You become fully engaged and boredom flees.

Hints for Practice and Mastery

This meditation process has two parts to it. The unbroken sequence creates an intense, effective meditative experience. Each part works with the other parts to achieve the final result. The first part of the meditation locks us into the natural rhythm of the breath in the nostrils. We flow with it, effortlessly. The natural polarities that take us from poor to rich, from life to death, from confused to inspired are always with us. But as we meditate on the nostril breathing, we remain steady, no longer fluctuating between the polarities. As we meditate, we can still feel the winds and waters, the movement and turbulence of life. But as we follow our breath and attune to the mantra, our ever-present awareness allows us to remain open and intuitive. We engage our horizon. We continue forward; we live in hope. That is the grace and beauty of a human.

This meditation clears the emotional weight we accumulate through effort. As you may have already experienced, the constant push for growth and progress can be emotionally exhausting. This meditation establishes a new rhythm by integrating the actions of the brain's hemispheres. The second part stimulates the glands and gives you the endurance to sustain your meditation and reach your goal. It resets the patterns and habits of your autonomic system. As you stimulate the nervous system, the music of the snake dance moves the kundalini energy up through the spine and the chakras, the body's energy centers. The hidden corners of your mind are illuminated and the cloaking emotions are cleared so you stand exposed and engaged in your life. This meditative process integrates the changes and establishes the Self as you relax and surrender to what is.

As we go through the various stages of meditative practice, we confront layers of emotions and resolve many of the conflicts in our minds. Playing a gentle gong aids in this process. An ideal diet to accompany this kriya is melon, papaya, pineapple and cantaloupe. These foods will support you in being calm, contained, alert and self-healing.

Stage Three
Irritation

Irritation

Each mantra carries awareness.
It is a template for feelings,
A seed for an entire pattern of energy.
It has its own character.
It has its own frequency, projection and quality.
Jappa provokes it.
And it impacts your mind.

But the subconscious too has cherished
thoughts and feelings
Challenged to choose between the two,
you get irritated.
This conflict distracts you.
Outwardly the sound of a single birdsong can muffle
the mantra into whispered forgetfulness.
Inwardly you fall prey to your own visions
You drift along aimlessly lost in your own inner story.
Allow the subconscious to dump.
Acknowledge your irritation and release it.
Simply come back to the mantra
Return to the awareness inherent in its
pattern and rhythm.

Like a pearl produced from the irritating grit
of a grain of sand
Like soothing nectar it will heal you and remove
unnecessary conflicts.
You fall into visions or drift along with an inner story.

Thoughts come from the subconscious. They are irritating and out of your control. Some thoughts interlock with each other, others support in a parallel way and others penetrate directly. Keep walking. Do jappa steadily. The thoughts that dump will peel away the layers of the subconscious.

In meditation the stage of irritation is different from just irritation itself; it is a process in which the irritation arises and is triggered from the meditation. In this way, irritation becomes a conscious state, which naturally arises as we refine our minds and shift our thoughts away from the normal, everyday attachments and sensory entanglements. We begin to sense a little of our Self within our experiences at which point our subconscious objects and our habits resist. They get irritated. The stage of irritation represents a particular skill we develop to recognize and handle irritations as they arise while staying in touch with our senses and our self-awareness.

Stage Three: Irritation

We must learn to handle our irritations by figuring out how to use them in positive, powerful ways. As yogis, we master the polarity; we neither run from irritation nor toward pleasure. Both are emotional energies that make up the entire spectrum of human emotion we all share. You might be under the impression that meditation is a process of throwing aside irritation and seeking only peaceful thoughts. But any experienced meditator knows that the meditative mind opens one up to all the sensations, feelings and realities of life. Irritations are simply a part of that.

We know when we are irritated because we overreact to things. We react out of proportion to what's actually happening. Over time, irritation can gradually distort our feelings and behaviors, leading to frustration, anger, aggression or withdrawal. How much we react, how irritated we get, depends on our nervous system, the quality of our mind and our expectations.

During meditation we concentrate on a thought, a feeling, a goal or simply awareness itself. As we continue our meditation, the mind may begin to disagree. It refuses to dwell with us in our contemplative state. It wanders away from our focus. It generates negative, positive and neutral thoughts provoked by our subconscious, our environments and our emotions. In meditation, just as in life, some thoughts support, some oppose, some distract and many divert. And it is all-too-easy to become entangled in them. And once entangled, the thoughts interlock with feelings in our subconscious and the spiral continues with increasing intensity. The distracting thoughts become more frequent and present themselves as important or real, even if they are not. The meditation and jappa seem irritating; the world seems irritating; and we are often irritated even by ourselves. But it is just the mind reacting.

When this reactive energy builds up in the mind during meditation, as it does throughout our life, it is called *rajasic*, referring to the *rajasic guna*, and that energy can surge like a fire within us. We become impulsive. And worse still, we confuse intuition with impulse. Poor decisions become the norm. That same fire can be used to burn the whole house down or it can bring about great change and transformation.

The source of irritation can come from our thoughts or even something as mundane as a new diet regimen. It is up to the mind to redirect it. We often mistake the energy of irritation for vitality or strength; but that's like confusing an adrenaline rush with actual core strength, which comes only from training. In the same way, we must train the mind; we must sit with the irritation and transform it, not identify with it.

> *"The human body is the most competent and perfect machine you can ever experience or create. It has the capacity to adjust to anything. I am talking about a*

universal truth. We know it as a medical law. If we have too much uric acid in our body, say from non-vegetarian diet, we will be more irritated. And that irritation is really a non-settlement of the Self, which they mistakenly call energy! Now what should we tell them when they say, 'Oh, I have got a lot of energy to do things.' If you can't run around and do something at least you can fight with somebody? When you have a lot of energy, do what you want to do? What do you want to do? You want to talk to somebody, to go somewhere, to do something, and to feel something. It's very difficult to sit down and meditate or think when you are like this. It is very difficult. The highest achievement of human mental and physical activity is to calm down your body and mind. It is the hardest possible task to calm your body and mind at the same time." [21]

These irritating thoughts and feelings are reactions that originate within our own mind. These thoughts are all ours. They are not the world's; they are ours and ours alone. We are only aware of a few of our thoughts. The vast majority are subconscious, fleeting or passing somatic waves in our muscles and viscera. The waves we react to can be triggered by various things, challenges to our habits or beliefs to changes in perspective or function.

A change in our body's rhythm, especially in relationship to our chakras, will create an irritation that we must deal with. Commonly the impulses of the lower body conflict with the upper body in a battle for control.

"I am trying to tell you that you have to understand that your socio-psychological behaviors change when the impulsations between the lower area, that is the Second Chakra, and the upper areas, that is the Sixth Chakra, differ. When there is an irritation from below, then the pituitary impulsation will change. Now, normally the pituitary and the Sixth Chakra, have to pulsate in a certain definite way; it goes according to the rhythm of the breath. When that becomes controlled by the rhythm and the irritation from the sex organs, you freak out. You feel defenseless." [22]

Many yogic habits such as cleanliness, moderation in sexual appetite, good nutrition and daily exercise form a foundation that calms the body and mind. These habits synchronize us with our own natural rhythms. Fluid is another key component to keeping the body's rhythms in harmony. This is one reason we emphasize that practitioners drink enough water when they meditate and often recommend an extra liquid flush after certain kriyas. In that meditative calm, we can process the irritations, connect with our consciousness and direct the Self.

Stage Three: Irritation

"It has taken me sixteen years and I admit my failure; I am not successful in training you to clean yourself properly. As a Yogi, I know, when the first chakra area at the base of the spine and anus is not cleaned right, it creates an irritation in the entire meridian system. I know it as a matter of fact.

"There are three problems in your life as a male and a female: there is a first chakra, a second chakra and a third chakra. If you do not know the dos and don'ts of those three chakras you cause a lot of irritation. You create unseen, unknown irritation to your entire body, your mental attitude and your mood. That irritation causes a lot of turmoil in human behavior. When the basement is shaky and leaky, it can create a lot of headaches." [23]

"There is hardly any difference between a man and an animal. The basic difference is when we master these senses. Touch is a sense, sight is a sense, smell is a sense, hearing is a sense, speaking is a sense. A blind person can learn to read through touch. All these senses complement each other; if you are open to them, you open to a greater level of awareness. The basic law on which your whole sensitivity is based is to develop and magnify your sensitivity so much that you can absorb all, every irritation. That capacity will give you very smooth sailing in your relationships and in life." [24]

All these sources of irritation and our reactions to them distort our perception. They are the basis of many of our emotional projections. This upwelling of associations and thoughts cloak our reasoning and perception so we cannot see the other person clearly or directly. We see them instead through our own projections and feelings. That lack of clarity and the discrepancy between perception, expectation and action irritates us further. Something is off. We sense it and struggle, somewhat vainly, against it. What we are focused on is not what it seems.

In meditation our task is to stay fully present and aware. We neither react nor insulate our Self in defense to the irritations. We specifically do not let irritation steal our sensitivity. We redirect our reactions and stay true to our Self. We do not let our mind magnify the irritations into anger, fear or hate; nor do we let irritation become the lens through which we see our Self or the world. We don't deny the energy; we channel it into the *sattvic guna*, a neutral attitude of mind which sees things clearly and allows us to act effectively.

"It is very funny that we do not know how to distribute our energy. In our life there should not be any problem. There is x-amount of energy and if we distribute that

> *x-amount of energy according to our use and need. If we simply retain it and let it flow as we need, then we can be intelligent enough to handle our life. If we can handle our life, things can be all right; but what we do is we overdo. Sometimes, in time and space, we experience setbacks and problems. Then you are low in energy and you can't decide right. You feel forced to decide; it's a deadline and the decision will cost you a recurring loss or a recurring irritation and problems. We humans, who can be simple and perfect and instead, we just suffer. It is a lack of knowledge, lack of experience, lack of teachings, lack of given values, and not being taught the meditative process to control ourselves. We do not have a reservoir of energy, a reserve capacity; we have energy, that's not the problem, but we don't have a reservoir of energy."* [25]

In this stage of meditation, the practice develops our ability to expand our sensitivity. For this reason many of the techniques in Kundalini Yoga and Meditation are designed to create irritation; an irritation that comes as our old awareness gives way to new structures; an irritation that comes as we begin to grow and expand. One of the most powerful irritants in this tradition is the practice of jappa, repeating a mantra. The mantra is a seed, a sample of something more than our usual awareness. We rotate our mind on the axis of the mantra. We pass our feelings and thoughts through it. We create an irritation even as we stay still; in this state of shuniya, our body and mind use the irritation to expand and heal rather than simply react. Bearing witness to this irritation as we meditate calls on our consciousness and sensitivity and ultimately on our intuition.

One of Yogi Bhajan's favorite metaphors for irritation is the formation of a pearl:

> *"Five tattvas make your shell. And within that shell is the mind, which is the muscle, the real power of God. It is negative, positive and neutral. It is triple just like Father, Son and Holy Ghost; Brahma, Vishnu, Mahesh; three minds. And with all that there is a pearl, the soul. And what is that thing which has a shell and a muscle and a pearl in it? An oyster. So you are a human oyster!*
>
> *"A human oyster with very worked out muscles; and when those worked out muscles have no balance between positive, negative and neutral, then as a human oyster you cannot make the pearl! If the muscles work, you still need the seed—the sand. That seed has to go into the oyster and create the irritation. It is only with that irritation that the muscles of the mind are made to rub and create the pearl around it.*

Stage Three: Irritation

"In meditation that seed is the Guru Mantra. That is the touch of the Guru, the touch of wisdom. Without that touch there shall be no pearl. And without the pearl what is the value of the oyster? Then it's only meant to eat or to destroy or to be left behind. The oyster which has to create the pearl has to have the seed, the touch. And that touch in your life is the Guru's words. In our life, the touch of those words is very beautiful, huge, vast, and wonderful. You have 'Gur,' formula; 'Guru,' which tells you the use of formula; 'Sat Guru,' which tells you the strength—the satya—of that formula; 'Siri Guru,' which tells you the universality of the power of that formula; and 'Wahe Guru,' which merges you into the Infinity of God because of that formula. And we have the Siri Guru Granth Sahib which tells us, talks to us, relates to us, and makes us understand again and again the same thing. That it boils down to Sat Naam, again." [26]

Fortunately, we have many techniques that work to penetrate through the irritations and the projections. We can provoke an irritation using jappa and evoke a new level of strength and clarity within our Self. When, in a state of relaxation, we can call up and face our irritations and clear our reactions to them effectively, we open up our sensitivity to our real Self and begin to see what is—and not be blinded by our own projections.

"Normally, you will meet many teachers who will say, 'Don't be angry, try to control the anger, try to control this.' I am one exception. I say, 'Don't control it, channelize it.' You can't eliminate anger from you; you can't eliminate the creative force of sexuality. The entire creative force of the being is in the sex force. After the divine force in you, the second most powerful force is the sex force. You use it positively or negatively, use it or throw it out as you like. The option is yours; you have free will. But remember one sentence of mine: 'Everything, if you do it in moderation, is good.' Fanatic souls become ghosts; they cannot go beyond space, this is the cosmic law.

"Therefore, what you have to acquire is a basic perfection of skill so that when time is short, the sooner you become you then the better it will be. The fundamental master key to everything is to keep consciously breathing and know that it is a divine blessing for you. It will not take days for the effect. It will work so fast and wonderful that you can't imagine. I am going to teach the entire science today. If you can develop your eyesight to be fixed at the tip of the nose, and you can sit in an easy, meditative pose and apply Gyan Mudra for the magnetic current to follow and charge you, you can concentrate on your spine as you breathe deeply. Breathe down into the tail of the spine and then circulate your breath up. Yogi Bhajan, the

> *Master has said (I, the man, have not said), 'That person can ask the God to come to Earth and do his work.' That is the power of the man. Now, are you better than God or is God better than you?"* [27]

A powerful method to develop this stage of meditation and channel our irritation is *traatik* meditations. As our irritation clears, we gain a better sense of our Self. We do not wander lost in our reactions and distortions. We invite a sharper sense of our Self as we release irritation, control the flow of thoughts and become content, conscious and contained. This process of focus, irritation and clearing can happen swiftly, gradually or sluggishly. Yogi Bhajan gave this particular *traatik* meditation exercise in class and then instructed me in its therapeutic protocols. We used it in couples and groups, not only individually. If it is practiced individually, focus the eyes on a horizon point or on an appropriate *traatik* picture.[†]

This meditation will produce profound depth and calm. It will increase our mind's ability to see past the jumble of distracting thoughts. It will help sort through which thoughts support you and which do not. It will help you recognize you instead of your mind.

[†] See www.kundaliniresearchinstitute.org for information on the Traatakam Meditation and photo of Yogi Bhajan.

Eyeglass Traatik

February 11, 1972

POSTURE: Either individually or with a partner, sit in a meditative pose with your spine straight. If in pairs, sit facing your partner.

MUDRA: With both hands in Gyan Mudra, the index fingertip on the thumb tip, bring the hands up to the eyes as if looking through eyeglasses or binoculars. The thumb and index finger form the eyeglasses you look through. The other three fingers are straight but relaxed; do not touch the fingers of the opposite hand.

EYES: Snake Eyes. Open the eyes wide, then narrow them by lifting the bottom eyelid slightly; the top lid will follow automatically. In this way, you can look and not blink. Look straight into the eyes of your partner. As you look at your partner, see him or her as a unique individual. At the same time, see your individual partner as All People. Your partner is a cosmic occurrence, with you in this moment, for this opportunity to meditate. Your meditative stance is impersonally personal. You sit and look at your partner who serves as a mirror of all your subconscious relationships. Penetrate past all the reactions and clever machinations of your mind and see the immediate presence and radiance of your partner. You will become increasingly sensitive to your own presence and the effect of being in relationship.

A) In this posture, breathe long, slow and deep for 10 Minutes. The pace of the breath should be about four times a minute. You need not match your partner though your breath usually synchronizes naturally. When you exhale be sure to complete the

Stage Three: Irritation

exhale with a gentle retraction of the Navel Point. Your task is to sit still and to be steady. When irritations arise through your body or in your feelings, let them pass. Synchronize the rhythm of your attention and your thoughts to see your partner and to feel your own Self present, calm, content, contained and focused.

B) In the same posture, continue looking, eyes fixed, and begin alternately chanting the sound **Whaa-hay Guroo** out loud. One partner speaks, while the other listens; then switch. Establish a rhythm. Listen to the sound when you chant it. Give full attention to the sound when your partner chants, while simultaneously sensing the shifts in sensation and energy in your body as it is uttered. Sound itself plants a seed of new energy patterns. The chant and its subtle echoes flow through both of you; you become musical instruments of consciousness. Feel the sound in its subtle infinite origins as well as from your lips. 11 minutes.

C) Once again breathe long and slow. Keep a steady gaze with your eyeglasses mudra in place. 10 minutes

TO END: Inhale deeply, close the eyes. Roll the eyes upward and focus through the brow as you suspend the breath for 15 seconds. Exhale in one rapid breath through the mouth. Repeat this process for a total of three breaths. Then inhale and stretch the arms up. Move the shoulders and arms vigorously. Thank your partner.

TIME: 31 minutes total

Hints for Practice and Mastery

Pay attention to sitting still, keep the three fingers on each hand from touching and fix the eyes steadily. These simple things create the seed for your own pearl of awareness.

Stage Four
Frustration

Frustration

You are frustrated because some things need
to be rubbed many times before they become
smooth and they give way.
You fight the irritations.
You project your thought, your mantra, to cut and
intercept the thoughts released by your subconscious.
It is a confrontation.
Sometimes you want to stop.
You feel like going another direction.
Jappa.
Repeat.
Patience lost.
At that moment don't fight.
Resist the impulse to anger and rage.
Be neutral.
Allow the thoughts to flow.
Counter them with mantra.
Jappa.
Repeat.
Do not try to pit mind against ego.
Let the power of the mantra itself,
Calling on it,
Allow it to guide you.
Let it do the work.
Jappa.
Repeat.

Frustration will change to optimism.

You did not create the mantra.
You are simply borrowing it.

Thoughts flood into your mind. Some weaker some stronger. Sit still. Meditate on the mantra from the navel point. That is the point of Infinite vibration. You add your heart to it. Then as you cross each thought the power in the mantra supports you and dissolves the frustration of your limitations.

As we persist in our meditation we become more and more still. Our minds challenge that stillness; and that challenge gives us the chance to practice stillness once more; to become a witness to our own mind, our own feelings and sensations. Being a witness does not mean being passive. We retain our intention; we project toward a destination. But we need the ability to keep our awareness open and expansive, even as we attend to a selected thought or event in our consciousness.

Stage Four: Frustration

A common distraction that hijacks our effectiveness at this stage is frustration. Frustration comes as we face our limitations: We desire everything, and we demand much. Our ego assumes that if we can imagine it, then we must deserve it. But everything in life has a sequence and a consequence. Each action, every thought, has an arc, a narrative of action and reaction, beginning and end, responsibility and consequence. As we become fully present and in conscious relationship to our thoughts we instinctually begin to assess our resources, motivations and potential actions. Do we have the energy? Do we understand the sequence, the organization and the steps that must be taken? Even when we know how to be still and surrender our intention to the infinite, the question remains, are we sensitive enough to know when to do our part, when to move and when to be patient? As we meditate, we begin to separate our desires and demands from our values; we take into consideration our past thoughts and actions and our current capacity and energy level; and ultimately we confront what is necessary in order to manifest those values.

As we sit to meditate our mind confronts us. We can choose to either avoid the confrontation (and not have a very successful practice) or use a mantra to stay present and put our whole heart into the moment, each breath, each syllable. Through our awareness, we gradually shift our source of energy from the ego, and its attachments and beliefs, to the clarity, commitment and subtle flow of the infinite Self.

To deepen our meditation and become present and still in the face of conscious or subconscious frustration we can practice the following kriya, *Self-Hypnosis to Dissolve Frustration*, which will help dissolve the sense of frustration and increase the awareness at the Heart Center. Through *praanayam*, this kriya stimulates the energy of the Navel Point, and then guides that increased energy to the Heart Center, where it combines with a state of shuniya, to intensify the sense of presence and awareness. Finally, the natural potency of this still presence is beamed through a single thought. In this way we untangle our emotional interlocks with the past and lower our sense of frustration, clearing the way to create from a sense of Self.

Yogi Bhajan defined what he meant by the frustration in this way:

> *"In our life we are all playing the game of polarity and balance, just like an atom with a proton, electron and neutron. We all experience this contrast and swing of polarities. Sometimes we have something known as frustration. I would like to explain to you what frustration is. You must understand basically what it is. Frustration is when you have the energy and you do not know where to give it an outlet. Energy is there. Outlet is not there. It is a frustration. And the second*

major source of frustration is when you do not have sufficient energy and you have a huge outlet; you do not know where you can tap the energy you need. Frustration is generated that way." [28]

If we fight frustration with frustration, it doesn't end. It generates more of the same. It also leads us to impatience, anger or hatred. From the Neutral Mind, beyond ego, we can see that as things progress, as situations mature, often what seems like a block at first becomes an opportunity. When we stay still and open, and allow frustration to pass through, we can see our situation, actions and opportunities clearly. However, this state of inner frustration is common and causes many reactive behaviors.

"In life, what you want to do, if there is spirit, then there is a strength, there is an energy behind it. If not all your wishes become true then your dreams will become your subconscious frustrations. . . . 'Hey! He didn't fix my jeep and I am already ten minutes late.' And that frustration becomes negativity which becomes anger and splits the personality. That's as simple as it is. You never suffer, you are not meant to suffer. There is nothing which can make you suffer. It is your own anger which makes you to suffer. You don't have to be angry at somebody but you are badly trained. You feel you should let the anger out, but letting the anger out does not solve the problem. It is the inside anger which will split your personality and tire you down in life. When Hatha Yoga was developed it was developed out of pure necessity. We wanted to find if there was some way that there can be happiness. Where is happiness? In Vedanta Philosophy they knew that as above so below; the formless creates the form. The yogis thought we could clean up and fix up what is below and reach the above." [29]

"The majority of people do things out of frustration. You will be shocked to know that a lot of people do a lot of harmful things—and that eighty percent of those people do things out of frustration. Twenty percent [of the time] people do things out of love, and about ten percent of people do things out of understanding, five percent do things out of compassion and only two percent do things because of their own consciousness or God. To be cooperative and creative, the scriptures say, you need a merger of the Moon and the Sun." [30]

That merger of sun and moon refers to the many ways we balance the parts of our nervous system in order to handle frustration and stress. We need to be flexible. So, we use praanayama and meditation to take charge of our nervous system, balance our emotions and relax our reactions.

Stage Four: Frustration

We must also accept that frustration is natural; it's an expression of our temperament. This practice is not meant to get rid of frustration in life; frustration is part of life. However, being able to confront it and knowing how to dissolve it will strengthen our focus as human beings. It will help us become present, open and creative.

> *"Frustration becomes a temptation. But frustration is also a blessing. Man will never change without frustration. The course of a river is changed by a mountain. Frustration is the only such mountain in the life of a man. It gives you a last chance to change course. Frustration is called the last hope of man. People say frustration is very bad. [They say] why be frustrated, [I say] why not? I am frustrated with my work all the time. I don't get to do what I should get to do. It motivates me to move; to keep going."* [31]

Dealing with frustration is easy; just recognize the sensation of frustration, raise the energy and stay in stillness, then release the energy of frustration into a creative thought, which projects like a beam. The projected creative thought could be a mantra or a thought deeply imbued with the heart and spirit.

> *"There is no solution with you. You don't know what your problem is so how can you solve it? You do not have a method to analyze your frustration. If you do not analyze the root of your frustration, how can you pull out the root of your frustration? All you are hitting against is one wall or the other; that's not the way to live. The way to live is to accept that the situation is adverse, and that every situation of adversity can be replaced by prosperity. That's the simple way of moving through your frustrations in life. When your mind is frustrated, depressed, and angry, you don't find any solution. All you have to do is to sit down and start giving yourself energy. What you have is energy in the Breath of Life. You can expand it and make yourself strong so you can cope with the situation. Sadness, depression, self-hatred, self-anger, frustration, hopelessness can all be wiped out by energizing your inner being. And then after that you can join into anything you want; that is not my problem. If you stay basically weak and basically depressed and basically negative and then you expect everything to become positive, it's not possible."* [32]

So, we must change our energy and guide our frustration toward creative projections of prosperity and committed sequences of action which will serve our future.

Self-Hypnosis to Dissolve Frustration

June 12, 1990

POSTURE: Sit in a relaxed meditative pose.

EYES: Closed.

MUDRA: Relax the hands in Gyan Mudra, resting on the knees.

A) Inhale through rounded lips. Take the breath into your lungs and mentally feel you are drawing it down deep into the navel center. Exhale slowly from the navel to the nose. As you exhale through the nose completely, pull the Navel Point in firmly. Consciously build the energy and power of the navel center. 15 minutes.

B) In the same posture, breathe naturally. Feel your Heart Center. Combine the energy of the navel with the Heart Center. Meditate on the sense of nothingness and zero. Enter into a state of absolute stillness in body and mind—shuniya.

Stage Four: Frustration

Meditate on the following visualization: "All is zero. I am zero. Each thought is just zero. My illness is zero. My frustration is zero. My blocks are zero." As negative thoughts come, your pains, commotions, disturbing problems or conditions, personal or impersonal, multiply them with the feeling of zero into zero itself.

Think of any sorrows or unwanted things in your life that seem to limit you physically, emotionally or mentally, situations or feelings that frustrate your intentions. Let them become zero. See each frustrating thought or problem as an image. Take each image and move it gradually into a small, distant, single point of light, insignificant and far away. It should look and feel like it is zero. If a positive feeling or thought comes, simply witness it, sense it, and let it go. 11 minutes.

C) Lock your mind on a single word that captures one significant quality or condition you most desire to manifest in order to fulfill your own happiness and growth. It may be something like "health" or "knowledge" or "intuition" or "wealth" or something more personal. Do not hold back. Identify the thought you want to project and manifest. Put your heart into it. Beam the thought in a continuous stream beyond boundary, without limitation. Synchronize that thought into your higher Self. Let your thought reflect and echo through your formless infinity. Put your mind into deep self-hypnosis. 15 minutes.

TO END: Inhale deeply and move your neck, shoulders, arms, spine and entire body. Loosen all the muscles. Exhale. Do this three times. Now lift the arms straight up and stretch the fingers tight. Continue stretching as you breath in and out. 2 1/2 minutes. Inhale deeply, suspend the breath for as long as you can and then relax.

Then deeply relax on your back for 15 minutes. Let everything go. Relax with a gentle gong or uplifting mantra music.

Hints for Practice and Mastery

This potent meditation sequence uses self-hypnosis. We entrance the mind's attention into a single thought or projection. This is the foundation for developing your basic creative and intuitive abilities. It clears the way, beyond frustration, and aligns you with your focus.

Yogi Bhajan's comments on this meditation:

> *"We are trying to get into self-hypnosis. To put yourself under a hypnotic trance is very essential. It is very curative for the person doing it, not for anyone else. Meditation gives you this capacity. A good meditator can totally switch his or her gears to put themself in a self-hypnotic trance. They can then act effectively to deliver the goods. This capacity is a requirement of meditation, it's not a gimmick. That's why if you have the strength, grit and projection for this, then understand you do not move your Self and at the same time you move the entire environment. In older times someone would say, 'Yeah, that person will be there.' Another person asked, 'How do you know they will be there?' The reply was, 'He will be there!' They were certain and beyond frustrations because in their meditative projection they had already locked into that person. We have to understand life like that. I don't know how you live without this meditative capacity. Without it, I know you miss and crisscross many things in your life. It's unbelievable! We must develop our intuition to lock in the totality with our projection."*

First secure your posture and the pattern of your breath. Recall that each breath is the gift of life; that each breath gives you a choice. The breath represents the energy of life and the movements of life. The movements of your body, cells, thoughts and feelings all flow with the rhythm, depth and pattern of your breath. When you control your breath you interrupt the automatic impulses and projections of your mind. You can become immediately, if only temporarily, conscious and in command.

This meditative process requires your full involvement. Direct your mind and touch base with the zero point—neutral—shuniya. Then filter your thoughts. You pull up thoughts and feelings and open to them freely. They may be pleasant or unpleasant, relevant or irrelevant, but you stream them through the filter of your consciousness and the point of shuniya. Finally as you become crystal clear you can project a creative thought and create a future.

Do this meditation with an attitude of gratitude. Do it confidently, knowing that when you focus your mind and clear your conflicts and depression, you can make an impression on your own infinite consciousness and locate your Self amid all the distractions, temptations and confusions.

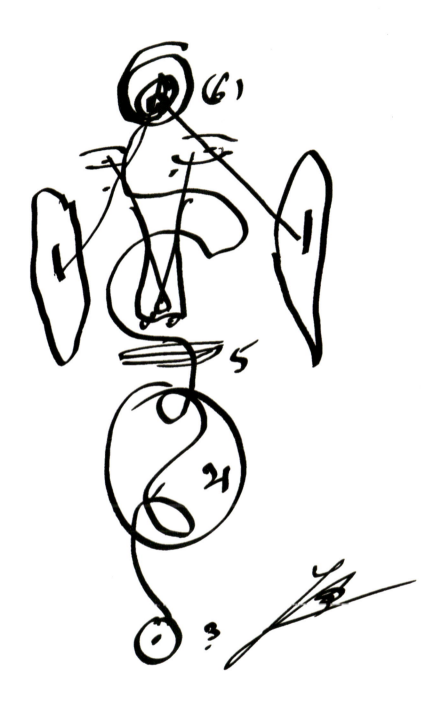

Your inner flow begins. You focus at the sixth chakra by looking at the tip of the nose, where the two channels of breath come together. Your jappa and breath synchronize. The navel energy flows upward and awakens the fourth chakra, the fifth and finally up to the sixth. Body and mind come together. You can command and project through the other chakras from the agiaa chakra.

We are now ready to realize the presence of the Higher Self within us. The first four stages have cleared the way and quelled our inner conflicts. These next three stages—focus, absorption, and experience and crystallize the Self—build our primary contemplative virtues and make way for the crystallized Self.

Stage Five
Focus

Focus

Without all the distractions what you focus on gains a finer grain.
You start to get into the mantra.
Your attention stays on its energy and character.
You start to feel its projection.
You can sense its virtues and qualities in you.
Your feelings have more detail.
The implications of each action and thought seem transparent and stretch ahead of you like trails into the horizon.

Stage Five: Focus

The first of these three stages is Focus. This stage represents a profound deepening and shift in our meditation. In this stage the control of the breath and use of sound creates a flow of energy from the Navel Center to the Heart Chakra, then upward through the Throat Chakra and finally to the Brow Point. The Brow Point is the command center—the base of the Sixth Chakra. From there we observe, project and command all the other chakras. Focus is a potent partner of the Sixth Chakra.

The word focus should be understood: Focus is when the mind dwells voluntarily on a realm of the senses, the domain of an object or on the sensation of the Self. Focus does not connote force of any kind. It does not imply suppression or fighting in any manner. Rather focus emerges as we allow the thoughts and feelings that arise to pass through. If we entangle ourselves with them, fight them, they only become stronger and more resilient. In that tangle we lose focus and we lose our clear sense of self. Effort is not the way. Instead, focus is gained by gathering our attention, energy and love around something and letting go of everything else. It is not attachment. It is not habit. It is right effort.

When we chant a mantra mentally or out loud and synchronize it with our breath, we become neutral. We stop chasing the passing thought; stop being enmeshed by the compelling emotions of subconscious memories, dreams and fantasies. Mantra becomes the fulcrum to our meditation, adding power and elevation to our focus. The steady pulse of a mantra allows the full spectrum of thoughts to creatively and safely pass through.

Focus usually means attending to a selected area of concern, filtering out other thoughts so as not to be distracted; yet welcoming those thoughts and feelings, no matter how disparate, if they relate to, illuminate or mature the focus we've selected. Our mind gains an alert nature; alert to the implications, sequences and consequences of our thoughts, and lets us know when something degrades our focus, lowers our value or takes us toward actions and consequences that are not congruent with our goals or our identity. Practicing focus cultivates the facility to follow our intuition and to act with expertise and ease. When intuition is activated, we move with little effort and we trust the outcome, without trying to control it. With focus and intuition on our side, we remain true to our Self. If we find we're not reaching the results we intended or we are acting out of character, our mind sends a signal, and we get to make a choice. In this way, we can navigate our lives from a place of truth and not be carried away by our own whims and subconscious agendas.

> *"Sixty percent of the time it is your subconscious personality that persuades you into action. Forty percent of your actions start with some conscious activity. Out of this twenty-five percent are direct biases, prejudices, and beliefs. Only fifteen percent maximum is initiated and directed by the conscious mind! Now if you understand this classical division of your personality and mind, then you have a chance to improve. Then it is required that you learn to meditate on one thought. From that focus all your subconscious patterns should be very correct, supportive and righteous. We call that an alert nature. What is an alert nature? Alert nature is well defined in psychology. Alert nature is a subconscious pattern of behavior, a deep training, which gives you a warning before you even begin the sequence of actions that will give you specific consequences. We also call it your intuitive nature. What is an intuition? Intuition is a premeditated awareness of any sequence you want to pick. It doesn't mean positive or negative; it is basically as neutral as energy. Energy is neutral, creative energy has no bias, it can create anything. So your inner happiness lies in your mental training. In your mental training, your inner happiness comes as you harness the sixty percent of thoughts and actions which are from your subconscious mind."* [33]

Focus requires training. The mind will always need training. As we relate to a focus, our alert mind gives us signals to notice what we would normally have missed, to open to the unfamiliar, to see anew that which is habitual and to check the unintended consequences of actions that we start.

When the mind streams its many thoughts, we often wonder if we are failing. Shouldn't we be thinking about nothing? Focus is much more active than that. There are meditations where the focus is zero or nothingness, but when thoughts arise, as they will, we process them. We stay present. We develop the neutral, conscious witness and see the thought, emotion or action for what it is. We experience its impression, or sensation, but we also sense all the connections and implications of each thought so that we can discern and select the thought(s) we want. Ultimately, we open to the interconnectedness, the oneness, of all things—the Ek Ong Kaar.

> *"Suppose I find a thought, that is, a desire deep in me to rob a bank. Two things could happen: either I should really go and rob a bank or I should get rid of this desire. Otherwise there is no way out. I will be stuck on that desire, compelled to act in some way or be distracted from what I am actually doing. For a yogi it is very easy. He or she will sit down and stab the desire to rob the bank: 'All right, which bank? Why? Who is going to participate?' He will rob that whole bank in*

Stage Five: Focus

meditation, pre-robbery! At the same time the yogi is using the mantra and the controlled breath, which cuts down the reactions right along with the thoughts because the bij mantra is repeated on the breath. In meditation, with each inhale and exhale your bij mantra runs. Let the thought go free. If instead you let that thought settle in you and you react to it, then it will never leave you and it will prime your subconscious to act instead of you. A bhogi† has to release himself with a positive polarity or with a negative polarity instead of becoming neutral. Positive polarity is the future; negative polarity is the past. Or the release is through fantasy or the opposite side of the coin, a life of dreams. The mind has to work hard in a dream and that upsets the nervous system totally. Dream is a very heavy process. But if a yogi has the same thoughts as in those dreams but he meditates with the breath, then he will go through it, let it go, and not worry about it at all. His breath is there, in and out, Saa Taa Naa Maa, Sat Naam, 'The bank I'll rob, so and so will go with me, I'll ask such and such people to convince me, buy the rifle, we'll time it like that, I saw that thing . . . the whole thing from beginning to end.' His mind will go through it but be alert, present and not get caught. You will be the cleanest personality and you will be the happiest being. Try this with any desire or wish. Once you meditate, focus and put any desire through this test, you cannot re-desire and react to that at all; you may try your level best. That's the only difference between a yogi and a bhogi. These are very important things, deep, deep, down in your life."

In order to accelerate the inner development of the Self we need to bring the two major channels of the breath together. They must synchronize and balance. We use the breath and the mantra to allow our thoughts to pass through instead of reacting to them or diverting them into our subconscious.

---

† someone tied to the emotions, without a meditative mind; this quotation is a continuation of the one on page 104. See footnote 33.

Praan Naadi Shabad Guni Kriya

November 20, 1973

POSTURE: Sit in Easy Pose or Lotus Pose, with a straight spine, and apply Neck Lock.

MUDRA: Place the right hand into the left with both palms facing up. Connect the thumb tips and press them forward. Hold the hands in front of the chest at the level of the solar plexus. The elbows are relaxed.

EYES: Fix the eyes on the tip of the nose. With each pulse of the breath, mentally focus through the Brow Point at the root of the nose. The eyelids remain 9/10ths closed. Fixing the physical gaze on the tip of the nose creates an automatic pressure and a convergence of praana flows at the Sixth Chakra.

BREATH: On the inhale, divide the breath into six equal segments. In six equal strokes fill the lungs completely. Each segment is a distinct inhale, sharp and conscious. On the exhale, divide the breath into two segments, two strongly whispered breaths through the mouth.

Stage Five: Focus

MANTRA: On the inhale mentally vibrate Sat Naam with each of the six segmented inhalations, Sat Naam-Sat Naam-Sat Naam-Sat Naam-Sat Naam-Sat-Naam; on the exhale, whisper Whaa-hay Guroo; first exhalation Whaa-hay, and second exhalation Guroo.

TIME: 31 minutes

TO END: Inhale deeply, suspend the breath as you focus your entire energy through the Brow Point. Then exhale through the mouth powerfully. Inhale again as you stretch the arms up, suspend for 10 seconds, and then exhale. Repeat this twice. Relax.

Hints for Practice and Mastery

The effect of this meditation relies on attending equally to the breath pattern, which regulates the praana and meridian flows, and to the sounds of the mantra. It is this synchronized combination of breath, sound and rhythm that gives such power to Kundalini Yoga Kriyas and Meditations. On the segmented inhalation, it is as if the sound of the breath whispers the sounds of the mantra. Focus on hearing the sounds. If we hammer the sound mentally, on top of the breath, it can seem like there are two separate flows of sound. Instead, the relaxed steady focus of this meditation should feel as though it arises from a single source of awareness. Focus, as a stage of meditation, is not about effort; locate the sensation of your Self and give your full attention to the sound, in its gross and subtle aspects.

Stage Six
Absorption

Absorption

Lost in the mantra, self-consciousness fades.
Attachments and fears drop away.
With your limiting beliefs left behind you enjoy the
present. The moment becomes unique.
A time and space like no other.
You experience the mantra as one Infinite ray of your
Being, a small universe in itself.
No longer foreign its qualities are part of you.
You need nothing.
You are satisfied.
You dwell with it as if you are in the presence of
someone you love.
You begin to sense what is real.

Each negative thought is changed to positive. Each gross is changed to subtle. As you hold the positive it becomes multiple positive. It awakens feelings in the body and the head. As you absorb it, is processed through all the chakras. You absorb, adjust and direct that energy in totality.

The process of absorption is all about our ability to transform, learn, acquire virtues and co-create with the universe. The efforts that characterize the struggles of the first five chakras are transmuted and their energy informs the subtle flow of the higher chakras. As our meditation process deepens, we begin to recognize and engage all the negative thoughts and impulses from the shadow self, which seem to challenge and oppose our intentions. But now we see them not as something foreign or outside ourselves, but instead as a part of our own larger process; we view them with compassion. We no longer respond to them with anger and defensiveness. Each negative thought, each gross thought that impels us to act with force or from ego, is synchronized with our higher, intuitive Self.

Stage Six: Absorption

Force is replaced with the power of our totality. Absorption into that totality changes everything. In each fragment of our mind, we feel the One who gives us the thought, not just the thought alone. We feel the creative energy that composes the qualities and characteristics of the thought, and we use those components to increase our own lightness, energy and flow in each and every part of the body.

The Navel Center and the Brow Point become completely attuned to each other. The force of the navel transmutes to the power of the Third Eye. Identity and intention combine to project a thought in partnership with the Unknown. The throat center is the crucible, the point of transformation and transmutation. Long Sat Naam is the sound that vibrates and switches each thought to a higher frequency. As we chant, that elevated energy begins to embody and pervade every cell. Our sensitivity is magnified. Everything is amplified by the energy that comes from the spontaneous flow of our real Self, our totality.

At this stage, every effort seems effortless. We become absorbed in the formless aspect of the Self. As we fully embrace all parts of our experience within a single awareness—as One Awareness—the conflicts between all the perceived parts of the Self begin to fade. What was once a dark shadow, an opposition, becomes a support. This is a central idea in yoga and meditation. The works of Patanjali discuss it in some detail:

> *"Many writers who have written in English about yoga have translated samaadhi as trance. But trance is not the correct equivalent in English. Just as medical science and engineering science have their own technical terms, similarly spiritual science also has its own special technical terms. Trance means an unconscious state but samaadhi, which one gets in yoga, is not an unconscious state. One remains conscious and that consciousness is in his control. So for that reason its correct name is spiritual absorption. It's one type of absorption. The mind is spiritually absorbed. In the first chapter Patanjali has described samaadhi or absorption. In the second chapter he has written the means to achieve that."* [34]

Much of the work of Patanjali as well as the commentaries on his work describe the gradual training of the mind in order to enter a stage of spiritual absorption, which can be described as follows: With the barrier of ego removed, our consciousness uses the mind to stay centered on a stream of thoughts that dwell in a single domain of experience so the reality of what exists is realized. Simple, right?

Absorption relies on focus but takes us beyond the action of focus and into the object of the focus. Absorption eliminates the boundary between the object and you, them and us, now and eternity. Opening this space of experience prepares us for the final stage wherein we can crystallize a sense of Self that is authentic, unique, and though finite, finely attuned to the Infinite.

The meditation for this stage can banish depression and energize us. It builds our caliber so that we can project our Self to conquer and attain things. To do this we have to have a crystal Self, a Self that is energized, clear, relaxed and non-conflicted. The hidden self in us, the oppositional self that projects negative thoughts and clings to the power of maya and ego, must be cleared out. We need to chew it up and turn it into energy, which can be used for the presence and projection of our subtle Self.

When we become crystal clear, we easily absorb into and merge deeply with our higher Self. It is then that we begin to experience flow. Flow requires focus, which we cultivated in the last stage. Flow, when combined with absorption, allows us to become aligned with our own Self and our witnessing consciousness. If we are fully engaged in what we are doing, effort becomes effortless. It is like jumping into the current of a fast moving, deep river, it carries us without effort if only we would dive in. In this meditation, we dive into the deep river of our being.

The first part of this meditation requires intense effort. It uses a powerful deliberate chopping motion, which stimulates our nervous system. It challenges our capacity and provokes our caliber. It strengthens our resilience so that we can be present and whole under the pressures and distractions of life. Then we expand our energy and our mind with a sequence of praanayams that open up the energy channels (the naadis) and release the power of the chakras. As we increase our alertness and elevate our energy, we can clear out the flow of negative thoughts and break the hold that our grosser dependencies have upon our consciousness. Our capacity for directed absorption empowers us to replace those dependencies with the power of clarity and the presence of Self.

Finally, we immerse into the fundamental bij mantra, Sat Naam. Its sound and quality has the power to balance the chakras and refine our sense of Self. Meditation into the sound current of this particular mantra invites us to merge into our own Infinite Self. It invites us to experience the horizon with each step we take; to honor our purpose in each decision we make; and to feel our own heart within each person we love. Absorption lets us release the struggle with the finite sense of Self and allows us to embrace our formless unbound Self. Sound conquers the thoughts more elegantly than breathing alone can ever do. Breath expands and energizes us, giving us an energetic lasso to reach a new frequency of emotion and thought. The sound current, or naad,

Stage Six: Absorption

and absorption into its subtle pattern of energy makes us co-creators of our bodies, our minds and our Self.

You and your unknown become known to each other. Deep meditation, absorption into naad reshapes the aura, radiance and projection. This simple effective kriya is an opportunity to attune the mind to the Self, your crystalized, subtle Self.

For Absorption in the Crystal Being

July 31, 1982

PART ONE

Sit straight with an erect spine. Place the palms together in front of the chest. The base of the palms is at the level of the diaphragm. The hands move in a powerful chopping motion—from Prayer Pose in front of the Heart Center rotate the mudra until the fingers are angled down, below the solar plexus, then back up—the elbows and arms stay very stable as the hands move. The eyes can be open or closed.

Interlock the thumbs to stabilize the mudra. The motion is powerful; it should feel like an earthquake. The hands do not separate even though the movement is forceful and fast.

The breath is driven by and synchronized with the hand motion. Inhale as the hands rotate upward, exhale as they go downward. The pace is similar to Breath of Fire, and the motion is steady and strong.

Continue steadily without slowing or decreasing in effort for 7 minutes.

TO END: Inhale deeply, press the palms together in Prayer Pose at the Heart Center. Suspend the breath gracefully for 10–60 seconds. Do not strain as you hold the breath. Suspend the breath, be still and be completely alert and steady. Suspend and then release it in a single strong stroke. Repeat the breath suspension two more times.

PART TWO

Sit straight. Extend the arms out to the sides; elbows are straight; and the hands are flat and stiff with the palms face up. Concentrate at the Navel Point. Begin a powerful Breath of Fire, moving the Navel Point strongly.

Continue for 3 minutes. Continue this mudra throughout the following exercises: Part Two through Part Seven. Move immediately from one praanayam to the next.

PART THREE

Keep the same posture and begin Cannon Breath through an O mouth. Breath of Fire through the mouth is equal in and out and puts pressure on the cheeks, lips and throat.

Continue for 3 minutes.

PART FOUR

In the same posture, begin Breath of Fire through the nose; move the Navel Point. Continue for 1 minute. Then inhale deeply, and suspend the breath for 10-15 seconds.

PART FIVE

In the same posture, begin a conscious, steady, slow, long deep breath through the nostrils. Keep your mind focused on the breath, its path and its energy. Trace the path between the Navel Point and the Brow Point with the inhale. Guide the breath from the Brow Point down to the Navel Point on the inhale, and from the Navel Point up and out the Brow Point on the exhale. Synchronize the breath to connect the gross and subtle elements.

Build a feeling of strength and expansion. Be fully present and alert. Continue for 5 minutes.

PART SIX

Keeping the same posture, inhale deeply and suspend the breath. Consciously find your hidden self. Provoke the parts of your subconscious and your sub-personalities that oppose your intentions. Find the commotional parts of your hidden personality that have their own agenda, their own flow of limited, negative and ego-driven thoughts. Consciously become aware of it; feel it; visualize it. Let the power of your suspended breath chew it up, break it up and swallow it. Then exhale powerfully and with the exhale clear out those thoughts and feelings. Release them and use your energy for your own intentions and purposes. Continue this visualization; clear it all out. 3 Minutes.

PART SEVEN

Continue the same posture, breathe in deeply and suspend the breath. Hold it lightly. Visualize your Self like a clear perfect crystal. You are full of light. You are clear in all directions. Gradually sense the light filling all areas in and around and through you. Any area of your body or aura that is tense, relax it. Any area that is dark, fill it with light. Expand the light in all directions at once, as far as your mind can go. Radiate simultaneously in every direction.

In a single, focused thought, dwell on your purpose, intention and commitment. Then exhale completely and rapidly inhale again. Continue to meditate in this way. Become a perfectly balanced crystal of light. Feel wholeheartedly present, strong and devoted to your intention.

Continue for 3-5 minutes. Then inhale deeply. Stretch the arms up and shake the hands and arms.

Stage Six: Absorption

PART EIGHT

Sit in a comfortable posture, spine straight, with an attitude of relaxation. Put your hands in your lap; the right hand on top of the left, both palms facing up. Touch the tips of the thumbs together. Close the eyelids or keep them 1/10th open.

Feel every bodily sensation, small or large, pleasant or annoying, elevating or grounding, passing or steady. Sense the skin, the entire surface area of your body. Once you have fully allowed the sensations of your soma and brought them into your awareness, imagine you are a yogi with a body that is so vast, so expansive that it contains all the planets, stars and galaxies. The universe and its many forms of being are like cells in your vast body of light. Let your mind absorb the feeling of this vastness, that your body is so full of light, and so vast. You are transparent. Absorb the universe and let it absorb you. It is a mutual existence.

In the vast ocean of consciousness that you are, sense the vibration. There are waves of sound. There is a naad that constantly creates. As you absorb into that subtle sound and merge into its essence, you and the cosmos, you and God, you and your infinite Self are blended. You are the manifestation of that Being.

In this hypnotic trance, meditate on the sound of the Bij Mantra: Sat Naam. Absorb into the sound deeply to feel and hear its subtle dimensions and flow. Take a deep breath. Breathe all the way into the navel. Then chant:

Sa-a-a-a-a-a-a-a-a-a-a-a-a-a-a-t Naam

Sat is steady and extended. Naam is short. Sat is a full sound, vibrating from the chest, the skull and at a moderate to high pitch. It should feel like a projection to unlimited horizons. The complete mantra is chanted at a pace of about four repetitions per minute.

Continue for 31 minutes.

Flow into the sound. Let your Self be alert and at the same time completely absorbed into the sound. Savor the flavor of your creative being.

TO END: Inhale deeply, suspend the breath as long as is comfortable, and then exhale. Do this three times. Then relax for several minutes.

Hints for Practice and Mastery

Although there are several parts to this meditation process, it has a strong internal structure and a single integral syntax which takes you through the process of change and refinement of your mind. Do each part from a place of stillness within yourself. Witness the changes that naturally occur with each step. To absorb into any sensation or quality that you choose is a primary capacity of the mind. When directed to the sense of your consciousness or to energetic qualities in your experience, this absorption helps you overcome the pull of the mind toward emotions and attachments. When this stage is mastered you easily select and direct the projection of your mind.

Absorption centers you and opens your perception like a panoramic window. As you meditate, note each thought that vies for your attention and allow it to pass through as you stay present.

The arms are held extended to the sides for a long time in this series. This is an opportunity to experience how mental absorption can relieve physical discomfort. If you react to the initial discomfort of holding the posture, it will only increase and endure. If you acknowledge it, choose to accept it, relax your muscles and shift your attention to your breath, to the infinite source of your breath, it will dissolve and be replaced by a stable, calm experience. You may even enjoy it.

STAGE SEVEN
Experience and Crystallize the Self

Experience and Crystallize the Self

Deep within lies the wellspring of intuition.
Wisdom and awareness arise within you.
At last an experience of what is real.
You have touched your Self.
With new clarity attained, your reactions cease.
The past is gone, no longer an issue.
The future to come, no longer a threat.
The present to be, aware and alive.

Consciousness, heart and passions of the sex organs and lower chakras all act together. You can feel you as animal, human and angel. You are present and can feel the reach and the containment of you. You are very awake, very human and open to experience.

The final stage of this first journey is essential to being human, being happy and being prosperous. The crystallized Self in Kundalini Yoga is not the ego and despite the name, it's not a fixed thing like a rock or a tree either. It is a dynamic creation of all that we are. Our personality and persona are only parts of the Self, which hold our projection and our sense of integration. But the Self is equally informed by the formless and unknown aspects of our being. The center of gravity of our psyche, the Self, is a concept which constantly changes; it's in constant flux. Clarity of Self depends on our state of consciousness, which chakra we primarily live from, and our level of development and maturity. This stage of meditation crystallizes our sense of Self at our current level of development. It becomes the base on which we develop further. It has elements of the formless and the timeless, as well as the easily recognized parts shaped by our memories, relationships, activities and thoughts.

Stage Seven: Experience and Crystallize the Self

From the Self we can witness, experience, assess and direct our actions. It is the fulcrum on which our consciousness acts effectively. The first job of meditation is to "conquer the mind." We must command the mind to act with us and for us. Otherwise, on its own it simply operates automatically and mechanically, running about in all directions. With the Self, the mind serves to help us claim our true identity.

Meditation helps us reclaim our foundation. It invites individuation—the Self as a realized human being. It recognizes the Self and empowers us to act as a purposeful agent in our own lives and in the lives of others. However, the Self is not an object or a thing, it is a dynamic reality that leverages our consciousness to act through form from our formless Self. Yogi Bhajan repeatedly explained that the changes of the coming Age could easily overwhelm our sense of Self. The Aquarian Age, globalization, and the maturity of the human psyche, beyond its adolescent impulses, will challenge our core sense of Self along with all our current ideas. In the extreme he saw our failure to confront the times with an intact and solid sense of Self as leading to a pervasive "cold depression" and an "info-dementia" that would detach us from our core identity and from humanity. On the other hand, the maturity that comes through this transition—either by our practice or by the passing of generations—will launch a new era of prosperity, creativity and collaboration.

The crystallized Self is critical to embodying our humanity and spirit beyond the constraints and confusions that religions and other political institutions have left us as a legacy. Through all of human history individuals have found a way to crystallize the Self. With that crystallized Self we can stand before the depth and mystery of our being and act with dignity, integrity and creativity. It is for that vision of humanity and the miracle in each individual that Yogi Bhajan shared the technology of so many teachers and from so many traditions. It is his gift to the Aquarian Age and our legacy to carry forward.

> *"The tragedy, which you are facing today as a human being, is going to end in the Age of Aquarius. It will be a mega-facet, multiple-conscious conception, a projective society formed by people. If you won't fit in, either you develop to that level or you get lost. Which religion will survive, which won't survive, I don't know; I have nothing to know, it is not worth knowing. There is no need to waste time. Which human being will survive, which will not survive, which will take whatever comes to him and still stay sober, conscious, and intuitive? Will you have an applied intelligence to have an answer, or will you be emotional and commotional? In you is the most pure essence of God; you all contain it in a very*

dormant manner. Some people call it nectar, some will call it Allah, some Yahweh, some call it God, some call it kundalini; it is called many things.

"Actually all you really have is a personal concept and experience of the infinite and God. Practically, God is your Self. When, having millions and millions and millions of weaknesses you still survive and sail above it, that is the character of the Self. Normally you say you can't control a situation, you can't control an environment, you can't control a relationship, you can't deliver anything! Having two hundred million weaknesses and feeling all the fears of the planet and feeling totally rotten to the bottom of the bottom, if you still rise up and chant 'Hamee Ham, Brahm Ham' that is what God is." [35]

When we begin to crystallize the Self, we gain perspective on our egos and emotions and open the heart to being human. In that humanity we embody whatever God is; whatever spirit creates. Up to now, we have been able to avoid the responsibility and potential implied by the coming shift, but it can no longer be avoided. The coming Age is no longer on its way—it is here! Crystallizing the Self is an essential step toward maturing the elevated human consciousness, which is needed and required to move forward in prosperity and peace.

In this next process, which is a longer meditation, Yogi Bhajan emphasized that effort and discipline are necessary in order to crystallize the Self. We get a sense of the Self not by letting go of all effort or responsibility, nor by isolating ourselves from the outside world. Instead we find it in our awakened consciousness, through action, alertness and in community with others. A solid cycle of 2½ hours churns the Self out from the emotions and ego like butter is churned from milk.

Opening the Heart Center is the key to the culmination of this first journey. The mantra, Hamee Ham Brahm Ham, is ideal for that. There are many mantras that work on the Heart Center. The sound "Ham" and the sound "Hoo" are used in many wisdom traditions. The mantra we are using is complete. It has a tantric structure embedded within it. Hamee Ham is earth; it is the sense of Self we get in our connections with other people, places and things as well as our own self-reflections. "We are we." It affirms our total interconnection and confirms the source of our authenticity, which is that same connection. Brahm Ham is the heavens, the ether and the subtle aspects of our Self. "We are God." It is the formless creative witness within us; the part of our existence that is beyond the rational, it is the ineffable reality of our being. Combined they act like a heartbeat: existence-nonexistence, personal-impersonal, part-totality. The energetic form and flow of this mantra works the Heart Center, Navel Center,

Stage Seven: Experience and Crystallize the Self

throat and Brow Point together. They act as a harmonic chord that engenders sensitivity to the Self within the body. This mantra crystallizes the experience of the Self and the God embodied in our uniqueness.

> "You never understand religion; you have to understand by experience. After you visit planet earth, where do you have to go? The beauty is that once you realize, from your visit to planet earth, where you have to go, you don't need to go anywhere! That's the beauty of it. That is the salvation. That is realization. 'Jeevan mukt hoye so jiva.'† Then the problem is solved.
>
> "First thing that is a problem is that we don't believe in God; we don't believe that God is with us and within us. Second thing is that we do not know where His house is. Where does God live? Does anyone among you know? Realize by experience that God lives and you can hear Him. It is the beat of every heart. You don't have to do anything so that your heart beats. It has a subtle sound: Hamee Ham, Brahm Ham, Hamee Ham, Brahm Ham.
>
> "That sound is always and ever. We created this music to match up with that inner music—that is mantra and the naad. Why do we always want to imagine things beyond us; imagine distant heavens in order to understand what our soul is hearing. The heart is the instrument which sends the vibration and message: Hamee Ham, Brahm Ham; Hamee Ham, Brahm Ham; Hamee Ham, Brahm Ham. That is exactly the sound which you can hear. Spend some money and take a stethoscope and put it on your heart. Listen alertly for a few minutes. You will be surprised to find that your heart chants; this guy chants continuously for your whole life.
>
> "Someone said to me, 'Sir I meditated for two full hours!' I said, 'So what? The heavens fell? Your heart not only meditates, it chants harmoniously and its flow keeps you alive.' What a friend we are to the heart. We never listen. A doctor listens to another's heart but needs another doctor to listen to theirs! Listen to your heart and in this chant realize God with you and in you." [36]

Yogi Bhajan shared his experience of the transcendent Self as immanent within our form, soma and presence. We don't need to imagine or fantasize about what the heavens are or are not. We don't need one religion over another. We need only a crystallized Self, one that can experience itself and ultimately transcend itself.

---

† Trans.: You are liberated, realized while living in your Self.

Transcendence is part of what nurtures our uniqueness and matures our spirit. It also supports our form, the vehicle through which we experience everything in our lives. A crystallized Self is an integrated sense of Self that operates from stillness, openness and awareness. A crystallized Self makes room for compassion; and that compassion begins with your Self. Compassion allows the whole Self to become present: all the parts that we affirm and all those we don't; all the parts we know and all those we don't. Opening the Heart Center is the first step to being fully human. Transcending the animal nature and realizing our human dignity means we can direct our passions by tapping into their qualities and energy in order to serve our consciousness. The first sign of an open heart is the ability to recognize our own emotional patterns, our automatic behaviors, and step back from them, even when they feel intense or seem just and right.

> "We are going to talk today about the Heart Center. The story of the Heart Center is very funny. A majority of the time people do not know anything about it. They know it has some petals, some energy, this and that; you can read that in books and I leave that to you.

> "What is this fight between heart and head? An open heart center means warmth, compassion, passion, kindness, hatred, anger; everything which is wonderful in the world and everything which is rotten on the planet. They all come through the Heart Center. If you set your heart on something, your head will give in, that's why it is the most powerful center and extremely dangerous. On the other hand, this is the only center worth living with.

> "It has a physical side to it. On the physical side of it, you have a heart, its electromagnetic field is its own, you can put a pacemaker in it and still you can help it to beat for you. This center is very enduring. It is made of two parts. One is physical muscles and nerves. It pumps the entire blood and nurtures your every organ. It is responsible for getting back and supplying your lifeline and it works constantly until it gets tired and says goodbye! The other one is its electromagnetic nature. It is one organ which has its own electromagnetic wavelength and composition.

> "There are a million words we use for this heart. We say, 'Open your heart.' 'I hate you from the very bottom of my heart,' now what will you do with the top of the heart? I don't know. 'My heart goes out to you.' There are millions of expressions which relate to the heart, but we still mess up our life mostly because of that same heart. This is because this center controls passion. Any time passion is not controlled for use by consciousness and human intuition, it will bring destruction.

Stage Seven: Experience and Crystallize the Self

It's a law which I can't change. Mind you, I am not against passion! But ninety percent of pain in your life comes from passion that is misused. That pain does not come from your compassion. Without meditation, ninety percent! You have no intuition with your passion either. Passion you must have; but passion minus intuition is nothing but self-destruction, period, there is nothing more to it.

"You start condemning yourself. Sometimes you overleap with your passions. This magnifies human miseries. It can intensify and magnify quickly and seem that people have gone lunatic.

"Now it's a common thing to say, 'Have compassion, be compassionate to others.' What is your understanding, your realization? What are you trying to do by saying that? It can be a very stupid thing to do. If you ever want to be compassionate, first be compassionate to yourself. You shall not understand another person's feelings and behaviors accurately, intuitively, if you are not compassionate to yourself, period. Others can handle their life. It is your life you are supposed to handle—and that is called the dignity and divinity of God. You are connected, but your friendship won't last, your relationship won't last, your marriage won't last, if you do not have both passion for life and compassion for the Self." [37]

When Yogi Bhajan initially discussed this project, he sketched the diagrams that accompany each stage. The *tantric* sketch (see page 125) which captures the feeling and process of this stage is simple and exact, and shows the wholeness of the experience of the Self as a large circle or oval. Hanging down toward the earth are genitalia that represents the gross passions, instincts and feelings we all have in common. They are the connection to life and the natural world. Slightly above is a spiral, the energy of the navel center and our normal consciousness as earthlings. We are creatures of a creator and we live practically. Above that is a face. It is the angelic touch within us. It is feminine and creative compared to the lower symbols of masculine genitalia. It is consciousness. It is our inner witness. The sketch shows that all these areas work together as one, as a crystallized Self; we are contained, content, conscious, creative and sensitively intuitive in our actions. As he put it, "You are present and can feel the reach and the containment of you. You are very awake, very human and open to experience."

The following deep meditation series is powerful. Respect it by doing the deep relaxation afterward for at least 31 minutes. Then take some time to notice your own experience and share it with others. Do not leap into activity, work or play, and especially don't leap into your car!

The series forms a complete cycle that guides the kundalini energy and the aura to open the Heart Center and establish Self-recognition. A sequence of mudras is used to direct and synergize the effects of the mantra through the chakras. This first step is essential to later stages that express the Self in action and that mature the experience of the infinite Self. As Yogi Bhajan used to say, you need a coin to cross the river; that is, there is always a toll, a price to be paid. That price—that coin—is a well-developed and integrated sense of Self, which we can later mature and transcend. Once the Self is crystallized in the Heart Center and we consciously allow self-compassion, then we can begin to fully engage the world, our bodies and minds, and other people authentically.

Meditation Series to Experience and Crystallize the Self[†]

Becoming the Sound Current

POSTURE: Sit in Easy Pose or Lotus Pose, with a straight spine, and apply Neck Lock. The spine must be erect, with the chest lifted, and the lower spine tucked slightly forward to create a perfect effortless posture.

MUDRA: Gyan Mudra, thumb tips touch the tips of the index fingers, resting over the knees.

EYES: Focus through the Brow Point at the root of the nose. Eyes are either closed or 1/10th open.

MANTRA: Hamee Ham, Brahm Ham; translated We are We, We are God.

Chant these powerful sounds; they will alert you and connect you to your Heart Center. Your task is to open your senses to every feeling that the mantra awakens in your body, emotions, and thoughts. Attend to the more subtle aspects of your aura and arcline as well. Simply attend to the sound of the mantra. Keep your mind on the sound, the space it creates, the flow of the tongue's movements and the way the sounds resonate at the lips, brow point, chest, heart and navel. Hear the sound as you produce it. Listen to the subtle energetic echo of the sound throughout your body. Gradually establish your sense of Self as a witness. Be present. Be aware of your own awareness; sense the flow of all your sensations. Notice when you are present and engaged and when you drift. Experience the mantra directing the flow of thoughts. Experience the stillness becoming intensified and relaxed in the center of all that you are.

[†] Instruction given to a group of clinical practitioners in Los Angeles in the 1970's. The instructions for this meditation are from the contemporaneous notes of the author and could not be verified by KRI Review.

Stage Seven: Experience and Crystallize the Self

You can meditate on the meaning of the chant. The words remind us that we are interconnected, one with all we know and all we don't know. Just as the heart circulates blood and nutrients to every cell, the sounds of this mantra are the heartbeat which circulates the healing praana and consciousness throughout your being. As you relax into the subtle form of the chant, you will notice waves of openness, relaxation, connectedness and healing.†

You see all that you are: the plus and minus of your personality; the play of light and dark of your karmas; the constant shifts in your environments and relationships. The mantra builds your compassion for your Self so that you can be whole; it allows your Self to be and to BE. Go deeply into this chant; partner with your Self.

TIME: 31 minutes.

TO END: Inhale deeply and suspend the breath for 10-20 seconds. Release it. Repeat three times. Then sit absolutely still for one minute. Sense your presence. Sense your sensitivity. Allow all the motions of the universe to come to the shore of your stillness. Move immediately into the next meditation.

---

† Use track 2 on the "Humee Hum Brahm Hum" recording specifically created for this process by Gurucharan Singh Khalsa and Gurusangat Singh.

Open Lotus Heart Meditation

POSTURE: Remain in the same seated posture.

MUDRA: Bring your hands into an open Lotus Mudra in front of the Heart Center. The base of the palms come together. The first digits of the pinkie fingers and the thumbs touch their corresponding fingers along the sides. The remaining fingers are straight and spread open, much like a lotus in bloom. The palms face each other are open to the heavens.

EYES: Focus at the tip of the nose.

MANTRA: Continue chanting the mantra, **Hamee Ham Brahm Ham**.

Many feelings will pass through you as your Heart Center strengthens and old wounds begin to melt into the sound current; once hardened parts of your heart and old defenses will begin to drop away. Trust yourself. Immerse yourself in the presence of the open heart. We are most aligned with our real Self when we have the strength to stay open and connected to all people, everything and everyone in the universe. It is in this connectedness that we realize our uniqueness. Be real and be present as you chant and dwell in the sound current.

TIME: 31 minutes.

TO END: Inhale, suspend the breath and exhale three times. Sit absolutely still for one minute. Sense everything. Then move your shoulders and arms or massage each other's shoulders for two minutes to prepare for the next part of the meditation sequence.

Traatik Dhyan to See the Unseen

POSTURE: Sit in Easy Pose or Lotus Pose, with a straight spine, and apply Neck Lock.

EYES: Focus your eyes straight ahead. You will see a triangle within a triangle.

MUDRA: Bring the fingertips of each hand together, with the palms apart, making a teepee. With the fingers pointing upward, curl the index fingers and the middle fingers downward between the palms so that the backs of the first and second digits come together. Keep the thumb tips together but bring them down so they are parallel to the ground and pointed toward the body. Raise the mudra 6-8 inches (15-20 cm) in front of the face, so that the tips of the ring fingers are at your Brow Point and the tips of the little fingers are directly in front of the eyes. The thumbs will be at chin level.

This mudra represents the subtle within the gross. It represents the opening of intuitive communication, seeing beyond the surface of things to its causative flow. Psychologically it adjusts the conscious persona with the subconscious temperament and impulses. The two fingers that are curled downward represent the connection to the earth, to the impulses and feelings that normally dominate us. They are seen within the triangle formed by the thumbs and the curled fingers, which represents stability in the turbulence of emotions and feelings. The upper part of the mudra combines with the lower part to create a tantric balance of polarities. The mudra itself is neutral. It forms a lens or gateway to sense the presence of your dynamic real Self amid your many roles and activities.

Stage Seven: Experience and Crystallize the Self

MANTRA: Continue chanting the mantra, **Hamee Ham, Brahm Ham**. Ideally, we slow down the sound current, using track number four on Gurusangat Singh and Gurucharan Singh's new CD *Humee Hum*. Be fully present, mentally absorb yourself in the sound and sense your Self and the gradual dissolution of the barrier between you and the focus of the mudra.

Keep the mudra still. Do not close the eyes or let the arms down. Establish the mudra, and then relax the shoulders so that you can hold it with as little tension as possible. The wrists are flat and the elbows are relaxed, not lifted, and make a larger triangle. If the arms feel tired after a few minutes simply stay still, focus on the mantra and let it pass as you stay present to all the sensations and energy this mudra evokes. This is a *traatik* meditation, a meditation with eyes fixed and gazing. The mudra creates the form that focuses the gaze, which brings energy to the Sixth Chakra. This completes a connection between the Heart Center and the Sixth Chakra, which makes you steady. From this stillness within the crystallized Self, you become a witness through the eyes of your unique Self rather than becoming dissembled by your actions or the emotions they evoke. You can feel and do everything and still be present within the Self.

TIME: 31 minutes.

TO END: Close the eyes, inhale deeply and suspend the breath. Visualize the mudra; penetrate beyond the finger tips to the formless, which gives the fingers its tips. Briefly dissolve yourself in your infinite Self. Then exhale through the lips. Repeat this three times. Then inhale, stretch the arms up, opening and closing the fingers. Relax the breath. Run your palms from the brow in a downward motion, one smooth stroke over the heart, a few times.

Relax in silence for 10 minutes. Stay in silence. Stay present.

Meditation of the Two Teachers to Balance Karma

POSTURE: Select a partner and greet each other. Then come to silence as you face each other in a meditative posture.

MUDRA: This mudra is the polarity of the Traatik Dhyan in the last meditation. Bring all of the fingertips together, pressing their corresponding fingertips, with the palms apart, to form a teepee. Curl the little finger and the ring finger inward and down between the palms with the backs of the first and second digits together. Point the mudra toward your partner; keep the wrists straight. The forearms are at the level of the solar plexus. Touch the tips of your middle fingers with your partner's. The touch is light but certain. The thumbs point upward, pads together.

EYES: Fix your eyes toward your partner and gaze steadily. Become very still, with an alert attitude, spine straight and chest lifted.

MANTRA: Continue chanting the mantra, **Hamee Ham, Brahm Ham**.

Stage Seven: Experience and Crystallize the Self

TIME: 31 minutes.

TO END: Inhale deeply and suspend the breath. As you hold the breath close the eyes and see as though the eyelids were not there. See beyond the surface of what you see. Use your heart to feel all. Then exhale powerfully through the mouth. Repeat this three times.

Then inhale and stretch up. Thank your partner. Without music stand up and move your body. Shake, stretch and move; move and dance authentically. Distribute your energy to every cell. Keep the atmosphere of the meditation and the mantra. Move for 3-5 minutes.

The two teachers are traditionally represented by the extended fingers. The index finger represents Jupiter, which teaches through knowledge, expansion and opportunity. The middle finger represents Saturn, which uplifts and gives perspective. It teaches through discipline, focus and the correction of pain or karma. It grinds your ego to a point of precision and strength. They are extended and connected through the Saturn tip in this mudra. Old karmas and new opportunities are moderated by the compassion of the Heart Center in this lovely meditation.

The Heart Center gives us the gift of Self; the sensory perception to recognize our own emotions and witness them from the still center of the Self. It gives the capacity to express love beyond fear. As it connects us with our Self, we can connect with others as well. As you deeply meditate with this mudra, many relationship karmas will adjust. When you are authentic and present in your Self, your relationships reflect that. Relationships that you experienced or handled in a manner that occluded your sense of Self or entangled you in a haze of commotions flow through this timeless moment of meditation. Relax into the flow of the sound. Be real and be present. The sound and the mudra will guide the change. There is no need to try. Your awareness nurtures the Self as you distinguish between ego, emotions, reactions, memories and authentic presence, the voice from your heart.

Heart Seal Meditation

POSTURE: Sit in a meditative pose.

EYES: Closed; focus through the Brow Point.

MUDRA: Bring the hands to the Heart Center. Cross the right hand over the left, in the center of the chest. Feel your heart beat. Keep the chest lifted slightly.

MANTRA: Continue to chant the mantra, **Hamee Ham, Brahm Ham,** using track four of Gurusangat Singh and Gurucharan Singh's Humee Hum.

TIME: 31 minutes.

TO END: Inhale deeply, suspend the breath and press the hands firmly on the chest. Exhale in one powerful stroke through the mouth. Repeat three times.

In this meditation, seal the sense of your Self at the Heart Center. Sit still and consolidate your Self. Welcome the unknown infinity of your being and synchronize with every action, thought and cell. Meditate and become aware of all sensations. Become aware that you are aware; aware that you are present and observing; aware that all that flows through you is not you; aware that you are created and creating in this moment; aware that each moment records your thoughts, acts and feelings as a ripple in infinity and for eternity. Before this vastness, become humble, joyous, contained, content and conscious. Rest in simplicity; practice alertness, with a full heart, and bless all. Bless your Self; bless your friends and enemies; bless all that is known to you; bless all that is unknown. Be clear, crystal clear.

Stage Seven: Experience and Crystallize the Self

Deep Relaxation

After this meditation series, relax deeply. It is required to relax for 31 minutes.

Lie down on your back. Relax each part of your body. Feel your Navel Center, Heart Center and Brow Point. Gradually relax your mind into a positive uplifting vastness. Go beyond being. Let go of all effort. Listen to a gently played gong or relaxing mantra music.

SECOND JOURNEY
The Expressive Self

Stage Eight
Rasa

Rasa

Life becomes juicy.
No longer flat, it is three-dimensional.
It sparkles with energy.
You sense the beauty and the many flavors of life in every situation.
That "Rasa" is healing.
Your one-pointed concentration activates the higher glands in your brain to release,
optimizing neuro-chemicals.
Those special chemicals are called "Amrit," the nectar.
That supports the feeling and energy of Rasa.
You have no doubt.
You do not suffer from a lack of meaning.
You are clear, certain, involved and awakened.

The first four stages of this second journey are all linked. Each contributes to changes in energy, awareness and mindfulness that together create a stable base for the remainder of the journey. The word, *rasa*, has a long tradition in both yoga and Ayurveda.† Rasa means essence; it connotes the juice of something as you begin to process and digest it. When rasa is used properly it becomes rasayana, an element that rejuvenates the body and mind. The highest form of rasayana is generated from meditations and kriyas that stimulate our own glandular and cellular secretions. This inner elixir is called *amrit*. In mythology amrit was known as the "water of life," or the "fountain of youth," created in the beginning of the world, the elusive nectar which bestows immortality. Yogi Bhajan frequently referred to amrit and rasa in a more practical way. He said amrit and rasa are natural secretions that can be cultivated; however, they require the optimal functioning of the pituitary, pineal, hypothalamus and frontal lobe, and originate from the raised vitality of all the cellular and nervous functions. When this inner nectar flows we are less reactive and impulsive; and we respond from an elevated consciousness. In this sense, the rasa simply opens us up to the delight of life and to the perspective which produces maturity, wisdom and grace.

† An ancient and well-respected healing tradition in India

Amrit opens up spiritual insight as well. With amrit flowing we naturally feel and act from compassion; we don't talk about it, we live it. This stage of meditation transforms us both physically and mentally. It balances the flow of life in our body and mind. To enter into this deep stage of meditation, we must stimulate the glands, align the body and then beam the mind; and meditate on the Self as a vehicle for the infinite flow we are all a part of. Once this inner aliveness and purification are established, we can use our own inner rasa, or juices to heal others. We become rasayana—rejuvenated. And with this renewed energy we are ready to fully express the Self. As rasayana, our creative presence will heal; our radiant energy will uplift. In this way we fulfill Yogi Bhajan's words: "Your presence should be a healing."

Traditionally, rasa included working with the properties of metals. Mercury represented changeability; and even today you hear people say, "He has a very mercurial nature," meaning unpredictable. And although mercury is a poison, in Ayurveda it was used in small amounts in many different formulations. *Rasa Shastra*, an ancient text, described two major categories of elemental transformation and rejuvenation: alchemy and rasayana. Alchemy described how to transmute mercury and other elements into gold. But it also alluded to inner transformation. Rasayana was the use of food, herbs and healing techniques to rejuvenate the body and mind and increase longevity. Both approaches were explicitly spiritual in their invocation of the grace of God.

Over the years, Yogi Bhajan shared many Ayurvedic formulas for rejuvenation and the cultivation of rasayana. He personally tested them and identified those he believed in. He included them in the herbal products he promoted and in the daily lifestyle habits he taught. From Yogi Tea to the traditional *chyawanprash*, he emphasized the need to stimulate all the rasas of the body in order to be healthy and to support our meditative practices and personal saadhana. His gift to all of us is the experience of healing as a natural process available within each of us. When our rasas are balanced, and the amrit is flowing, our radiance can induce a state of self-adjustment in ourselves and others. That is, if we first meditate on our Self and balance our own energy, then expand our sense of Self and practice a conscious, contented, neutral awareness, then we can heal others by word, look and touch. He called this process Sat Naam Rasayan when it was done through expanded awareness; Healing Hands when it was done through touch and somatic adjustment; and blessing when it was done through prayer. After working on Stages Eight and Nine, explore the praxis of healing with another practitioner. Experience what it means to heal through our presence, through our touch and through our prayer (See pages 410-411 in the Appendix.).

We will use a sequence of three separate kriyas to work on this stage of meditation–Rasa. In the first kriya, we meditate on the Self and establish an open state of sensitivity and balance. We become alert and maintain a steady awareness of every cell of the body, fiber of the aura and field of sensitivity. In the second kriya, we stabilize the ability to beam the mind and to hold steady under the flood of thoughts and feelings that come from our Self, our environment and other people. In the final kriya we stimulate the Seventh and Eighth Chakras (the aura) and the higher glands as we break the limitations of ego and impulse. We use the Guru Mantra (Whaa-hay Guroo) to guide the mind into an expansive state that drops the ego and in a simple, sacred way erases the pride and vanity that is often a major block on the meditative path to an authentically expressive Self. These three kriyas build on each other and are to be practiced in this stage as a seamless sequence. Move directly from one kriya to the next without any breaks.

Meditation Series for Rasa

Invoking a Meditative State

February 26, 1979

POSTURE: Sit in Easy Pose, with a straight spine, and apply Neck Lock.

MUDRA: Make a solid fist of the right hand. Raise it to shoulder level with the forearm vertical and the palm facing forward. Raise the left hand up so that the forearm is vertical. Extend the left wrist so the palm faces upward and the fingers point to the left. The fingers are straight and the palm is flat.

Consciously hold the hand positions. The left hand will tend to relax from its position, but keep it steady. Honest effort will bring the best results.

EYES: Look at the tip of the nose

BREATH: Long, slow deep breath. Inhale and exhale consciously, with control. On the exhale, suspend the breath out as long as you can, with the Navel Point pulled in firmly and the diaphragm lifted. When you can no longer hold the breath out, and before you experience any strain, inhale deeply and slowly. Continue this breath pattern.

TIME: 11 minutes. You can gradually extend this time to 31 minutes to deepen its effect.

TO END: Rapidly inhale and exhale twice (2 seconds inhale, 2 seconds exhale) and then inhale, and suspend the breath for 10 seconds, stretch both hands up and tighten the body. Exhale and relax.

Hints for Practice and Mastery

As you hold the breath out become absolutely still. Feel the spine as a staff of light that extends to infinity and attracts the flow of the whole universe and the blessings of all the saints, yogis and healers. The key to this meditation is the pressure that arises when the systematic breath combines with the polarity established in the mudras. It initiates the pulsation of the sixth chakra, and the pituitary, and we become more intuitive. The two hands create a cross flow in the ida and pingala. The steady gaze at the tip of the nose holds the mind. Stay consciously conscious and open the feeling of space and equilibrium in every cell and part of the body. Anywhere there is tension release it. If there is tension, fill your body with energy when you inhale and go into a neutral, content and contained state as you hold the breath out. Consciously let go of any tension, block or fear in the body. The upper glands will gradually adjust and you will go steadily into a deep meditative state.

Stimulate the Chakras

December 20, 1999

POSTURE: Sit in Easy Pose, with a straight spine, and apply Neck Lock.

MUDRA: Place the fingers of the left hand on the forehead. Align the fingertips up the center of the forehead. The little fingertip is on the Brow Point at the base of the nose, between the eyebrows. The other fingers stack upward on the midline. The thumb rests naturally on the side of the head. The fingertips touch lightly without any additional pressure. Extend the right arm forward from the shoulder with the palm facing left. The arm is straight and parallel to the ground.

EYES: Closed

BREATH: Breathe slowly and deeply. Meditate silently. Focus on the energy and flow of the breath throughout the body and at the Brow Point.

TIME: 11 minutes. The time can be extended gradually to 31 minutes for individual practice or when teaching.

TO END: Inhale, suspend the breath for 5-10 seconds then exhale. Inhale again and suspend the breath, then exhale. Then inhale and interlock the fingers, suspend the breath 10-15 seconds as you stretch the interlocked fingers up over the head. Stretch up and pull up the spine. Then exhale and relax.

Hints for Practice and Mastery

Focus first on the posture. The extended arm often feels heavy or painful and the mind protests the idea of holding steady. Instead, do not move the arms at all, and focus on the breath. Make the breath steady, slow and gradually deeper as you continue. This long deep breath will stimulate the Brow Point and relieve the sensations of pain. You will transcend the pain as the glands secrete and the rasa is balanced. You will develop a sensitivity to stay steady even as your thoughts begin to jump.

The left hand is the heavens and the right arm is extended to the earth. Your consciousness processes both through your awareness. The steadiness that comes with this meditative state is the healing state. We are all experiencing the pressure of this highly connected Information Age. The information from the body and mind of the person you heal or bless disturbs your own body. This meditation creates a steadiness and a stillness that releases all those reactions and serves as a lever to shift the energy toward wholeness and healing.

Because this is the second kriya in this sequence, the meditative space has already been established. In this meditation you begin to beam the mind. You create a profound stillness and within that stillness you focus and connect to anything you think about. As you open up to the flow of thoughts and sensations in yourself and others, that focus allows you to stabilize the space and dwell in consciousness. From this space, you can project a thought, connect to another person at a distance or, as a healer, induce a resonance within a person who needs your healing energy. Beaming is a basic skill that helps us reach our goals despite the pressures and distractions of life.

Haumei Bandhana Kriya

September 1, 1978

POSTURE: Sit in Easy Pose or other meditative posture, with a straight spine, and apply Neck Lock.

MUDRA: Make the hands into fists and extend the thumbs up. Bring the hands, palms facing the body, in front of the Solar Plexus. Relax the elbows. Press the pads of the thumbs together with a steady strong force.

EYES: Closed

MANTRA: Take a deep inhale and exhale completely as you chant, **Whaa-hay Whaa-hay Whaa-hay Guroo**, 4 times on the breath, in a steady monotone:

Whaa-hay Whaa-hay Whaa-hay Guroo

Whaa-hay Whaa-hay Whaa-hay Guroo

Whaa-hay Whaa-hay Whaa-hay Guroo

Whaa-hay Whaa-hay Whaa-hay Guroo

Stage Eight: Rasa

The repetitions are chanted on one breath. With practice this can be extended to 8 repetitions. We are using 4 repetitions as our base, which makes a rhythm of 16 pulses. To practice this meditation most effectively, listen to the sound as you chant it. Be conscious of the fact of speaking and listening. Speak each word distinctly so the lips move on the "Whaa" and "Gu" sounds. The pace is moderately fast: the inhalation and four repetitions take about 10-12 seconds. As your energy shifts and expands, inhale intentionally and remain alert; keep the rhythm and pace steady, with precision.

TIME: 22 minutes. In practice this can be extended to 31 minutes.

TO END: Inhale deeply, suspend the breath and mentally repeat the mantra. Then exhale. Repeat. Then inhale and stretch the arms up, open and close the fists. Exhale. Shake the arms and hands until the fingers relax.

Hints for Practice and Mastery

If you're feeling stuck, this meditation un-sticks you; it frees your spirit. It breaks the normal, everyday bondage of your ego, which constrains the consciousness and over time, limits your awareness and narrows your perspective. When bound to the ego, your rasa reflects those emotions. Driven by wave after wave of attachment and impulse, you gradually begin to think of yourself in those terms. The finite sense of Self then obscures the unlimited possibility that is always within us—the infinite.

We acquire *haumei*, that sense of egocentricity, without any effort. Haumei means reliance only on what we know, what we want, what we control and what we have. This reliance on ego, on I-ness and My-ness, blocks the sense and experience of Thou. We foolishly think we can walk, without the foundation of the earth to walk on, or that we can breathe, without the spirit of the Infinite giving us breath. We do not trust our own infinity; we do not know our own unknown. We falsely believe that we must know how something works before we can rely on it. But of course this is impossible. We rely on the unknown every day; our hubris simply blinds us to it. The ego believes we are not connected to All; it feels we must rely only on our Self and not allow the hand of God or the touch of the unknown. Yet, Spiritual Teacher after Spiritual Teacher has told us that we can have a strong sense of Self and still be humble and delighted by life.

A core spiritual insight is that every human being is inherently valuable and shares the same Creator and inherits the same creation. No matter how accomplished we may be, our normal experience is limited, finite and narrow. We cannot know or sense the infinite and be complete within our Self without some form of devotion, surrender or love. The infinite within us competes with the finite within us. The ego battles to make the infinite finite, for even in surrender we compete: who is the most devoted, who has the greater surrender, who has sacrificed more. This basic blindness, error and ego create so much suffering. We cultivate one rasa, one taste, over all the others instead of finding the One Taste in all tastes; we experience the gross rasas but miss out on the subtle, the bliss of the amrit. This meditation helps break that bondage. Yogi Bhajan said:

> *"Nothing disturbs me, because all those negative things that you tell me do not exist! I know this by experience. When you talk negative things to me, [I know that] they do not exist in you, they exist in your ego, in a separate pocket. Ego is not you; it was given to you to exist. Yet you have totally left your Self aside, and you have totally put ego in the forefront, as you; that is a misplaced identity.*
>
> *"We'll talk under the concept of misplaced identity and the contract of consciousness in conscious life. I am going to pursue this series slowly and gradually so that you can understand through the virtue of knowledge that God is, God was and God is what shall be.*
>
> *"To get rid of haumei, the mantra for meditation is Wahe Guru. There are millions of mantras. Nothing else can work for that.... Haumei Bandhana Kriya is a very, very sacred thing that looks very simple but it's very powerful. Well, the time has come when the change of Time has to be recognized. We recognize that the change of Time means that people will not survive with only the facets of their beliefs; they need to live by the facets of their experience. In the Piscean Age, we knew it, we lived it, and we believed it. Out of our beliefs we continued. Unfortunately that era is over and now is the Age of Aquarius. The Gods have changed; the Heavens have changed, and now life will go by the test of experience."*

In the Sikh tradition the concept of *haumei* is frequently addressed. It is seen as the root of many human problems for without it we can easily find contentment, confidence and courage. In the Sikh scriptures, the second of the ten masters, Guru Angad, wrote about this:

> "SECOND MEHL: This is the nature of ego (Haumei), that people perform their actions in ego. This is the bondage of ego, that time and time again, they are reborn. Where does ego come from? How can it be removed? This ego exists by the Lord's Order; people wander according to their past actions.

Stage Eight: Rasa

Ego is a chronic disease, but it contains its own cure as well. If the Lord grants His Grace, one acts according to the Teachings of the Guru's Shabad. Nanak says, listen, people: in this way, troubles depart. || 2 || PAUREE: Those who serve are content. They meditate on the Truest of the True. They do not place their feet in misdeeds, but do good deeds and live righteously in Dharma. They burn away the bonds of the world, and eat a simple diet of grain and water. You are the Great Forgiver; You give continually, more and more each day. By His greatness, the Great Lord is obtained." [38]

In this same tradition, the Sufi saint, Kabir, reminds us that the hours of meditation, and the efforts we put in to create a deep experience are essential. "Mere words achieve nothing; one finds inner peace only as *haumei* flees." [39]

Haumei is normal and has within it a path to its own balance: recognize that the One that gives you your Self and your bliss also gives you the ego. Go beyond the gifts and the challenges to the infinite oneness, which is the giver of all.

Please see *Witness Your Consciousness from Within Your Self on page 402* before moving on to Stage 9.

STAGE NINE
Delight

Delight

Delight is more than pleasure.
It is the charming attractive force of pleasure.
In delight you enjoy your own pleasure.
It is a rapture that holds your attention without effort.
Like a dancer who enjoys the dance and
the act of dancing.
Like a dancer who is grateful to the intelligence
behind the dance.
Your mind is aware and enjoys its
own awareness.

When the realm of pleasure, the sex organ and feelings, reaches up to the cosmos and becomes vast, there is nothing but delight. Pleasure without fear, spontaneous and fulfilling your reality is everywhere. Below you gather the thoughts and let them flow precisely and powerfully to the central channel. Every thought blooms and gives many seeds. What a spring-like delight.

This stage of meditation is about the way we attend to pleasure. Do we find pleasure in sensations from things or do we find pleasure in the expression of the Self? Can we sense the flow of the Self in the act of creation? Can we feel our vastness and enjoy the pleasure of existence without fear? Can we consciously attend to the process of the Self so that we do not just feel a passing pleasure but a constant flow? Can we meditate and move ourselves beyond simple hedonistic pleasure to a point of delight? Can we savor our experience, not simply taste it?

To consciously initiate thoughts and feelings from the Self rather than simply reacting to thoughts as they arise is powerful. It makes us feel alive. Initiating our own thoughts breaks us free from the ruts and patterns created by habit; we experience a new freedom and a broader horizon as we quit reacting and instead, start expressing from within the Self. All our pleasures begin within the Self. We manifest our own joy, no longer tethered by attachment or worldly sensations, we engage the neutral mind and grow more sensitive to the full spectrum and dimension of pleasure. We stay present to the Self and awaken the delight of life.

The experience of delight brings a natural though somewhat paradoxical and often unexpected outcome. We become more disciplined. We begin to align our consciousness with what we do. With all the pressures and distractions of our environments and our immediate emotions and sensations, we find a way to cultivate and express our authenticity and creativity. In fact, when we stop attending to life's sensory free-for-alls of pleasure and pain, cognitive discernment and discipline emerge naturally. Our minds attend to the pleasures of consciousness and engage in the meaning and connections of things. We become steady and embrace joy and sadness equally. We develop the meditative habit of being consciously conscious. No matter the circumstance, we embrace it with openness and sensitivity. We make space for it.

I once saw a chef taste soup. He first looked at it; then watched it as it was poured into a small cup. He swirled the mixture and observed its color, patterns and textures. He then took a few quick breaths through his nose to clear his senses and become present and focused on this moment. He then smelled it, taking in its aroma, without tasting the liquid. He smacked his lips and tongue as he let his feelings and reactions to the aroma settle in his mouth. Then he sipped it. Just a little, to alert his body to what was to come; then he quaffed the rest of the sample luxuriantly. He paused briefly. Then described every flavor, every impact on his palate, the variation of the taste over time, how it combined with all the other parts of the meal, and his energy and mood as he sampled it. He expressed the feelings that arose and what they revealed to him about the significance and meaning of the soup as a culinary creation and its relationship to the food culture of his particular city. This is a basic example of savoring. The chef's delight in the soup was more than in its taste. It was in the consciousness of tasting the taste. It was in the entire act of creation and the many layers of feelings and sensations that unfolded as he let the sample reveal itself under his full attention.

What if we did this with every thought? What if we could tell when a thought truly expressed our heart and served our intention? And what if we then matured that thought over time? What if our creative pleasure, our core sexuality, were engaged in the expression of our thoughts as co-creators with the universe? What would it be like to feel the flow of the universe without fear and to consciously select each thought and each feeling before bringing it into our central channel to travel through our consciousness and experience it as the Self? This is delight. This is the art of meditation, which is creativity at its highest octave.

At this stage of meditation we are often misdirected by the collapse of delight into simple pleasure-seeking or pain-avoidance. Neither creates freedom in the Self. When we chase those sensations instead of cultivating our capacity to savor our own experience of consciousness, we create duality, which in turn creates tension and splits the mind and the Self into us and them, mine and yours, ego and spirit. That inner split is what the yogis called fate. Our ego, like a shuttlecock in badminton, is bandied back and forth between the polarities. We cannot avoid the polarities, but we can keep them from falling into duality. Fate is an uncontrolled duality, while destiny is a controlled duality in which your consciousness guides you. Destiny is not a fixed destination but a true course, a North Star, which guides your consciousness to its fullest expression and development. When we create these dualities within the Self, we become the source of our own limitations. Because the split Self doesn't allow us to use the full creative capacity that is our birthright as a spiritual beings; instead we operate on partial power, flawed insight, and dimmed fragments of the mind. The culprit is of course the mind itself. Untrained, it is reflexive and reactive and like a dog will follow any scent. Without consciousness and the development of the frontal lobe, we become hypnotized by our own activities and the environments we find ourselves in. Too often people experience profound insights when they practice contemplative techniques but don't have the resources to apply them to their daily lives. We become angels at the retreat but remain devils in the world. This stage of meditation stabilizes our identity and our ability to attend to the flow of life, to our creativity and to our destiny.

Experiencing and mastering delight is essential to a fulfilled life. Yogi Bhajan spoke to this important stage of meditation:

> *"Kundalini Yoga gives you what you call 'the delight of life.' You can have life but you may not be delightful about it. Every human must understand and recognize that they must have an identity and each identity must have a status. A person who doesn't find his Self, his identity and his status, it doesn't matter how rich he is or how poor he is, he is born and dies in vain."* [40]

> *"The fact is, in the beginning we were, now we are and always we shall be in the same spirit. Wherever we are, we are born to conquer time and space. We are born to bring delight, happiness and grace to the human race. There is no goodbye."* [41]

Stage Nine: Delight

The ability to experience and share the delight of life is independent of status and circumstance. It stems from our depth and dimension:

> *"The delight of life is in the life. Not in your games, not in your fame, not in your name; in the light of you, in that light. It is to experience that spirit, that humble little thing in you. When the psycho Self marries the psyche Self is when Self is born.*
>
> *"That normally happens through bhakti—devotion. But with status and accomplishment, sometimes they become so rigid, they are trapped in their own cobweb and never come out of it. If the Self has no rhythmic logic, no realistic reasons and no flexibility, humility and flow, then it is dead."* [42]

In this stage of meditation we awaken delight. We use our attention to savor the experience of our Self in all its subtlety. We dwell in the stillness, feel the openness and guide the creative focus with the mantra. We experience delight as we recognize the creativity of the Self in every action and in the actions of the universe at large as if they were our own.

Delight is to be a light of the Self. It is the experience of God; divinity embodied. Living lightly with delight in all that is—that is living to our fullest as a human being. One who can embody consciousness practically and intuitively is not limited by circumstance nor aided by cleverness or strategy. It requires only a fearless simplicity that connects with and accepts all that is.

The duality that separates our finite and infinite Self is removed by the flow and structure of the mantra, Haree Naam. The two realms become one in consciousness; things seem to run to us. We do not need to chase what we are already part of.

> *"We human beings are very weak because we cause the cause of duality in our everyday life. It is not something we want to do. But nobody tells us not to do it, so we do it. We have a body, we have a mind and we have a soul, three things; but we exist like a shell. That's your life. Like an oyster, you have muscles, you have a shell but you couldn't put the grain of discipline in it to make the pearl. It's a very sad story.*
>
> *"Now mind is infinite, body is finite. Right there is a rupture. If the soul and mind get together, then that's Infinity. Then you can bring the body along with it. In our rational thinking, we only understand the earth and earthly needs. We do not understand our heavenly needs. Without the touch of our infinite Self, the delightfulness in life is missing. And when light and delightfulness in life are not there, then there's a lot of pain.*

> *"You have to understand something. There is nothing more precious than you! There's nothing more precious than how you can enjoy within you your very you. It's a very fabulous gift! You worry about other things. You can keep on worrying but there is no solution in worrying; you can only worry. The solution is, when you relax and don't worry instead of trying to run after things. Keep going, but if you can, also sit and meditate and let things run to you."* [43]

When we do not recognize the source of our duality within our Self, our own inner split, when we continue seeking for Self without recognizing that the distance is created by our own fears, when we act from duality instead of our totality, we miss the delight of life. We miss the light that shows us the way forward. Our duality looms as a shadow between our sense of Self and our consciousness.

To experience the delight of our entire experience—our tattvas, gunas, chakras, Ten Bodies, mind, organs, glands, feelings and sensations—our meditation needs to be an alert, magnetizing filter for the natural flow of impulses and actions in our life. We hone this contemplative capacity again and again because we must be able to apply it automatically, when we are unconscious as well as when we are aware. We practice in order to attain an intuitive alert nature that abides naturally in all of our activities and that serves to express our consciousness and character. Mastery is when we experience this sense of delight both when our mind is focused as well as when we're simply allowing the unattended flow of thoughts and feelings.

> *"Controlled duality is called destiny, uncontrolled duality is called fate. Elephant is very good. It can bring the biggest log home and go where no machine can go. But when an elephant goes wild, my God! You have no place to hide. You understand what I am saying? Elephant is what an elephant is. Destiny and fate are controlled and uncontrolled duality. They are what they are.*
>
> *"The soul is Infinite. One is always one: Atma Amar Hai. Soul has no tragedy, no feeling, no facet, no contribution, and no retribution. That's why we say, 'Ek Ong.' The mind creates and shuttles between body and soul. Kaar is the physical existence and actions. So we say, 'Ek Ong Kaar.'*
>
> *"When you do not live to your status as a human, you are not human. The word, human, means this: Hue means halo; Man means mind or mental; being means the existence, now. Human means: You are a mental halo of the being now! That's your status. In other words, you are the light, so in everything which you do, think or feel, delight yourself! Light! Delight yourself in the light of it, that you are the light. That's one simple principle.*

"It's not: Oh, watch my muscles. Oh, look at my blue eyes. Oh, look at my money, look at my purse. These adjectives and attributes do not matter at all. So the waves of the brain, the thoughts and feelings, must be viewed by consciousness, tested by intelligence and executed under the total control of your own standard and status. Then you will have a state, then you will have an empire, then you will be the king of kings." [44]

Meditation for Delight, Destiny and Creative Flow in Life

September 25, 1978

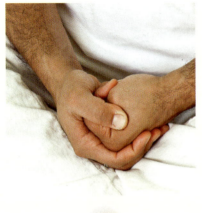

POSTURE: Sit in Easy Pose or other meditative posture, with a straight spine, and apply Neck Lock.

EYES: Closed or 1/10th open

MUDRA: Make a fist of your left hand with the thumb tucked inside the fist. Keep a firm but not painful grip on the thumb. Wrap the fingers of the right hand around your left fist. Lock the right thumb on medial side of the left fist sealing the left thumb and fingers. Rest the mudra in the lap, keeping the hands firmly locked throughout the meditation. This mudra is a tantra; it is a controlled combination of polarity that acts as a seed for the mind to become still and observe itself.

MANTRA: Inhale deeply and chant the mantra 3 times on one breath. It can be done in a monotone or a slight tonal variation. The pace is quick; lyrical or extended musical patterns are not appropriate.

Haree Naam Sat Naam Haree Naam Haree,

Haree Naam Sat Naam Sat Naam Haree

TIME: 31 minutes

TO END: Inhale deeply and suspend the breath briefly. Then exhale. Repeat this three times. Then inhale and stretch the hands up, opening and closing the fists. Exhale and relax.

Stage Nine: Delight

Hints for Practice and Mastery

With this meditation we cultivate our creative consciousness and savor the delight of the Self. Yogi Bhajan often said that without this sense of delight life is without taste. Kundalini Yoga and Meditation delights and awakens our sensory Self so that we can feel the subtlety, movement and expression of our own consciousness. Life is a challenge of distraction and diversion. We can better enjoy its variety and relentless change if we cultivate a consciousness and an attitude that controls the polarities, which create the texture of our life.

This meditation uses the Ashtang Haree Naam mantra. With practice you can immerse yourself into its rhythm and its breath pattern for 11 minutes, 31 minutes or much longer. As you master it, it can bring a state of delight, rapture and turiya.

The mantra is a perfect experience of flow and precision, creativity and discipline. It uplifts the mood. It counters the negative self-talk that builds up emotional fortresses of self-limitation. The hands are locked in a mudra that feels very contained and solid. During the entire meditation, the feeling is one of ease; it is a state of *sahej* or easy flow. There is no great effort. It is a rhythmic relationship, which has great impact, one breath at a time, like waves striking the shore.

As you chant stay aware of the sounds. Keep a sensitive field of consciousness and be alert to the subtle movement of energy and play between your still center, your soul, and your mind. Notice how the *naad* of the mantra constantly shifts the energy in your soma. Let go of any feeling of effort. Savor the sensation of consciousness and the feeling of each moment as it matures and blooms into full flower.

The practitioners of this mantra declared it a liberator. They said that even if your karma denied you a human birth, and you were to incarnate as a donkey, simply hearing this mantra in your heart would liberate you and elevate you to a human birth. As you enter deeply into this mantra, you reach a natural state of self-rapture. This is turiya, the ultra-consciousness; a state of total neutrality and awareness.

This stage of meditation sensitizes you to the rasa, the delight of consciousness itself. That profound delight orients you to act from your consciousness instead of from unconscious habits. Through graceful self-regulation you mature and authentically embrace each moment.

Please see *Healing, Mental Beaming and Delight on page 407*, before continuing to Stage 10.

Stage Ten
Politeness

Politeness

*You begin to reach beyond the small you.
You act beyond the boundaries established by the
beliefs and concepts you hold about yourself.
You gain the manners of consciousness.
You realize the reality of all other beings and creations.
Your mind does not stop at a thought about yourself.
It is just a thought.
You draw on the more fundamental reality of your
spirit and commitments.
You are deeply satisfied and self-sufficient.
Politeness is your capacity to act with automatic
habits that serve your consciousness and your
extended sensitivity in every action.*

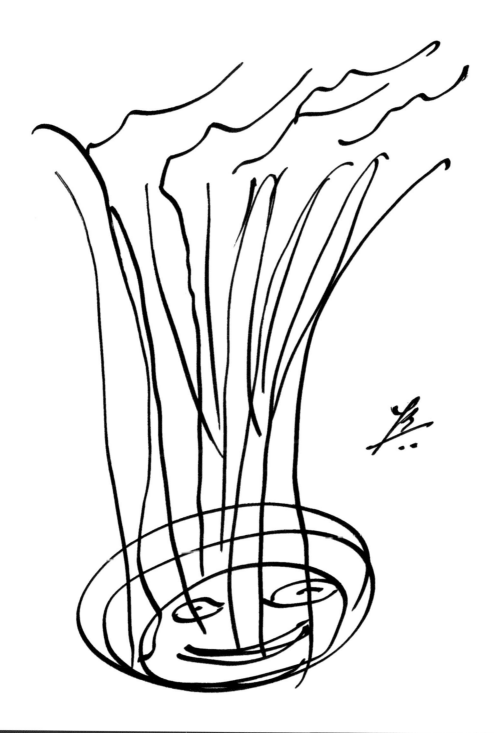

You are at the base of everything. Imagine the vast ocean of life. It pours into you through the crown chakra like a massive waterfall. You can feel the beginning, middle and end of everything. You act knowing every result and sensitivity. Politeness is respect of your self.

𝒜t this stage of meditation we expand our sense of connection to all things. We act beyond our self-imposed limitations acquired over the years. For beyond that finite Self is our identity—a conscious living truth—which we call "Sat Naam." Our identity is the truth of what is; and when we experience this identity, we are able to love all that is for it is no longer separate from us and how we experience ourselves. We break the ego's isolation. As we expand in consciousness, we must cultivate the manners and mannerisms that serve our status as human beings. We deepen our relationship to the traditional yamas and niyamas and act from a place of integrity. We become polite and never take advantage of anyone.

Stage Ten: Politeness

We establish our projection and our actions in our meditation. We understand that we are at the base, at the core of everything. We begin to sense the consequences and implications of every action. We realize in the most profound and noble way that politeness comes from a deep respect for our Self. We become gracious and committed to what we do. We act with politeness, which is supported by authentic direct communication. Without the clarity of who we are, our Sat Naam, politeness can be irritating and insulting. The other person senses our politeness as a game instead of a reality and they become defensive; their survival instincts will kick in. However, once our meditative stage reaches politeness then this gap between projection and reality vanishes and others will relax and sense our sincerity. Trust is established.

This stage of meditation fully integrates the connection between our core identity in consciousness and the vastness of life in experience. A solid identity not only gives us flexibility but also the capacity to be polite. It is a position of strength from which we can fully commit our Self, in action, relationship or discipline. Polite simply means nonreactive; to be polite is to take a non-reactive stance.

Meditative experiences are difficult to capture in language, but an image that captures the sensitivity and awareness of this particular stage is the vastness of the ocean. It seems unlimited. Driven by invisible tidal forces and stirred by waves and winds, it is filled with many forms of life and many types of people, and they are all interconnected. Each existence shares the ocean and creates waves that are sensed and responded to by others. In the same way, everything we sense pours through our crown chakra like a great wave. We feel the Self. We feel the beginning, middle and end of everything, every process, every life, every action, and every flow in the ocean. We act from our heart knowing our effect. We respect our Self and demonstrate our respect for others through equanimity and politeness even under difficulty or opposition. We act and speak for now—and for the future.

The practical behavior that accompanies this stage of meditation is conscious communication. Secure in our identity, we can speak straight but politely. We can confront someone without making war. We avoid slander and gossip because it lessens our own value as well as the others and dilutes our projection and intention. People often avoid speaking clearly and directly when trying to help someone. Without politeness, directness can miss the context, be misunderstood or get reduced to simple criticism and ultimately a fight. The strength we acquire at this stage lets us speak truthfully with confidence and kindness.

Teaching to women one summer, Yogi Bhajan explained, *"If a woman's mood is rude or crude you are automatically sixteen times minus; when you are bright and polite you are automatically sixteen times plus. So please understand your impact."* [45]

He also reminded us that the body and the mind are seamlessly connected. One always moves and shapes the other.

"If the tongue is sweet the world belongs to you. What does that do to you biologically? It keeps you young and healthy. Polite language gives your skin all the secretions and vitamins you need. If you are impolite and upset, your skin becomes rude, too. Try to understand. I am telling you the glandular game. When you talk rough and obnoxious it affects your skin which is the most sensitive organ and has to compensate for it. If the skin has to change cells faster than normal it won't change enough cells, so your skin will become harsher and rougher to the touch." [46]

Our mental habit, which we train in meditation, affects our health, beauty, alertness and vitality. The reactivity of the skin, as it blushes, sweats and shivers, embodies our connection to our environment and the responsiveness of our emotions. This stage of meditation expands our sensitivity and allows us to respond to everything in the world politely and with sophistication.

This stage is not strictly about the behavior we would normally call politeness. Instead it is about a discerning consciousness, the relationship between our core sense of identity and all the conditions and contexts of life. We are polite because we are real. We are polite because we maintain self-sufficiency and self-satisfaction. We can afford to behave politely because we are secure in our realized identity. We may have things to win or lose, but we act with integrity despite the outcome, and we handle any gain or loss with grace.

To activate this capacity we need vitality in order to be resilient and to act consciously. We also need an inner sound current that effortlessly supports our identity, roles and goals by connecting to the Infinite within us.

Sat Kriya Variation to Merge with the Sense of the Infinite

February 3, 2000

POSTURE: Sit in Easy Pose or Lotus Pose, with a straight spine, and apply Neck Lock.

MUDRA: Raise the right arm straight up. The palm is open and faces toward the left. The fingers of the right hand are spread open. The right shoulder is slightly lifted as you fully extend the arm upward. The left hand rests over the left knee.

EYES: Closed.

MANTRA: Sat Naam. Chant **Sat** from the Navel Point, pulling the navel in as you chant. With this sound, the diaphragm will lift, which automatically stretches the spine upward a small amount. As you chant, **Naam**, relax the navel and keep the spine steady and straight. Imagine the sound Naam is released from the Brow Point. Concentrate on your straight spine, and imagine that the upper hand connects you to the flow of the infinite.

PACE: Repeat this mantra in a steady rhythm of about 8 times per 10 seconds. Concentrate on the sound.

TIME: 31 minutes.

TO END: Inhale deeply, suspend the breath as you squeeze the muscles tightly and stretch the right arm up. Concentrate on the flow of energy along the entire length of the spine and through the Crown Chakra. Exhale powerfully. Repeat this sequence two more times. Then relax and move the shoulders.

Hints for Practice and Mastery

The energy that builds and is released from the Navel Point gradually fills the central channel of the spine. Create a steady rhythm and meditate from the base of the spine, up each vertebra, to the top of the head and unto infinity. Once that channel is established, merge deeply into the sound current of the chant. Simultaneously focus on your sense of presence and the sense of the infinite with equal intensity; an awareness will emerge that is neither. When you become present to all things and all things become present to you, the stage of politeness is yours.

In this stage of meditation you establish your self beyond a primary polarity of the mind—me verus nature—that separates us from everything else in the universe. You simultaneously become stronger in your sense of Self and more aware of your interconnection with everything that exists. You see how your creative thoughts and projections are mirrored in the world; we see what we are, what we project and what co-creates our reality. Through a nondual lens the world is organic, familiar and sentient. All that we see is a reflection of who we are and what we are part of. Politeness is an expression of that nondual experience. All the world is us and we are all the world. Or as Yogi Bhajan often said, "If you can't see God in all, you can't see God at all."

This is the state of *patantra*, where your projection is perfectly reflected in the universe. It has always been so, but you now realize it in awareness and reflect it in your actions and speech. Yogi Bhajan refers to this state of perception in this way:

> *"The universe has a law of equal projection. It is called, patantra, and it is a simple law. As you look into the mirror it looks like the object is outside. The mirror image is a reflection of equal distance: accurate and exact. If you put an object ten feet from the mirror, in the mirror it will reflect ten feet. That is true in your mind and the cosmos. Question is, if you desire something, either that can be fulfilled or it can't be. Nobody is desireless. Even to become desireless is a desire. So in the cosmic law of nature, God has created us in exactly the situation where we are equidistant from every thought, from every action and from every reflection."* [47]

As we encounter our own reflections in the world, let us be conscious and polite for they are simply a reflection of ourselves. Politeness is the manifestation of nonduality.

STAGE ELEVEN
Humility

Humility

When the rapture of the ninth stage mixes with the
polite receptivity of the tenth stage
it takes you beyond your own expectations.
It creates the eleventh stage.
You become very humble.
Guru Nanak, the great yogi and saint,
embodied and expressed this.
He saw the vastness of the Creator and
experienced that delight.
He said he felt as small as an ant.
He was happy to be even the dust under the feet of
those who walked to some sacred place to have the
chance to repeat the Names of God and be elevated.

Humble, here, means a lack of pretentiousness. You
have innocence from self-acceptance.
You need no distinction other than the reality of you as
a creature of the Creator.
Humility is modesty filled with the power of
innocence.
Guru Nanak and other saints realized
how much is unknown,
How much exists beyond the furthest horizon of the
mind's capacity to imagine.
In humility you can form a relationship to
that Unknown.
When that happens, you awaken the ability to teach,
heal and serve humanity relentlessly.
Your mind gains the fearless openness that comes
with true humility.

Humility comes when you use the rock (triangle) of wisdom to balance your perception, relationships and life. The seesaw of balance has the small ego, womb-like from earth, on one end. It has the greater ego, spiral and cosmos-born, on the other. Wisdom changes from the small to the large. When you are small you can only hear your own talk. You are petty. You don't hear the other person. Humility is a gateway to the vistas of Infinity.

Humility is the gateway to the vistas of infinity. The meditative mind that masters humility is unbreakable. Humility's gentle expansiveness and graceful receptivity is the vehicle to see the unseen. It gives us the capacity to open up to our intuition. Normally we are locked in our ego, which by nature is small and limited and which by habit, only sees what it believes (and believes only what it sees). It acts automatically and defends its routines. To see beyond the hoary walls of habit and ancestry we need humility. Humility takes us beyond our own expectations of our Self and invites the hand of God to bless. Through humility we learn quickly and profoundly. It is a state of immeasurable strength.

Stage Eleven: Humility

Cultures around the world rarely praise this virtue. Self-promotion is often seen as the only path to success and adoration. And yet, this is the secret of humility: when we become consciously conscious before our own infinity we are promoted without effort to heights we cannot even envision. Humility moves the horizon beyond the limits of our imagination.

As a meditative capacity, humility is so central to growth and transformation that Yogi Bhajan talked about it in his very first lectures here in the United States, when in 1969 he shared his vision of the future:

> *"The Aquarian Age, the New Age, is an age of truth and love; an age of tolerance and service. It will be an age of humility and equality. It will be known by a few things. The people who will cross into this age will not possess what they should not, and they will possess everything they should, but under no circumstances will they be possessed by anything. It will be an age where for the first time people will recognize God not as a person but as a primal truth and energy. The worship will change from a personified God to a relative, more subtle truth, that is energy itself. It will not be a solar energy or a lunar energy it will be a basic universal energy; the creative energy which is known as the cosmos."* [48]

Humility has nothing to do with passivity; nor does it give status or power to another over the Self. Instead, humility comes from putting the infinite above any status. When we are humble we see the God in all. We see the infinite in every finite. We realize that we all come from the unknown and go to the unknown; we all come from God and go to God; we embrace and honor who we are and express it freely, without hesitation.

We are all too satisfied; we stop short of optimal; we settle for what we know. Why? Because It diminishes our anxiety about the unknown and the fear we experience because of our lack of control. Humility takes us beyond what we know as we embrace who we are as human beings presiding over both finite and infinite domains. When we are truly humble we have the habit to bow, to surrender our finite self before our infinite Self. We become still in the face of awe; we delight in the free fall of the unknown, which restores our innocence and renews our courage. We are enraptured.

Humility is often defined negatively as meekness, self-deprecation or inferiority. That is not what is meant here. Instead, humility is the absence of arrogance, conceit, or the feeling of superiority over others. A more profound connotation of humility is an openness to what is: Are you humble enough to accept your light and your gifts and act on them without inner conflict and duality? Humility is a condition of the mind that lets us merge with another person; it is a merging with God.

"Practical humility or humility in action is not saying, 'humbly yours,' and then taking off the head of somebody. Humility in action is a stage of universal consciousness." [49]

"Your mind is clean, your consciousness is clean, your character is shining and radiant; and you have achieved the purity of humility. What is the nature and purity of humility? You become zero. Zero multiplied with anything makes zero. To receive knowledge and to become a vehicle of that knowledge, to promote and give it to others is called the continuity of God. That is a life which is worth something. That is called the purity of meditation." [50]

Humility is a central capacity that allows wisdom to guide our life instead of intellectual positions or ideologies, which only abstract us from our Self and disconnect us from each other. Humility perceives the subtle; it experiences the awe of infinity and sees beyond the surface of things; it is associated with the Sixth Chakra.

"Wisdom cannot come to you if the sixth center of humility and the fourth center of compassion do not work together in your personality. I don't care if you study Hatha Yoga, I don't care if you study Kundalini Yoga, I don't care if you study Raj Yoga, I don't care if you study at all. If your compassion and your ability does not flow and reflect your personality, you are a nut to begin and to end. You can intellectualize things or justify in your ego or with your power you can go on a trip, but that doesn't make any sense, in the long run you will be defeated without humility and compassion." [51]

"Nobody can be perfect in every aspect of life. But if you become intuitive and perfect and know everything, you cannot do anything except what is the humble way. So basically, ecstasy, wisdom, transcendent experience and success and all [those things] you talk about don't make any sense. It all depends on one thing—how humble you are.

"If you are very wise and you are not humble, you have no wisdom, because humility and wisdom cannot be separated. Divinity and humility cannot be separated. Infinity and humility cannot be separated. Because it's a statement of facts: God is the owner and God is the Infinite. The only Infinite. We are all part of that Infinity. Recognize the fact that you have in your life that Infinity which is in charge. That Infinity is such a vast Infinity that It Itself does not know how huge, big and what jurisdiction this Infinity is.

"Still you waste your time trying to know everything. The self-sensory system, which God gave you, doesn't need to know, it knows. In a feeble way it tries to let you know as well. You are not humble enough to listen to that feeble, humble voice.

Stage Eleven: Humility

> *"Death is as inevitable as life is. Passage of life is as inevitable as day and night is. But your commotions and reactions to life are inevitable and will kill you. You are not being genuinely humble enough to even let your wisdom exercise itself. A person who is not humble cannot understand the subtlety of the soul because he cannot understand the Infinity of the God.*
>
> *"You know, when you cannot tolerate yourself, you cannot tolerate others. When you cannot love yourself, you cannot love others. Because you are not humble, you are not vast."* [52]

This is a very important idea to understand within yourself. In Stage Ten we used Sat Kriya. Its power and effectiveness opened us up. Many of us feel we have to seek a great opening of the Third Eye, filled with visions, in order to signify a spiritual awakening. But those experiences can easily be misused and confused with imagination and subconscious dreams. Humility is key:

> *"The majority of you might be thinking it's good if the Third Eye is open. Do you know that it was open the very first day you did Sat Kriya? Do you know that? I know we never told you. If anybody can do eleven minutes of Sat Kriya right, absolutely all the centers, all the naadis and all the chakras are penetrated. Do you know when you chant Sat Naam with Sat Kriya you project your aura in absolute and radiant form. Your radiant body becomes one foot wider?*
>
> *"Then what is wrong? You expand your Self through praanayam and you come back to normal with pratyahar, meditation. The idea is that you should experience all greatness and still become humble as a human being. Then where is your problem? Your problem is when you cannot maintain humility. The problem is not in Shakti, the energy change. None who practices Kundalini Yoga has a problem with Shakti [whose energy is natural to us and within us]. Then where is the conflict?*
>
> *"The conflict is in humility. You cannot continuously maintain the humility. Why? Because as long as you do not experience the Infinity of God, your image is very limited; you hold the wrong image of yourself which you believe or imagine."* [53]

Humility as a state of consciousness is essential. When we chant the Adi Mantra, Ong Namo Guroo Dayv Namo, it is done in a state of humility so we are not limited by our own image nor inflated by our own need for recognition, aggrandizement or popularity.

> *"There are certain lines, which I cannot cross, excuse my handicap and I want to keep it the way it is. We do not initiate. We ask our inner being to initiate, we never, ever start a class, without mentally chanting or loudly chanting, Ong*

Namo Guroo Dayv Namo. This is one line we always begin with. In this Raj Yoga, Kundalini Yoga, the higher you are the more humble you are.

"Humble doesn't mean that you are timid. Humble means you are very strong, very courageous and always come through. Humility doesn't mean what you mean by humility. We are very humble that the impossible will be accomplished as possible. That's humility to us. I don't know what it is to you. To you humility is to lie down and let them take me away. No, that's not humility, that's cowardice. There is a big difference. Humility means there is nothing impossible in your life. Humility means you are humble before the light of God, and get the power to accomplish what you have to accomplish. When the call of duty is the beauty of life—that's humility.

"In the West, humility means giving up. In the West, surrender means defeat. In the spiritual scriptures, surrender means victory. I surrender to my inner will to accomplish when I have to. I take my personality, my commotion, my neurosis and put them to the side and do the job. Words have been totally misinterpreted here. Please understand that when we say we are meek that does not mean we are mean. Meek means we are accommodating, we are giving, we are comforting and we are enlightened. In spiritual language meek means only four things: We are humble peacekeepers." [54]

"I'll ask you once in a while not to play the game of your mind. Sit down, meditate and see clearly. Then you will recognize the strength of the mind and the soul behind the Infinity of the action. In your mind you know everything. You are very wise, very beautiful, but you do not know how to totally merge.

"The highest game which the Western mind has played with the Western man or woman is they do not know merger. They do not know the basic ingredients of merger, which is humility. You do not know how to be humble before God, you do not know how to be humble before Guru, and you do not know how to be humble before the Infinite and before truth. When you are not humble you cannot receive.

"Humility is not needed to show that you are weak. Your weakness is just that you have to receive the strength. Humility is to let the ego go and open the heart. Then you can receive the strength of God. It is humility which lets you open yourself to receive the ever living truth.

"The East has produced all the religions and created the timely stars on the horizon of spirituality. It is my best effort to come here so that tomorrow the West may break that tradition. We may be blessed with saints who have totally recognized mind to *relate to the soul and not the traditional tragedy of the Western mental intrigues which bring nothing but pain and impurity."* [55]

From this perspective everything that comes to us is part of our destiny and has been given to us so that we may experience it and mature because of it. The divine will and our will meet as one in humility. The feeling of separation and inner conflict only arise when we lack humility and demand control we can never truly have. Instead, bow and be still.

Almost every wisdom tradition has a discipline of bowing. The Christian tradition of genuflection has us bend a knee or bow to show respect in prayer. Buddhism uses prostrations to clear the Self and become zero; put aside all things and become present; show respect to the Buddha, the teachings, and the sangat. Bowing is integrated into the prayers of the Muslim tradition throughout the day. On and on, we see that bowing is one of the most common and effective ways to reduce one's constant preoccupation with ego and status and open ourselves to humility, gratitude and grace.

Though not meant to diminish, efface or control us, bowing connects the practitioner to the Higher Self, beyond self-imposed limitations. Yogi Bhajan gave many meditations that used bowing combined with a sound current in a mantra or a *shabad*. The technique of bowing rhythmically with the musical recitation of Jaap Sahib, the beautiful and powerful writing of Guru Gobind Singh, is a potent kriya for courage and humility in the Sikh tradition, and was incorporated into many kriyas. On a purely physical level the act of bowing, whether from a sitting position or a standing position, is excellent for strengthening digestion, circulation and spinal flexibility. Its most important effect, however, is on the emotions and mental attitudes which follow the act of bowing. With that said, we can bow physically but not mentally. Every tradition asks us to bow in our hearts—not just for social face. If we practice bowing as a ritual or a sign of religious membership, it loses some of its potency. But when we practice it as a technology and a living ceremony, in consciousness, we embody true inner piety.

Meditation Series for Humility

Bowing before the Infinite

October 12, 1971

POSTURE: Sit in Rock Pose, on your heels, with the spine straight. Keep Neck Lock applied throughout.

MUDRA: Interlace your fingers in Venus Lock behind your back, keeping them relaxed at the base of the spine throughout the movement.

EYES: Closed; concentrate on the Brow Point at the root of the nose.

MANTRA: Har Ham

MOVEMENT: Begin bowing at a steady pace. Chant Har as you bring your forehead to the ground. Chant Ham as you rise up and sit straight.

The pace should be moderate and steady at about four complete bows every 10 seconds. Stay in rhythm and move steadily and smoothly. The sound Har is made using the tip of the tongue; focus on hearing the sound at the Brow Point. The sound Ham vibrates in the upper chest as the chest lifts and you sit up. Mentally sense the Infinite and surrender all thoughts and conflicts as you bow forward. When you chant Ham, experience your strength and an inflow of energy that lets you act with compassion, from the heart; to act as God or the Infinite. Your arms are relaxed behind you and will

Stage Eleven: Humility

move naturally as you bow. As you continue deeper into the meditation hear and feel the inner polarity of the sounds. Your awareness will hold a space for both sounds, simultaneously, as if the two echoed and merged into a single presence and clarity. You are a crucible that blends the heavens and the earth, the finite and the infinite, in your creative action and your steady stillness.

TIME: 11 minutes

TO END: Inhale deeply and suspend the breath as you sit straight. Remain sitting up and exhale powerfully. Inhale again; suspend the breath as you squeeze the muscles along the spine. Exhale powerfully. Once more inhale deeply, squeeze your muscles tightly. Press the lips firmly together. Exhale powerfully, let the hands go and relax.

After 5 minutes go on to the next kriya.

Speaking Humbly before the Creative Infinity

October 12, 1971

PART ONE

POSTURE: Sit in Rock pose on your heels, with a straight spine.

MUDRA: Rest both hands in your lap, palms up. Rest the back of the right hand in the open palm of the left. Touch the tips of the thumbs together.

EYES: Closed; concentrate at the Brow Point.

MANTRA: Haree Har. Repeat the mantra as if it were Ha, Ree, Har; that is, recite it in a clipped steady pace in three distinct parts. The tongue has three positions. **Ha**; the tongue is down. **Ree**; the tongue flicks the front upper palate. **Har**; the tongue moves up touching lightly. Focus on the movement of the tongue and the sounds; the pace is about 8 to 10 repetitions every 15 seconds.

Stage Eleven: Humility

This meditation works on the power of the throat center. Humility is in part the ability to speak directly, from your truth, but touched with compassion. First establish your posture, then hear the sound and become relaxed and very present. The stillness in your mind is immersed in the sounds generated by the tongue. You have nothing to do. All is done by the pulse of the sound current. Put aside the constant urge to do, to accomplish, and instead let the universe, your infinite Self, work for you.

TIME: 31 minutes

TO END: Inhale deeply, suspend the breath and press your tongue up to the roof of the mouth. Squeeze the muscles along the spine. Exhale powerfully. Repeat this two more times. Then slowly come out of the posture. Stretch the legs. When you are ready, go directly into a deep relaxation.

PART TWO

Relax on the back. Do a progressive relaxation of all the muscles and body parts for a few minutes. Then bring your focus to the Navel Point. Listen to a gently played gong or mantra music. Let everything go. The sounds you have chanted and the energy from the bowing will circulate to every cell and uplift you.

TIME: 22-31 minutes.

Bowing for Humility to Transfer Praana

January 16, 1972

POSTURE: Sit in Rock Pose, on your heels, with a straight spine. Place the palms on the ground alongside your legs. They should be completely relaxed throughout the exercise.

MANTRA: Akaal Sat. Akaal means beyond death or deathless. Sat is the existence; what truly is. Akaal Sat is undying existence or undying truth. This chant is a meditation on the infinite that is both beyond form and within every form. It is the constant flow of existence and grace. The sound of Akaal is about twice as long as the sound Sat. Sat is recited with an emphatic strong pull of the Navel Point.

MOVEMENT: Begin a steady bowing motion. The hands remain relaxed with palms on the ground as you move up and down. Chant the sound Akaal as your forehead touches the ground. The A in Akaal initiates the motion downward; Kaal completes the motion forward, ending as the Brow Point touches the earth. The sound Sat is done as you sit up, pull in the Navel Point and lift the chest slightly.

EYES: The eyes are closed and rolled up in Shambavi Mudra, focused at the root of the nose, as you bow forward. When you rise up open the eyes wide, looking straight forward; maintain your awareness and projection from the Brow Point.

VISUALIZATION: Visualize a huge white sun directly before your Third Eye. Though the sun is not that color, visualize it to be so. Build the brightness

Stage Eleven: Humility

so it becomes an infinite light equal to trillions and trillions of suns. Imagine this at the Brow Point. As you bow forward, feel the earth as a very little thing, sacred and sweet, within the infinite light. Bow with the trust of a child that expects and accepts all resources to be given.

TIME: 11 minutes.

TO END: Inhale deeply and sit up straight. Suspend the breath with the eyes closed. See beyond the brilliant brilliance of the sun through the Third Eye. Roll the eyes up gently. Project into that light without limit; dissolve yourself and let the infinite light bless, heal and fulfill you. As you exhale slowly, pull in the navel and feel the energy flow through your hands. They will vibrate with the release. Repeat this visualization; squeeze the spine strong and straight as you see the light and penetrate into it. Do this three times total. Then sit still and breathe slowly. Focus on projecting the flow of healing energy through your hands. From the infinite light through you to whatever needs to be elevated and healed.

Hints for Practice and Mastery

When you lock into the rhythm of this bowing meditation it is remarkably ecstatic. It takes a little practice to get the eyes to close and open in exact synchrony with the bow and the chant. Once this is settled in, change your focus to the sound itself. Notice how the sound, visualization and sensation of praana in your energy field each shift. There is a pulse of energy. At first you may be trying too hard to create an effect. Gradually dwell with the energy as a witness and let your humility before the infinite light increase the flow itself. Once you can do nothing everything flows.

The practice and perfection of this kriya can heal as if through miracles. It was said that if someone were to perfect this for three years, they could make the dead live, healing those without hope. When you have time, as homework or for personal practice, extend this healing practice. Do it with a partner, switching roles and practicing kundalini healing through the transfer of praana. Place your hands toward the person you want to heal. Stabilize yourself into the sun. Feel the vibration through the hands and soothe and smooth the space of that person. Let the light heal. Meditate on the miracle mantra: Guroo Guroo Whaa-hay Guroo Guroo Raam Daas Guroo chanted five times on the breath.

STAGE татTWELVE
Elevation

Elevation

Humility and its fearlessness let you drill even deeper with your mantra.
Continued practice takes you into the twelfth stage, elevation. Your horizons expand.
Your perspective changes.
Old limitations and beliefs drop away.
You examine each thought against the background of your whole life. You stay clear about what you want to accomplish and contribute.
You let go of many ideas from the past.
You renew and increase commitments that are meaningful.
Equally, you drop things that are not yours to carry.
Many of the deepest patterns that make life seem repetitious drop away.
The elevation gives new leverage.
You experience your feelings as part of the vastness you have touched and been touched by.
Change becomes much easier.
The hills and valleys of life all seem smooth as you fly over them at this new elevation.

With ease your consciousness rises like balloons. You are still you. Connected. But you see the trinity in every cell, thought and action. The play of the universe is easy to see. Positive and negative all serve a greater pattern.

In this twelfth stage of meditation we become very light. Although we still have a strong sense of the Self, we dwell in the Neutral Mind and observe the play of the Negative and Positive Minds. By opening our perceptions up and holding what we see lightly, at a higher frequency, we observe new patterns. We develop a new perspective. Like standing on top of a table, everything seems different from this new vantage point. Even the familiar things of daily life take on new shapes from this perspective. Or like elevating to a high peak, we can see the path we took, the village below, and the entire flow of activities in life. From this elevated perspective we can easily let go of things that once held us hostage. As we liberate our energy from these attachments, we experience the joy and pleasure of seeing things anew. We relish the creativity and insight this new elevation brings, which in turn, informs new strategies and approaches to problem-solving so that we can overcome our obstacles and reach our goals.

This practice is not simply to detach; it is to be nonattached. It is not simply to be mindful of what we see; it is to see the unseen in what we see. Elevation is a necessary step toward cultivating the capacity to see the unseen, which culminates in the final stage of this second journey. We plant the seed by stimulating this inherent capacity here, at this stage. We need a fully functioning Third Eye and upper glands, in order to continue our journey. Yogis became experts in developing these upper chakras, because they are necessary for the engaged observation, which is at the core of so much artistic perception, healing insight, and wisdom; as well as the capacity to see the unseen, which allows us to see the patterns and connections between the events in our life and our own soul's journey.

What is it like to master this meditative state and develop it in your life? Yogi Bhajan described elevation this way:

> *"Do you really want it? Test everything on your consciousness. The goal of this is not to just become conscious. The job of a very elevated person is that whatever you say you can compute it and all its consequences consciously; that's an elevated yogi. Do you really want to know what an elevated yogi is? I do not agree with any of the books I have read about it. It is a living person who can compute everything good and bad, said and not said, seen and unseen through consciousness.*

> *"That's a true definition of a yogi. Why do we talk about yogis as those who have powers and those who live four hundred and fifty years and never die? I never discuss it. Because I had the pain of having it and I understand how dangerous they are to you, how abnormal they are to you. These powers are so abnormal to the human body and human consciousness that you can't even enjoy your life.*

> *"Consciousness is the real power. It's the power of our power. It is the most ultimate power. If a yogi is a yogi he can compute everything through the scope of that consciousness. I call it conscious scope. Look at yourself and your life through conscious scope. This is the practice. Look at everything through the conscious scope. Don't bother to react, and don't think that this is your idea, or your feeling good or bad. They are simply ideas, thoughts; don't feel bad or upset about it. Whatever comes to you look at it through your conscious scope because once you can screen everything through the lens of consciousness you have the real power of the Self. Do you know what lens is? The more powerfully you develop this lens the more powerful you become. You learn to see. And with a lens with conscious scope you shall always see the truth. It is the easiest way; that is the master's way."* [56]

Elevation is the cultivation of conscious scope, which means that we develop the capacity and the habit to use consciousness and awareness as our primary tools. Consciousness is a light. It needs a lens: microscope, telescope, nanoscope, or conscious scope. When we observe the same flow of thoughts and begin to see the underlying pattern, we develop a level of discernment that is at the heart of the elevated human.

Most of the time we don't live from this elevated perspective; we get diverted by labeling thoughts good and bad, which excites our emotions and invokes our moral instincts. But still, we want to know what is what. What is unsaid in what is being said? Typically we take this idea of conscious scope and think "Oh, that is good. I have it, or I can get it. I can use it." But Yogi Bhajan exhorts us to practice it, apply it, but don't get caught up in it. Psychics and healers often fall into this trap. As they become more and more sensitive, they gradually take a superior position over others rather than an elevated position within themselves.

When we master elevation we recognize and forgive our own flaws and understand how to use them as lessons for ourselves and others, or as talents to regain our authentic voice. To experience true elevation, we must take this approach; otherwise we get trapped by the powers and lose sight of the goal, which is to observe, elevate the perspective, cultivate conscious scope, and be delighted by what emerges in the creative reality of life.

Elevation requires a limitless scope. The mind can never find the limit of God, or out-guess God. The mind believes that it can contain the Infinity we call God like a bird in a cage. However, when we are elevated we grow more comfortable with the unbounded creativity of existence and the delight of life—good and bad—than with the burden and weight of trying to control everything.

Yogi Bhajan felt that the capacity to elevate ourself and others trumped all other claims made by religions. In other words, he saw elevation as the basic human capacity, which gives rise to all other religious traditions and their traditional practices: worshiping together, creating opportunities to work together, meditating together, solving social problems and doing good works. With the change of the Age, returning to our innate human capacity is essential for each of us. For it is then that we can be elevated, elevate others and express our heart's true nature.

> *"Elevate. Always remember you have one religion, you have one purpose, and you have one situation to deal with. It doesn't matter what circumstance or situation you are in, you shall elevate it! Elevate, each day! Live to elevate yourself. Each day elevate one person. Each day talk to one person and elevate them. Make elevation your religion and you shall reach Infinity."* [57]

The other practice within this stage of meditation is neutrality. A neutral mind, which loves all that is, is unusual. Normally we love something and hate another. We avoid pain and seek solace in people, places and things or beliefs. But in the life of an elevated consciousness, we see more. We feel more—not less. We neither run from nor toward the vastness we experience; we allow it. We don't avoid the patterns we see. The unseen is seen equally in all of the creation, good and bad, poor and rich, blessed and cursed. Our ability as an elevated human being is to elevate another, to bless, and to choose the path that is in alignment with our consciousness.

When an elevated consciousness sees the pain of the world, people and their habits, it feels that pain and chooses to help even as it accepts it. Elevation does not hide pain; it reveals reality.

> *"Guru Nanak says God is all. But it is very painful to accept whatever God has created. Because when you are on the Fortieth Pauree,† the fortieth step of the ladder, to see somebody only at the third level is very painful. It's almost impossible. As an elementary soul, when such a person sees the complimentary and supplementary souls it cries! It is those cries which also elevate humanity. The higher you go, the more pain you feel. The higher you travel, the more dangerous it is. At higher elevations your breath gets shallower and you get sweatier. Isn't that true? That's why Guru Nanak said first have fear of God. You will become fearless from everything else and that's the first step to take fear out of people, out of this Earth, out of your surroundings. Put it instead in your heart as it is from God. Fear from God is a blessing. Fear from anybody else is a curse. Don't judge Him "* ⁵⁸

When we have the practice of elevating others, then that consciousness is felt by others. Just to connect with an elevated consciousness can uplift or heal. It can attract and create prosperity. When we have a crystallized Self, we expand our light, deepen our insight and create our reality in words and in actions, in this way our presence itself can work. We need no other aid. We elevate our self and others.

The challenge is to do it with humility, free from spiritual ego, to stay in the pure state of innocent delight and expansive awareness that comes with elevation.

> *"Unfortunately there is no gimmick which works, there is only one thing which will work: if you can relate to your consciousness and clean it out through some discipline. Then you can become radiant. This is the Law of Radiance, the law of the Tenth Body. The Law of Radiance is whenever anybody will have the arcline*

---

† Author's Note: The 40th of 40 steps on the ladder of consciousness described in the composition Japji by Guru Nanak; that is, the highest elevated state.

and aura in perfection of the radiance of the Self, the presence of that person shall work. The God intensifies Itself into existence with creativity.

"If you are a doctor be a doctor, but also be a healer. A doctor can cure; a healer can heal even by a touch. Now actually a human is, when you touch, it should elevate the consciousness. When you feel someone or something, it elevates that consciousness. When you are there, that itself is a miracle. That's the power. That's real." [59]

One of Yogi Bhajan's favorite formulas for teaching and learning was "Poke, Provoke, Confront, and Elevate." In order to learn we have to poke our old ideas and current perceptions, reactions and feelings. We have to poke our personality and test our reality. We provoke that reality by observation and conversation. We challenge our old ways of thinking and confront our ego. Life does this on its own actually. But when we're able to include the elevated consciousness, we're given an opportunity to witness the patterns and transform them in consciousness. Poke, provoke and confront; test the reality of what you see.

The last step is to elevate. Without this all the rest are useless—and even harmful. A bully can provoke. A critic can poke. Elevation means to elevate the consciousness of your Self or another to a greater perspective. It can be observed in many forms and in the formless. But essentially the task is this: When you communicate with someone, help someone, teach someone, ask yourself, "Did I elevate? Did I stay present to my soul and consciousness and bring them to that same level through my radiance? If I confronted or provoked was it out of right or wrong, or was it out of clarity, kindness and consciousness?"

The next meditation process gives you a chance to practice this refined sensitivity and experience your own consciousness and elevation. Every goal will be better served; every person will feel honored by your seeing their reality; the mind will become a perfect lens of the real Self.

We will use two meditations; one we'll repeat because it is the core meditation for elevation. The second meditation is a powerful meditation for the glandular system and arcline, which deepens the first meditation once it's repeated. The purpose of this sequence is to elevate our mind, stimulate our glands and consolidate our sensitivity and sensibility into an ongoing capacity to apply elevation in all of our actions, perceptions and creative expressions.

MEDITATION SERIES FOR ELEVATION

Meditation for Elevation

August 21, 1996

POSTURE: Sit in Easy Pose, with a straight spine, and apply Neck Lock.

EYES: Lock the gaze down, beyond the tip of the nose.

MUDRA: Cross the index and middle fingers. The Jupiter (index) finger represents positive expansive knowledge. The Saturn (middle) finger represents the lord of purity and discipline. The crossed fingers represent two things: First, that your knowledge is supported with the discipline to act on it and to keep it pure. Second, that these two linked energies cut your karmas. It is an ancient mudra of blessings. The other fingers are held onto the palm by the thumbs. Bring the hands up to shoulder height. Palms face forward.

MANTRA: Aadays tisai aadays, Aad aneel anaad anaahat, Jug jug ayko vays

I salute Thee, the Primal One, timeless, pure, beyond form and boundaries, Age after Age you are One.

Speak this mantra in a special way. Pull the Navel Point in rhythm with the words. Speak from the Navel Point with projective energy. Let the pull of the Navel Point move the tip of your tongue.

This mantra strengthens the Radiant Body and Arcline to elevate consciousness. You are addressing the infinite, and the company of those who have elevated themselves

Stage Twelve: Elevation

to serve and to heal. These words of Guru Nanak are a salutation to the Infinite—to the God beyond the Infinite God. If you master this pauree from Japji, it elevates and opens your insight, giving you intuitive knowledge of your Self and the universe. It is the yogi's humble obeisance to the Infinite in all. One repetition takes about 5 seconds.

TIME: 11 minutes. Do not exceed 11 minutes; its effect is slow long and deep; and slowly, gradually you will find that you are achieving something.

TO END: Inhale deeply. Close the eyes and concentrate in the center of the head. Suspend the breath and concentrate on the sense of your physical body. Let you and your body feel each other. Be still and radiant. Exhale. Inhale deeply and suspend the breath. Concentrate on the sense of you and your mental body. Feel the field of energy and radiance of your mental body's projection in relation to your core consciousness. Exhale. Repeat once more. Then sit still, relax in stillness for a minute or two.

Move directly into the next kriya.

Meditation for Rasa and the Inner Eye

January 5, 1995

POSTURE: Sit in Easy Pose, with a straight spine, and apply Neck Lock.

MUDRA: Take the left hand and place the center of the palm on your Navel Point, with the palm resting against the abdomen. Bring the right hand a few inches from the hair line, palm facing the body. It is in line with the arcline from ear to ear, around the head. Move the hand rapidly in synchrony with the mantra. The hand moves a few inches (7-15 cm.) in a fast, staccato pulse to focus you and energize the arcline and the aura; it's as if the hand were vibrating. Sense the temperature and sensations in the palm of the left hand; the exercise can create quite a bit of heat.

EYES: Concentrate at the Brow Point with the eyes closed. From there sense the energy released at the Navel Point. Trace its path along the spine and through the head to the forehead and pituitary.

MANTRA: Har

From the Navel Point and tip of the tongue, rhythmically pulse the sound Har. This is the sound of creativity, the creative power of consciousness. Listen to it. Be aware; speak and listen as you speak. Hear the inner sound of the sound. Sense the shift in your energetic bodies as the sounds prepare to arise and manifest on your tongue and through your chakras. As you continue, the pressure on your nerves will increase greatly. You are reshaping your central nervous system.

PACE: Chant Har about 3 times per second; it's a quick pace, but do not slur the pronunciation. Focus it, place it, and project it. Create a continuous sound current.

TIME: 11 minutes.

Stage Twelve: Elevation

TO END: Inhale very deeply, suspend the breath. Keep the right hand fixed over and above the forehead a few inches (5-10 cm). Meditatively focus on the energy between the palm and the head. Sense the energy in the navel area as you press the Navel Point tightly with the left hand. Exhale powerfully like a cannon through the mouth. Inhale deeply again. Suspend the breath and concentrate at your pituitary. Squeeze the muscles along the spine. Feel the energy flow like a snake along the spine from the base to the top and over the forehead to the pituitary at the root of the nose. Exhale powerfully like a cannon through the mouth. Repeat this breath and meditative projection once more. Then relax. Be still and relax for a minute or two, then move directly into the final 11-minute meditation.

Hints for Practice and Mastery

This meditation is incredibly powerful and its effects are immediate. Unlike many meditation practices that are about stillness and witnessing your own mind, this is an active meditation. Your focus is important. Keep the lessons learned in the first stages of meditation to locate your sense of Self and establish the still witness. Then direct your projection so that your physical, mental, and subtle bodies all work as a single rhythmic action. Put your whole Self into this. Be strong and precise at the same time; it is not a wild or exaggerated movement.

As you continue, your nervous and glandular systems are pressurized by the effort and stress of the action, which progresses in phases. The first few minutes are easy. You will sense the interlock of energy between the Navel Point and the Brow Point. Then the nervous system will object, align and adjust between minutes six and seven. During this phase you might receive messages from your nerves: pain, shakiness or even vivid images or sounds. Keep steady. If you feel suddenly tired, call on your inner wildness and put your energy, courage, anger, everything into it. The motion stays absolutely controlled and disciplined, but channels the emotional energy. After nine minutes the glands will respond powerfully. Your soma will open the rasas to create the potential for amrit.

The last few minutes can open the pathways of experience that otherwise take many years of sitting to access. After a brief rest go directly back to the first meditation. You will experience it more deeply and more intensely, with an elevated perception.

At the end of this class Yogi Bhajan was jubilant and said,

> "Hallelujah, God is not far away if you know this exercise. If you practice every day, it takes only eleven minutes. For the first three minutes it looks like a joke. After another three minutes to four minutes, about seven minutes, it hurts like hell! I know, because I practice it whenever I need to take care of my being. Then during the last three minutes, you must really do it hard, and that completes the eleven minutes. Then two times you just simply hold the breath to prepare yourself. The third time you hold the breath and pull all the spinal vertebras back to the back all the way here, up to the brow. When you feel here that little tingling it will start happening and you let it go. Now what can this do for you? This can make you see the unseen, know the unknown and hear the unheard for your elementary constitution of Self. You don't have to go to anybody to initiate and you don't need me to teach you spirituality. You are the spirit and you are the pure one. So be self-reliant."

Stage Twelve: Elevation

Meditation for Elevation

Repeat the first meditation for 11 minutes.

The second round of this meditation is an opportunity to take the practice deeper. Consciously let your Self rise as gently as a balloon. Sense the mantra, the changes in your energetic space and survey your mind. See the stream of thoughts, the beliefs you hold and the way your Negative and Positive Minds present things to you. Elevate into your Neutral Mind. The earlier stage, Rasa, is stimulated by the second meditation process. Now allow the Delight you practiced in Stage 9 to be with you as you enjoy the way your consciousness re-sorts your perception. The Neutral Mind sees all of your positive and negative streams of thought and observes new patterns that emerge from the higher perspective of elevation. What holds us back is often the emotional base of perception. Let flourishing emotions such as delight and savoring be part of your elevation. It is an auspicious moment to allow new insights to arise and new perspectives on your feelings, strategies and beliefs to naturally emerge. Let your real Self express itself through insight and perspective.

STAGE THIRTEEN
Graceful Enlightenment

Graceful Enlightenment

*Heart and senses wide open.
You embrace every movement and feeling.
You feel everything.
You sense everything.
You are open without condition and choose to act with
Grace. Supple and swift.
Refined and beautiful.
You walk steady and regal.
You walk lightly, enlightened.
You are the perfect witness to the Creation and the
merciful pulse of the Creator that gives you
life on each breath.
That gives you power in each word.*

The key to this stage lies in how we handle the polarities we experience. Life is filled with them. How gracefully we handle them is the measure of an enlightened human being.

Stage Thirteen: Graceful Enlightenment

In this stage our hearts need to be wide open, and our meditative capacity needs to be able to balance the fundamental impulses and energies of our life in both body and mind. When our emotions are experienced vibrantly and in alignment with our consciousness, then our thinking can be sensible, clear and creative. We do not drain our energy with unnecessary internal conflicts. We open our sensitivity to all; we feel all and welcome all. Enlightenment isn't abstract; it's when our presence lightens the load of each person we meet, work with, serve or teach. Gracefulness comes from the internal balance of our thoughts and feelings. The willingness to commit our Self to act with integrity, responsibility and care in every situation we encounter is graceful enlightenment in action.

In meditation it is not enough to observe and detach. True meditative skill is to feel what is going on and transmute it; to become an alchemist, balancing the play of polarities. It requires strength and the active projection of the heart while in meditation. This is an important concept: Many teachers accurately say that the enlightened state is to rise above the polarities of circumstance, gain and loss, claim and blame. But they often miss the plot, which is at the very heart of the human experience of relationship, which is to embrace responsibility. Buddhists capture this quality by vowing to stay committed to uplifting all sentient beings. Christians show it in acts of service and commitment to community and compassion. Sikhs express it in the practice of serving friend and foe alike. At some point every enlightened person gathers their resources together and commits them to grace in action.

> *"The greatest misfortune in the science of yoga is some idiots who called themself yogis. They start preaching that a yogi is one who is above all polarities. But they don't say at all the most important second sentence. A yogi is a person who is above polarities but picks up the action and results of the polarity. You should be above pain but you should pick up everybody's pain. That is what above pain means. Above pain does not mean that you should be gross and insensitive and nothing should move you. To be above the law of polarity is that you should totally pick up the bill from the effect of those polarities. These half taught scriptures are damaging, it is better not to even learn them. It is better to eat raw food than something half cooked.*
>
> *"Get your scene together so that you can face the scene that is coming. Stop your own game and be prepared to see the huge game that nature is going to play. Get ready for it. Can you understand me when I have to face a ten year old boy and he says, 'Yogi, will you betray me too or will you teach me more wisdom?' Should I not I cry, am I not a human?"* [60]

Graceful Enlightenment is a stage of sensitivity and responsibility. If we rise to the perspective of an enlightened being, then it is the natural impulse of the soul to lighten the load of others. When we become sovereign over the Self, we feel responsible to all because we are connected to all.

> *"An enlightened person is above time and space. Enlightenment is when your behavior, your conduct, your pros and cons, your guidance and your conviction reaches the point beyond time and space. There are ten Gurus in Sikh history. Guru Nanak was the one to whom every spiritual faction, every spiritual religion bowed. What a great sage, great enlightened being, and great person he was acknowledged to be. The one who is enlightened knows that there is a light in everything. He does not get messed up by darkness. The actual state of consciousness, if you are enlightened, is to live above time and space, though you are the time and space."* [61]

The example of Guru Nanak is well-known. He was accepted by all the traditions, from Hindu to Muslim to Christian to every Sant and yogi he met. He traveled from the Middle East, all around India and up into China to heal, bless and uplift. He lived a practical life and never reacted to the plus and minus of those he encountered. In this sense he was profoundly graceful and enlightened. He saw the light in others and passed his experience along. His most powerful message, in a time of kings, castes, tribes and social change, was that every person was equally sacred and had the infinite within them. There is no special one except the One in all. Because of this recognition within himself, he could speak and the words were both in time and space and beyond time and space. They are shared, chanted and studied to this day. Everyone desires this graceful realization. We cry out for it like a child, hoping it will be given to us. But therein lies the problem, instead of asking the infinite within ourselves, we seek it from the outside, other people, religions, drugs, you name it. We do not recognize that this one special consciousness is already within us; it's a part of our nature and must be developed through humility, discipline and refinement. Yogi Bhajan makes this point in his example of Guru Nanak,

> *"It is a virtuous fact that in this world we can get wealth and ask for goods from somebody else. The main difficulty is that we cannot ask for righteous living and good conduct by somebody's favor nor can we beg for it from somebody else. It is the primal instruction in the words of Guru Nanak that this work of raising this radiance of your spirit to full awareness of your spiritual Self and enlightenment you can only get through your own personal effort. It cannot be donated to you. It cannot come to you through the virtue, action, deed or concept of anyone but you. Guru Nanak says in his own words that just as every human being has a hunger*

Stage Thirteen: Graceful Enlightenment

for food in the body, so the spiritual longing for God is exactly laid very deep into every layer of consciousness in every human being.

"We take many different dishes made out of different kinds of food to quench the hunger of our body. In exactly the same way, to satisfy the longing for the merger of God into the radiance of our consciousness and in our mind, we use all kinds of different practices and saadhana. Each of these is to qualify our potential of life to be able to elevate and merge our finite into the Infinity and complete our Self into the Supreme Being. A human being is satisfied in himself, in his concept of fulfillment, when he elevates all aspects to the level of spirituality." [62]

Yogi Bhajan shared the techniques of Kundalini Yoga as a science and a path of knowledge, which gives you an enlightened mind so that you can use your psyche intuitively to relate to and invoke all the cosmic powers within and without. When he began sharing these techniques many people warned that they were dangerous. He countered saying they were not, because they are simply who you are. The energy is in you as you; it is part of your human nature. The only danger associated with this technology is individual enlightenment itself; you no longer need preachers or religious institutions who take advantage of you.

"Do you understand that someday you have to clean your weaknesses and gather your strength and be you? Don't you know what I am saying? How many times can you go to somebody else for an answer or for help? Are you ever going to be yourself? Have you ever had the confidence that you can drop your weakness and pick up your strength and simply be you? That is called awakening; that's called enlightenment; that is called reality, that is called being human. You are a graceful enlightened human when you can put your roots into Infinity and you can bring the fruits of Infinity. Life is Infinity to Infinity." [63]

We are complete to begin with. We have a discipline, a saadhana; we practice; we join in common efforts to uplift and express our creativity. The only barrier between us and God, between our confusion and pain and enlightenment, is a very thin wall of ego. Discipline and meditation, practiced honestly, with self-reflection, are not unique to Kundalini Yoga. With these same keys, you can enlighten yourself through any tradition or vocation you choose. The Infinite has no limit; and the fruits of the practice are the same, whatever the path, for the Infinite is within each of us.

"Man is a conscious, mature identity of God. Man is not a human. We are a light. Man is not to become enlightened. To seek and sell enlightenment, and all that, is a business in which man A, who is clever, tells man B about enlightenment to

steal their money. I call it spiritual cheating. It is very professional, and it has been done for centuries. But the reality and virtue is that each person is enlightened to begin with. The human being is divine to begin with." [64]

The final thing to understand about this stage is that it is completed in the third journey; graceful enlightenment is not the final destination; it is a rhythm, a way of living. Enlightenment, in and of itself, is not an experience, nor can it be grasped. It is in relationship to everything and everyone else, to all experience, in which you are engaged and humble enough to let the One be with you in all things, rather than grasping to become the One. It is a stage of dynamic evolution; one that realizes there is no end point and no beginning. There is no dimension that can capture the infinite aspect of our Self. So we must embody it in the grace of each of our words, the commitment in all of our action and the strength of our integrity. We demonstrate this enlightenment through the gradual constant expression of our ethical character; we sense what can be done and we act, creatively and courageously, to fulfill our duty. Graceful enlightenment is a flow that I embody but it is not mine; it is the expression of my authentic Self in action; it is what we mean when we say, "personally impersonal."

To agree to and understand the idea of graceful enlightenment is not the same as embodying it within our own consciousness and action. This is the challenge of this second journey: How do we embody, apply and deliver the consciousness of our elevated Self throughout the varied challenges and opportunities that life brings? Noticing a thought, selecting a thought and maturing a thought are essential meditative skills. But we often experience our mind as independent from our bodies, separate from our somatic state. We think the thought is enough; we believe that agreeing to agree, intellectually, is sufficient.

But to actually embody, live and express the stage of graceful enlightenment, the physical and subtle bodies must work in concert with the mind. Yogi Bhajan gave this particular meditation to help address this gap between head and heart; between consciousness and action; between intention and capacity; and between detached calmness and the nonattached, fully engaged, committed, graceful enlightenment of a Raj Yogi, which is demonstrated in the thousands of acts of seva everyday as well as in the lives of spiritual luminaries such as Guru Ram Das, Guru Nanak and those of service and compassion in all traditions.

Meditation for Graceful Enlightenment and Strength of Heart

August 27, 1975

POSTURE: Sit in a precise meditative posture with crossed legs. First take the left leg into the body with the heel close to the groin. Then move the right leg over the left. Place the right calf over the sole of the left foot. Slip the toes of the right foot into the crease between the calf and the thigh of the left leg, just behind the knee. Apply Neck Lock, straighten the spine and lift the chest.

MUDRA: Again, the position is very precise. Lift the arms up, and bending at the elbows, cross them behind your head. Grasp the upper left arm around the triceps with the right hand. Press on the point at the base of the deltoid muscle on the upper left arm. With the left hand grasp the upper right arm at the shoulder with the thumb tip on the dimple of the upper deltoids. You are pressing the meridian points at the origin and insertion points of this major muscle, which controls many lung functions and praana. Adjust your arms, stretching up and back from the shoulder so that you can fix this position steadily. Avoid resting the weight of the arms on the back of the head. Let the angels lift the elbows up and become weightless.

EYES: Focus at the tip of the nose. Look down; but do not cross the eyes.

Stage Thirteen: Graceful Enlightenment

MANTRA: Gobinday, Mukanday, Udhaaray, Apaaray, Hareeang, Kareeang, Nirnaamay, Akaamay

Sustainer, Liberator, Uplifter, Deliverer, Creator, Destroyer, Beyond names, Beyond Passions

Chant this mentally, in a steady rhythm.

BREATH: Sitali Praanayam. Roll the tongue and inhale through the "U" of the tongue in a long, slow deep breath. As you fully fill the chest do it consciously and gently so you do not strain the ribs. Practice gradually. As you suspend the breath lift the chest; do not put additional strain on the muscles. As you inhale mentally repeat the mantra twice. Then suspend the breath. As you suspend the breath mentally repeat the mantra two times at the same pace. Let the breath go in a steady controlled manner through the nose. Mentally repeat the mantra two times at the same pace.

This is often the hardest part to master. How gracefully you can release the breath depends on how well you mastered the inhale and the suspension. If your breath capacity is not yet developed, then practicing praanayama and other supporting kriyas that expand the lung capacity, along with breath of fire, will help.

There are 16 beats in the 2 repetitions; repeated on the inhale, the suspension, and on the exhale. Some practitioners systematically increase the breath to 32 beats on each part of the breath cycle, which is 4 repetitions of the mantra.

TIME: 31 minutes. If you are a beginner, try it for 11 minutes; rest briefly with the arms relaxed; and then start again.

TO END: Inhale through the nose, suspend briefly, exhale through the mouth. Repeat this three times. Then inhale and gradually stretch the arms up. Relax. Move the shoulders. Massage them and take care of yourself. Relax before doing some other activity.

Hints for Practice and Mastery

Balance is a key to experiencing the depth of this meditation. For some people it is easy; for others it takes some adjustment. So begin by adjusting the posture. Do your best. Relax mentally. The arms reach back unequally because the origin and insertion points on the deltoid are in different locations. That slight angular imbalance creates a pressure, which contributes to the positive pressure on the lungs and heart. It is a cardio-pulmonary healing marvel. The Heart Chakra is opened. The sixteen beat pace of the mantra multiplies the projective power of the breath and energetically engages the throat chakra, which supports the massive inflow of energy into the Crown Chakra and insight at the Third Eye.

It is an advanced meditation in many respects. The suspension of the breath is the cauldron that mixes the infinite and the finite. With practice, it brings you to the state of shuniya and then into turiya. The mantra, which you repeat on each of the three parts of the breath, becomes the sound current that guides your mind and in which you immerse yourself in stillness. As you inhale and exhale, it imbues a subtle pulse throughout all your creative activities in life. As you suspend the breath, it becomes the body of your consciousness. You are everywhere and nowhere. A very unique and special experience will emerge on its own terms within you. Then you will intuitively know how to use all you have sensed and analyzed to act in the creative dignity of your own consciousness. Nothing can shake you. In the Siri Guru Granth Sahib there is a slok that says "I received my breath in sixteen strokes, I held it, and I found God." So this practice has long been revered. Be present and patient; the sudden beauty of springtime surprises and delights us every year, in its own time.

Stage Fourteen
Express and Be Your Self

Express and Be Your Self

You experience being your own Self in enlightenment.
No matter what happens in life, no matter how strong
your emotions, no matter how extreme the changes
and dislocations of your life, you can locate
your own awareness.
You are alive, real and present.
This is the fourteenth stage.
You recognize your Self without any gap or doubt.
You exist with the motto, "to be, to be!"
Before this stage you struggled with the thoughts—
"To be or not to be?"
At this stage your meditation awakens your presence
and its power to create.
Instead of running around trying to make the universe
respond to you,
You become still and let the universe serve you.
You start to come from you as a creature of the
Creator
instead of you as your mind's idea of yourself—
your ego.

This is the final stage in the journey to the expressive Self. We enter this stage to master how to authentically express our Self in action; to be who we are in each of our actions. Every environment, every relationship, every goal and every task we engage in either expresses our Self or diverts us from our Self. When we stay aligned to our expressive Self in action, we are endlessly creative; we develop a depth of character and a trust in our Self that is priceless and universally attractive.

Stage Fourteen: Express and Be Your Self

Throughout the first stages of this second journey we developed and stabilized a preliminary meditative skill: the ability to beam the mind through a single thought, feeling and intention. In this final stage we need the ability to raise our level of consciousness, our Kundalini, through the chakras and consciously connect with the Unseen. When we suspend the normal chatter and impulses of our mind and absorb into the sense of the Infinite—the formless Unknown—we become profoundly still. We touch our deep Self. We invite our consciousness to be an abiding presence in all that we do. This is a step beyond simply resolving inner conflicts. Becoming still and feeling our unseen Self in rhythm with the laya chant is a kind of devotion to our true Self; it is an act of love that puts aside the conflicts in our mind and emotions so we can fully express our original true Self. When we attain this stage, nothing is gained or lost; we are original in who we are in every role we play. Our seen and Unseen; our known and Unknown act seamlessly together. We express our Self naturally like the fragrance of a rose. It is the bloom of character.

The Laya Yoga Kundalini Mantra Meditation does exactly that. Using the laya form of the Adi Shakti Mantra, Ek Ong Kaar Sat Naam Siree Whaa-hay Guroo, we will awaken our core kundalini energy and practice the powerful, transformational qualities of this mantra, which delivers the Infinite to us in practical experience. Our daily lives, with all the responsibilities we carry, demand an abiding strong connection to the Infinite. The mundane finite earthly tasks must be enriched by our ability to see the Unseen; for we must begin to sense the implications and consequences of our actions.

At this stage we also become more sensitive to the effects of our praana, our words and thoughts. When our Self is in our word and supports the word then our praanas and projections are one. We no longer create the inner conflicts that scatter and diminish our creative energy. We can express our Self and enjoy life. When we can express and be our Self, we awaken a powerful *tantra* between our lips and our life force: each word gives birth to worlds. Our voice can open hearts because our heart is in our words. Whether sweet or gruff our words ring true.

Many meditation practitioners stop short of this stage. Once they experience the delight that accompanies graceful enlightenment they find that is enough. But there is much more. We can and should be satisfied at each stage of the journey. However, if we continue to practice and hone the depth of our meditation, our sense of Self continues to expand in scope and quality. And in this stage the Neutral Mind takes us beyond being purely personal and reactive. We learn to be personally impersonal in all areas of life. We gain perspective. We easily see other people's points of view. Most importantly, we can step back from many of our own patterns that don't express our real

Self. We practice the art of embodying our consciousness creatively and consciously in all our obligations, relationships and environments. We align our actions to our destiny and no longer settle for the push and pull of fate alone.

Yogi Bhajan taught these kriyas, this science of sound, in the 1970s when he first came to the United States. He was conscientious to inform his students about the nature of Laya Yoga, its relationship to other disciplines and the conditions that were traditionally given for its practice. This critical stage of meditation and development of the Self is well served by the profound potency of inner sound invoked by meditations with the Laya Yoga Kundalini Mantra. At this stage on the path to realization we can express our true Self or take a detour through the ego of our accomplishments; stop half way up the mountain or traverse the rest of the journey. Instead of expressing our real Self authentically, uniquely, spontaneously and humbly, Yogi Bhajan cautioned us that some would become trapped in spiritual ego and claims to be special or superior to others in some way. The only remedy is devotion. We need to be devoted and to base that sense of devotion in an experience of our own Unseen; that spiritual experience helps us act with integrity, compassion and courage in the normal tasks and tests of our life. Spirituality in this sense is neither a belief nor an institution. It is a relationship between our known Self and our Unknown; our Self in form and our formless Self. It is both personal and impersonal.

The challenge is to express that true Self in our lives. That is the journey of these seven stages of meditation. This fourteenth stage—Express and Be Your Self—is the culmination of that journey. The Laya Yoga Kundalini Mantra Meditation raises our consciousness so it is possible to expand our Self, express our Self and stay humble and authentic. Without an inner current of connection to the Infinite, staying grounded is difficult. So the gift of Laya Yoga is that it's an easy way to clear our minds, increase our sense of Self in action, and experience our own enlightenment and fullest potential while living our own life. Yogi Bhajan taught that the experience of the Infinite is both immanent—now in everything—and transcendent—beyond any form or qualification. In the philosophy of yoga this is known as the relationship between *nirgun* and *sirgun*.

> *"Now this is a dispute which has never been solved up to this day. What is nirgun? Nirgun is formless, sirgun is with form. Bhakti Yogis say God has a form. He is everything; whatever we see is a God. Giani Yogis say, no, God is everything and God is nothing, the void. He is everything and He is nothing. Actually when you reach the stage of the mind of nothingness then you reach God, otherwise not. Less than that you are attached and attachment is a weakness. Now this dispute is going on and it will continue.*

Stage Fourteen: Express and Be Your Self

Someone is right in the sense that the individual mind is a part of the universal mind and it has to merge with the universal mind to achieve liberation. He is right. That is not wrong. That is a perfect truth. Ram, the great prophet and realized person, was as good a man as he was. But Ram is an example. Ram is one example that as an example one can raise his consciousness. Buddha is an example through which one can raise his consciousness. Krishna is an example through which one can raise his own consciousness. Mohammad is an example through which one can raise his consciousness. Guru Nanak is an example through which one can raise his consciousness. But people get stuck with it; they get stuck on the example." [65]

Above all, Yogi Bhajan taught that each of us, as human beings, embodies both of these qualities—nirgun and sirgun. We honor them through our creative action, expression and compassion. And he wanted us to share the technology of Kundalini Yoga from our own authentic experience; to become living examples of realized human beings. In order to do that, we must have our own experience of the Unseen, which will be understood according to our mental tendencies and karmas. We must know through experience that the formless can be seen in every form; and every form arises from the formless.

"You must basically understand, Laya Yoga, the most powerful and accurate yoga is when you get lost into the mantra, into the divine. It is really a powerful thing, that is true. But scientifically speaking, this develops from the Jappa Yoga. Jap is when we sing, when we chant out loud. Laya is when you get lost into the sound and rhythm within and without. Then it flows and prevails through us. Jappa and laya are two interconnected things."

"The idea of saadhana is that one has to be humble and to do service. It is seva, service without asking for a reward. There are three ways of doing service: one is physical service; second is to give an offering, it can be of any type; and third, is to practically do tapa, cleansing through inner heat or burning the karmas. Laya Yoga comes under the third form of service; it is a saadhana to the Self. To do that sadhana, we ought to have had a clean body and clean thoughts for some time. Then as the laya prevails through us it will not let us get polluted; it will prevail." [66]

We will explore this fourteenth stage and consolidate our experiences from this journey with two and half hours of the Laya Yoga Kundalini Mantra. We will do it in five sections of about a half hour each. These are all from a series Yogi Bhajan taught in the early 1970s. The combination will guide us through a profound, deep experience of the unseen Self within us.

The first laya meditation is a sophisticated priming of our inner sound current. We listen with the inner ear, with the Third Eye, and clear the praanic channels and meridians; we become flexible and open in our concentration and responsive to our sounds. The preparatory exercises let us practice and perfect the mantra. They establish our point of concentration in the center of the head and the crown, around the pineal gland. The sound is linked with visualization and an experience of light as well.

The second meditation, Sankh Kriya, attunes us to the most subtle aspects of sound. The posture helps this kriya increase our internal heat—tapas—to cleanse illness, impurity, tension and karma from the body. It is an extraordinary practice.

The third part of the meditation series works on the Heart Center and our ability to keep our Self clear and steady under any crisis, internal or external; it allows us to keep our authentic sense of Self present and creative.

The fourth part of the meditation series works on our focus, concentration, neutrality and ability to beam the mind. It gets rid of many blocks and inner conflicts in the subconscious that hold us back from expressing our real Self and our greatness.

The final part of this meditation series stabilizes our identity within our higher Self as we engage in normal activities. It is a group exercise that disturbs our mental projection as we interact with the environment. The provocation of the group dynamic invokes an alertness within us which extends our sensitivity and self-sensory body. The meditation solidifies the subtle body as our guide; it is that same subtle body that, according to the yogis, keeps our personal sense of destiny and purpose active.

If you put your heart into it, this meditation practice can give you a phenomenal experience. The energies released in this series will deepen your meditative capacity and your ability to apply the insights and skills attained in your life. It will enhance your enjoyment of life, your creativity, your communication and your charisma.

The Adi Shakti mantra, Ek Ong Kaar Sat Naam Siree Whaa-hay Guroo, is the foundation, the DNA of Kundalini Yoga. We practice this *ashtang*—eight beat—mantra every day in the Aquarian Saadhana and we use it during each of the three journeys outlined in this book. The practice for this stage is the Laya Yoga form of the Adi Shakti Mantra, which takes us into a powerful mental suspension of our normal attachments and attentions so that we can dwell with the unseen within us.

The unseen is the source of the seen; the non-existent is the source of existence. The experience of Laya Yoga places you at the gateway between these two profound aspects of our Self. It connects your creativity to your actions. It keeps you in touch with your subtle body under every condition. It is energetic and joyful. A once profound secret is secret no more. Now it is up to us to discover its inner gifts.

Laya Yoga Meditation Series

To Clear the Channels and Raise the Kundalini

August 23, 1970

PART ONE

POSTURE: Sit on your heels with the knees spread wide. If you are flexible you can drop into Celibate Pose with the buttocks on the ground between the heels.

MUDRA: Press all the finger tips of one hand to the corresponding finger tips of the opposite hand. Press firmly and evenly. The palms face each other but do not touch. The fingers are slightly spread and point forward, away from the body; the hands are held between the solar plexus and the Heart Center.

EYES: Close your eyes and concentrate at the Navel Point.

BREATH: Breathe in deeply through the nose. Then exhale completely. Hold the breath out and pump the navel rapidly, in a constant precise rhythm. The pace is about 3 pumps per second. When you must inhale do so in a long single stroke. Immediately exhale and continue to pump the navel and build energy in that area. The pumping motion is executed with a precise, firm pulse but without any extreme effort. The muscular movements are localized to the navel area and below. Energy will build naturally from the rhythm of the pumps.

TIME: 5 minutes.

Stage Fourteen: Express and Be Your Self

TO END: Inhale deeply, suspend the breath briefly as you concentrate on the crown of the head, and press the hands. Exhale. Repeat two more times.

This will clear your apaana, which will clear out all blockages. Anything that is stuck in you from this day can be cleared quickly so you can face yourself and your brightness, vastness and scope.

PART TWO

POSTURE: Stay in the same seated position.

MUDRA: Bring your hands behind your back. Grasp the elbows in a gentle lock. Stretch the spine and chest up so you are stable and alert.

EYES: Closed. Bring your attention and focus to the crown of the head. The eyes will automatically roll gently up as if gazing through the top of the head.

BREATH & MANTRA: As the teacher chants a long **Sa-a-a-a-a-a-a-t**, inhale steadily for the entire duration of the sound. As you inhale hear the sound in the center of the brain. Do not hear with just the ears as if the sound were outside; hear it like a point in the center of the skull. Stay aware of the dome of the cosmos, through the crown center above, the witnessing listener. When the teacher ends the mantra with a short, distinct **Naam**, exhale the breath through the nose in a single stroke. Continue to listen with this "third ear" and sense the shifts in vibration and energy throughout your body and aura. Like a pebble tossed into an absolutely calm pond, focus on the point of sound as it seeds sophisticated ripples throughout your awareness. The key to this naad exercise is to focus the eyes on one point—the crown. Feel the sound travel along the spine from the base, through each of the energy centers, into that single point. The flow builds along these energy centers with the inhalation and then releases through the crown center as you shoot the breath out on the exhale. Dwell consciously within the mantra. Do not let your mind wander into other thoughts and sounds. The movement of praana, which is guided by this sound, will open the six centers of consciousness on the long Sat and the seventh on the Naam.

TIME: 5 minutes. This exercise can extended to 15 minutes with practice.

TO END: Inhale once, suspend the breath and be still in silence. Exhale and immediately relax your posture. Stretch the legs, and refresh your muscles and body from being in this posture. You have pressurized and initiated the crown chakra and the pineal function to open your sensitivity to the subtle sounds of naad. Stay in touch with this vibratory opening as you take a break for a few minutes. Chat but do not gossip or speak about things that introduce a low vibration.

PART THREE

POSTURE: Sit on the heels again, or in Celibate Pose, with the knees wide.

MUDRA: Bring the hands into the mudra in Part One. This time, point the fingers downward toward the ground. The mudra is placed quite low, in front of the body between the sex organ and the root of the spine, the lower knot.

EYES: Closed. As in the previous exercise, center yourself at the crown of the head.

MANTRA: Akaal. Chant the mantra Akaal seven times; once for each chakra: **Akaal, Akaal, Akaal, Akaal, Akaal, Akaal, Akaal**. From the crown, pull the sound of this mantra along the spine. Pierce the centers as you open the flow and gather the flow at the top of the spine in the brain.

Keep the pitch steady and the sound strong for the first four repetitions. Then raise the pitch for the last three chakras in the upper centers.

Inhale deeply and repeat the chant, pulling the energy. The pace of the chant is about 15 seconds for the entire cycle of seven repetitions. It should resonate, pulse and pierce. (It is not long and drawn out as we do when chanting only one Akal per breath at someone's death.)

The mantra means deathless or beyond death, which is the Infinite Being Itself, God, all of the creative energy of existence and nonexistence. That is in us and we are in it. It is an intimate and responsive relationship. Meditation on this sound removes our fear of non-existence. It brings courage to express and act in the present moment. It invites wisdom and perspective, beyond our attachments, as we drop our commotional defenses against the vastness we are a part of. This series opens your sense of the sacred dimension of the Self in creative expression in the world. It prepares the central channel of the spine for the maximum flow of energy and consciousness from the Laya Mantra Meditation to follow.

TIME: 5 minutes.

TO END: Deeply inhale, suspend the breath and hear the mental echo of the chant from the upper centers. Feel it in every cell. Exhale keeping the pressure of the mudra and applying the locks. Repeat this breath and sense the vibration in every part of the cosmos. Exhale. Repeat and become still. Be aware of the unbounded space opened in you by Akal, which is always present. Be aware that you are being aware. Stay with this creative stillness as long as comfortable. Exhale and repeat one more time. Relax.

Meditation on the Laya Yoga Kundalini Mantra

POSTURE: Sit in Easy Pose, with a straight spine, and apply Neck Lock.

EYES: 1/10th open; concentrate at the Brow Point.

MUDRA: Gyan Mudra, thumb tips touching the index finger tips, resting naturally over the knees.

MANTRA: Begin chanting the Laya Yoga Kundalini Mantra. There is no break, not even for the breath, between the final sound and initiating the mantra again with Ek. It is a continuous rhythm and cycle of sound and breath. (See Page 384 for complete instructions on practicing this sound current.)

Ek Ong Kaar-(Ah), Saa Taa Naa Maa-(Ah), Siree Whaa-(Ah), Hay Guroo

TIME: 31 minutes.

TO END: Deeply inhale, suspend the breath. Feel the spin of the mantra and the flow of energy to the crown of the head and out. See the brilliant light of uncountable suns in pure white through the crown and everywhere. Concentrate. Then exhale powerfully. Inhale deeply, exhale. Suspend the breath out. Apply the locks. See light through the top of your head and beyond. Hold as you long as you can. Then inhale deeply. Exhale. Repeat this sequence and visualization two more times; and then relax.

After a few minutes, go directly into the next meditation. Drink plenty of water especially if you sweat.

Stage Fourteen: Express and Be Your Self

Sankh Mudra Kriya: A Naadi Sodhana Laya Kundalini Kriya

May 20, 1970

PART ONE

POSTURE: Sit in Easy Pose or Lotus Pose, with a straight spine, and apply Neck Lock.

MUDRA: Sankh Mudra is a conch. In this meditation we make a conch shell with each hand individually. Simply make a gentle fist. The first two fingers (index and middle) are moved slightly forward compared to the ring finger and pinkie. When you look at it, its shape is like the conch shell. The thumb locks on the medial side of the index finger. Keep the thumb straight; it acts as a seal to the mudra.

BREATH: Breathe consciously. Take long deep breaths through the nose. Mentally initiate the breath at the top of the spine in the center of the head; feel it in your sensory body. As you inhale, slowly guide the breath all the way down to the base of the spine. On the exhale take it back up the spine to the center of the head and out. Continue in this way to cleanse and prepare the channel of the spine and the subtle meridians of ida and pingala.

TIME: 3 minutes.

PART 2

MUDRA: Bring the Conch Mudra in each hand beside the ears on each side of the head. The hands are positioned 1-2 inches (2.5-5 cm.) away from the ears. The palms face the side of the head close to the ear. It looks like you are listening to the conch shell. The wrists are not straight. They angle upward.

EYES: Closed and rolled gently up. Concentrate at the center of the head.

MANTRA: Chant the **Laya Yoga Kundalini Mantra**, spin it up the spine. Witness this consciously from the upper center and crown. Sense the sounds of the mantra spinning and circulating around the head, reflecting from infinite conch to infinite conch and beyond. Keep the body still. But feel the spin of the sound. Be consciously conscious while absorbed in the spin of the Laya Mantra.

People mirror this mudra with actual conches to hear the echo-like sound of the sea. Symbolically, we are listening to the voice of the Unseen; the voice of the higher Self, or God. We are not listening to a finite sound. So as you chant you hear the sound within the sound; the sound from which the gross sound arises. The sound you hear vibrates everywhere at once and ultimately is heard by you at all points and from all directions.

TIME: 31 minutes.

TO END: Inhale deeply, suspend the breath and focus on the light through the Crown Center. Exhale. Repeat two times more. Then inhale stretch hands. Open and close. Relax.

Stage Fourteen: Express and Be Your Self

Laya Meditation to Beam and Create

February 12, 1972

POSTURE: Sit in Easy Pose, with a straight spine, and apply Neck Lock.

Extend both arms straight forward from the body. Interlace the fingers of the two hands to form a solid lock. Palms are pressed together. The thumbs are extended straight up, their sides touching. The thumbs form a "V"; this is your *drishti* or site line.

EYES: The eyes are fixed open, looking straight through the "V" of the thumbs to the horizon and beyond. This is a confident strong gaze; it is the drishti used by warriors to prepare them to be fearless and steady under all challenges.

MANTRA: Continue chanting the **Laya Yoga Kundalini Mantra**.

TIME: 31 minutes.

TO END: Inhale and suspend the breath with eyes open, mentally hearing the mantra. Exhale. Inhale again. Suspend the breath with eyes closed. Beam your mind to infinity. Project your intention, blessing or healing to your unseen Self to complete the cycle of co-creativity. Exhale. Then inhale and stretch the arms up, shake, exhale relax and massage your shoulders a bit.

It is this skill to mentally beam as you stay attuned to the Unseen Creative Infinity that strengthens your projection and helps you sustain your purpose within all the roles you play in the world. You can enegage and create with character and commitment. The strength it brings to you makes you radiant, bright and attractive. Like a magnet you align the surroundings to your purpose and unexpected resources come to complete your mission.

Relax for a few minutes. Massage and stretch the arm muscles. Take fluids. Then move into the next meditation in this series.

Sukh Saadhana: Peaceful Creative Projection with the Heart Center

June 3, 1970

To prepare for the meditation, practice Naadi Sodhana Kriya for 3 minutes: Sit in a meditative crossed legged position, or Easy Pose. Stretch the spine up. Focus at the Third Eye Point. Inhale equally through both nostrils, with enough force that the nostrils collapse toward the midline, flattening the flair of the nostrils. Feel the pressure of the inhale at the Brow Point. Exhale in a relaxed way through the nose.

There are two meridian points for *praana*—ida and pingala—that are stimulated. These two plus the Brow Point, which is also stimulated on the inhale, form a triangle. This cleansing breath is a *trikuti* praanayam; it is a balance of the three flows or three rivers. It can make you very peaceful and light. Stay steady and clear so that you can experience a peaceful full expression of your Self from the Heart Center. To end simply inhale, suspend then relax the breath.

POSTURE: Sit in Easy Pose, with a straight spine, and apply Neck Lock.

MUDRA: Bring the left hand onto your back with the palm facing away; the position is comfortable but up toward the heart center and over the spine. Bring the right hand onto your chest with the mound of the thumb and hand on the Heart Center; the fingers cover the left pectoral area. To make this precise, lift the chest and apply Neck Lock after positioning the arms and hands.

Stage Fourteen: Express and Be Your Self

EYES: Closed.

MANTRA: Laya Yoga Kundalini Mantra. As you chant locate your consciousness at the center of the head and Brow Point. From there guide the energy of the mantra counterclockwise up the spine. As it proceeds up the spine the sound spirals around the Heart Chakra as you proceed from the first to the second sound of (ah). The hands mark the magnetic field energy of the heart. This creates a delightful stimulation and imbues your projection with charisma.

TIME: 31 minutes.

TO END: Inhale deeply, suspend the breath, and meditate on the mental spin of the chant, the Heart Center and the brilliant light through the Crown Chakra. Exhale. Repeat two more times. Then relax.

Take a break for a few minutes; have a drink of water, refresh yourself and stay in the meditative space you have created. Then go on to the final meditation in this series.

Meditation to Express Your Real Self and Develop the Subtle Body

February 7, 2000

This meditation is practiced in a group; sit so that you can join hands with partners on both sides of you; or have the entire group sit in a circle. Sit straight in a cross-legged position with the eyes closed.

PART ONE

Bring the tips of your index and middle fingers and thumbs together. [Note: the ring and pinkie fingers should be extended up.] Bring the mudra in each hand up and to the sides of the shoulders. Palms face forward. 4 1/2 minutes. Chant the Laya Yoga Kundalini Mantra. Meditate on raising your energy up the chakras. Continue 3 minutes.

PART TWO

Keep chanting and simply hold hands with the person on each side of you. Hear the sound of the entire group as a universal psyche. Feel the waves of the sound through your hands, through your connection and through the entire space of the group. Hear the sounds. Hear the inner sound of the sound. Sense the Unseen, the sacred, the spirit pulsing in every voice and sound. Continue 3 minutes.

PART THREE

Now bring your hands palm to palm with your neighbor and interlace your fingers with the person to each side. Hold the lock gently but securely. Keep the Neck Lock applied and your eyes closed. As you chant, pull your interlocked hands toward you every time you make the "Ah" sound. Three pulls for each repetition of the mantra. Stay fully present. Be aware that you are aware of the Self; become sensitive to the sounds and each change within your mind, your aura and your physical body. Be still amidst all the disturbances, unexpected pulls and reactions of your subconscious. You will become very alert. This will bring extended sensitivity into play. Be open to everything that flows through your consciousness from the environment of the group. Keep your sense of Self and creative projection with the mantra steady. You will be able to beam the mind with a super-sensitivity to reach your goal and to sense what you need to know. It is a key to successful creativity, richness and authentic expression of your Self.

Continue 8 minutes.

TO END: Deeply inhale as you mentally spin the chant and pull the hands. Exhale. Repeat this four more times. Then inhale, stretch up, shake it out.

TRANSITION TO STAGE FIFTEEN: Deeply relax on your back up to 31 minutes.

Third Journey
The Transcendent Self

Stage Fifteen
Presence like a Beacon

Presence like a Beacon

Again your experience changes.
You become as still and silent as a lighthouse.
Grounded firmly on the shore your presence becomes a beacon.
Wherever you look, you can feel and witness its effect.
Your presence becomes effective.
Dignity and self-respect arise.
Spontaneous gifts from the knowledge that your presence affects everything.
Presence becomes part of the new vocabulary used to express your heart and spirit.

From your self-contained awareness you beam out from the heart chakra to the universe.

This first stage of our third and final journey relies on our ability to drop the ego. Dropping the ego, at least momentarily, is essential in this stage so that we can hone a particular skill, a *siddhi*: to project our presence without boundary. The ego requires boundaries. In this stage we practice the power to project our presence, beyond ego, to any place or person. We become limitless. We sense the Self, but without the normal boundaries that define and secure that finite sense of Self or the ego. We transcend the Self. We begin this dissolution of barriers by using the Heart Chakra to feel the Self and then forget the Self and beam out into the universe.

Stage Fifteen: Presence like a Beacon

Normally we live in our cozy ruts, comfortable circles and familiar neighborhoods. Yet our spirit and consciousness are as limitless as the horizon. In order to master this stage, we must first attune to our sense of presence and realize its potent effects. Presence itself is a powerful accomplishment of being human; but we take it further, we become a beacon that sends that presence out like a light to guide and uplift when all hope seems lost. This stage nullifies all negativity, in thought, word and deed. It neutralizes limitations and opens the diagonal path.

Yogi Bhajan was universally known for the power of his presence. Commonly, students would come to see him with questions, questions they knew well and had struggled with, ruminated and even obsessed over. When they would get within nine feet of him they would suddenly lose the thought. The question might have become suddenly irrelevant, or they might realize that they already knew the answer. The original question was often replaced with a new one, or they would just enter a deeply calm state. When asked what they wanted they would often become speechless.

In classes, Yogi Bhajan would meditate and his presence alone would elevate the whole class. He called it "flowing into the students" in order to uplift them beyond the conflicts that blinded them. At other times he would provoke people and create confusion in the same manner. In every case the impact was tangible and immediate. Driving in a car with him if he napped was difficult because everyone would go to sleep! Many of the lessons I learned from him were by direct induction. His aura and presence would imprint mine and I would simply know. This direct transfer is a well-recognized method certain teachers use to pass on what could not be easily put into words. Fortunately I had the opportunity to test what I learned later in direct conversations with him and to understand the mechanism and power of such transmission though presence.

> *"With your power of projection you can cut the auric body. It doesn't matter how strong a person is, they can become totally weak; and it doesn't matter how weak a person is, you can project energy and they will become very strong through the radiant body. This can happen as you just enter the room. Even if your makeup is no good and even if you are no good, if your radiant body is very good then its presence works, its grace works, and you uplift everybody. You have ten bodies not just the physical body you see."* [67]

As we release our limitations we begin to transcend our finite ego-self we begin to realize our basic nature: we are energy, light and consciousness. We can use and command that light to see our way through life. "I am the light of my soul," and we can sense, communicate and create with that light, through the soul. As that light increases, so too our presence becomes strong.

> *"What you call human actually gives you little more than being another, more sophisticated animal. You think you are an animal which thinks, feels and has the capacity to fulfill its desires. You do not experience and realize that you the human being are the living beacon of light. You can enjoy your own light! That is actually the purpose of your life. Enjoy your own light; you don't need a God, you are the God. You don't need to unite with something else; you are already united with your own little soul. Without that soul you are not alive, you are dead. Your mind can be so sensitive that it can know everything. If you have that little light of consciousness, of the soul going on, you are all right. Without that little light, you may have everything in the world, but you are still nobody. A dead body can be decorated with gold and diamonds and jewels and there can be a feast going around it for months or years, it means nothing more than something dead for the vulture in the desert. Death means that every possible sensitivity has stopped. That is what we are trying to do with meditation; to get that shadow out of you so that you can have your own life, your own feelings, and your own relationship between you and your Self."* [68]

To be aware of our own unique presence and the light that we beam around us and into the universe is essential to awakening our full human potential. Otherwise we live like shadows; like the images cast in Plato's cave. Our ability to sense who we are and to interact with every cell and every place in the universe, that subtle sensitivity, is part of our nature. We may use it or not. But still it operates. That realm of light has its own rules and processes. This stage of meditation uses the Law of Projection to become a beacon, one who uplifts your Self and others. Yogi Bhajan explained,

> *"There are certain systems in the psyche of a woman that if she can cut through the negative, depressive thinking and say, 'I am going to be a woman and I am going to be impressive. I have no reason to be depressive.' Then the matter ends, you win. You shall not lose. Your loss happens when you do not remind yourself who you are and that you are a woman. Under all circumstances you have to remember that your impact has to be foolproof. Let us achieve that.*
>
> *"Close your eyes and project light. Beam it out from you like a lighthouse. Become a lighthouse. Just a lighthouse! You know the lighthouse; it goes round and round and creates light! Just project that beacon. Become that and slowly, gradually, hypnotically, totally become that. Control your mind, hypnotize yourself. The self-hypnosis is, 'I am a lighthouse.' Slowly and slowly keep on reminding yourself until*

Stage Fifteen: Presence like a Beacon

you become it. You will start feeling it, seeing it and working it like a beacon. The mental effect of hypnosis is you become what you say you are.

"All of a sudden, open your eyes and relax. Assess how successful you were. Just create a spell: you are beautiful, bountiful and blissful; it will start happening around you. It's a law of physics: As the projection is, so is the psyche is. Whatever you are going to project, that shall be supported by your psyche. If you just project you are successful, you shall be successful. So if you project, you are a woman plus successful, then you shall be successful. Understand? From the very beginning until now, woman has been made, by circumstance or voluntarily, to forget that she is a woman first and then everything else."

"Success is very enjoyable, but with fear it may not happen. The solution is if you project you are a woman plus successful, there shall be no fear. It will all happen. Understand the environment, the circumstances, the friends; then the unlimited psyche also helps. Understand people are all humans but the majority have no human presence; no projection that they are human. There are women with no woman presence; there are men with no man presence. That's where the problem is. You have to be you and your presence must work. And if your presence is not yours, or if somebody can steal away your presence, then whatever you have means nothing." [69]

Presence is more than charisma. It is more than beauty. It is the power of a coherent projection from who we really are, within our soul, beyond our present roles and characterstics. Like a strong, invisible magnetic field, it radiates in everything we do and aligns all things around us. When presence is active it is a dynamic beacon, which calls on our Unknown to work for us. The Law of Projection and the Law of Attraction begin to work in harmony; other people and things, the entire universal psyche, work to manifest our potential.

With this innate capacity within us, how can we not know its power? How can we not use it? How can we become dependent on superstition, luck, drugs, other people and their schemes, when we can call on everything we need through our own presence? Presence is neither fantasy nor wishful thinking; it is a practical part of our existence. Although, it has its requirements: The greatest blocks to effective presence are from our own inner conflicts and inability to focus the mind.

"The problem with people who live with their hidden self and their hidden agenda and hidden personality is that they cannot act through their presence. They

cannot act through their presence and that presence does not affect things. If you throw a stone in the water, it must create ripples; there is no such thing that you put something into anything and it doesn't create waves. So it's impossible for your presence to not create vibrations. Instead what happens is your presence creates neither higher conscious vibrations nor lower conscious vibration. It has no committed focus. It creates confusing vibrations. You act and feel and project through your hidden agenda and hidden personality.

"The main problem in your life is that you cannot be yourself because you do not know what your self is. Neither your higher Self looks at the lower self nor the lower self looks at the higher Self because there is a block of the hidden self in-between. That block does not let your vibration cross. So you cannot come out with clarity of mind, soul and Self to gain trust. The greatest attraction and magnetic field through which your personality can work is when you are trustable. Without that life is very painful.

"Understand in your honest depth that you must please give yourself a chance to commit to yourself and to let your presence work. Don't go anywhere or meet anybody with the idea that you have to lecture, you have to convince, you have to argue, you have to reason. No, no, no, no, let your very presence create an effect from your divinity, your dignity, your grace, your character, and your consciousness. If you do this, there is nothing on this earth which you cannot surmount. Those who want to experience this most powerful and magnificent power within yourself, the dormant power of the enlightened kundalini, I have given you meditations." [70]

When we clear our hidden agendas and inner conflicts our presence shines. When we have conflicts, they are reflected in the shape and color of our aura. The conflicts contract and distort our muscles and blunt our ability to give congruent nonverbal messages. The meditation for this stage balances and clears the aura and reduces the long held blocks in the body. When the body is sensitized, when we can feel every cell and its connection with everything around it. The body becomes an intelligent, bright soma. Then the entire body can support a single thought that you beam into the universal psyche. We become effective and one pointed. A single thought becomes a lever to move the universe.

"The first thought in spirituality which was given by man to himself and herself was, 'I am, I am.' It means to accept your existence and project your spirit. Do not become a fanatic this or fanatic that. Just tell people, 'I feel very spiritual.' Half of your friends will leave you if you say that because it is very difficult to exploit a

Stage Fifteen: Presence like a Beacon

spiritual person. This phrase, 'I feel very spiritual today,' means no nonsense; it is a very polite way to get rid of nonsense around you. So build a thought that you are spiritual.

"First develop this thought, 'I am spiritual,' and communicate in everything you do that you are spiritual. Don't just start dressing up like you are spiritual. So what is presence? How you walk, how you talk, how you eat, how you live, how you communicate. Basically how you walk, talk, live, eat, and choose your habits should project your thought that you are spiritual. That's why I say, 'where presence works, nothing else works better than that; but when your presence doesn't work, nothing works.'" [71]

The meditation for this stage was once practiced by select healers to develop their ability to see with the Third Eye and to heal whoever came into their presence, even those who only saw them at a glance. In this stage of meditation compassion rules and the barriers between ourself and others thins. We see in our enemy and our supporters the same presence of the teacher and the God as in our Self. This is the game of the soul; play it by acting with character, dignity, effectiveness, fearlessness and divinity. Do not respond that you are good if someone tries to say you are bad. Instead act consciously. Create a beacon with your presence to uplift yourself and others without judgment or limitation.

Tattva Siddhi Meditation for Presence like a Beacon

January 28, 1972

POSTURE: Sit in Easy Pose or Lotus Pose, with a straight spine, and apply Neck Lock.

MUDRA: Gyan Mudra in each hand, index finger tip touching the tip of the thumb, resting over the knees.

EYES: Closed or slightly open, the eyes are rolled up gently in *shambavi mudra* with the focus through the Third Eye point at the brow.

MANTRA: There is no mantra specified. Let the sound of the breath be an infinite mantra of life.

BREATH: Segmented Breath. Regulate your breath so that the inhale is in equal segments. Begin with four equal strokes in through the nose. At the completion of the segmented inhalation, your lungs should be completely full. Exhale smoothly, slowly and consciously through the nose. As you inhale, visualize the breath and the cosmic praana coming in through the crown of the head. Fill the entire body, the spine and every cell with the inhaled cosmic energy. On the exhale visualize light and energy emanating from every pore of your body. Each pore sends out a blue-white ray of light, brilliant and coherent. The entire body vibrates with the energy you've accumulated and releases it from every pore. As the light extends you sense it projecting in all directions simultaneously. Feel all directions at once. Expand that light farther and farther to the furthest parts of the universe. Continue for 11 minutes.

Then increase the number of strokes on the inhale to five. Continue for 11 minutes.

Then increase the number of strokes on the inhale to 6, then 7, then 8 and finally 9. Each segmented breath is practiced for 11 minutes each for a total of 66 minutes.

Stage Fifteen: Presence like a Beacon

TO END: Inhale deeply, close the eyes and suspend the breath for 10-20 seconds. Exhale and expand your light. Repeat three times in total. Relax.

Hints for Practice and Mastery

For the best results, pay close attention to equalizing each segment of the breath as you increase from 4 to 9 segments. Each shift requires a conscious adjustment of pace, depth and pressure. The inhalations are drawn in by a movement of the diaphragm, not by powerfully squeezing the nostrils.

You visualize the light and energy emanating as rays all over the body, but keep the eyes focused through the Brow Point like a universal window which sees everywhere.

After the meditation, if you have time, sit very still. Let your mind see. Any place or anyone that comes to your attention, you will be there instantly and sense what you need to know. This meditation develops the siddhi to project your presence and your senses to any place. You will come to realize the effect of your presence. Understand that to use this meditation wisely, project from your heart as well. Conscious visualization is essential to yoga. It engages your imagination and creativity. It invokes your psyche to create with you. In the deepest stages of meditation this ability will also let you see the colors around things, the aura. These colors are actually in your own mind, but the energetic relationships they reflect are true. In those relationships you can sense and see the patterns of life. The color white represents a universal open consciousness, which is why as teachers we wear white. Blue is the effective relationship to personal soul and the ability to sacrifice for your consciousness. Green reflects a state of calmness and healing. A silvery white represents the positive power to create. A shiny, not dull, black can suck out any negativity. The blue-white light is universal creativity applied to your destiny.

Stage Sixteen
Radiance Everywhere

Radiance Everywhere

Your radiant body is everywhere.
You are felt everywhere.
You project your presence to every corner of creation.
You have no bounds.
Space does not contain you.
You trust creation.
You rely on it.
You are you. You are not entangled.
The Divine and your identity intermingle.

You are you. You are not entangled in any drama, emotion or commotion. Only your

This is a beautiful stage of meditation in which we rely on our radiance. We sensitize ourselves to the Radiant Body, which is the tenth body,† and rely less and less upon our own efforts and manipulations; the conflicts within the personality and the mind decrease as well.

† In Kundalini Yoga as taught by Yogi Bhajan® we recognize Ten Bodies: soul, negative mind, positive mind, neutral mind, physical body, praanic body, arcline, aura, subtle body and radiant body. To learn more see *The Ten Light Bodies* by Nirvair Singh Khalsa.

Stage Sixteen: Radiance Everywhere

The Radiant Body is universal. It is everywhere. Most of our lives we focus on our physical body, the small spatial and temporal confines of our most localized sense of Self and ego. As we transcend the finite Self, the doors of perception open. We are capable of much greater sensitivity. When we open up to that sensitivity we realize how many choices are available to us to be creative, meditative and original. We can work through radiance rather than impulses, hassles and conflicts; we can bless instead of stress; and we can attract instead of track our success and happiness.

> *"Impulse won't lead us anywhere, impulse is, 'I am under impulse, I must go.' Why should it make you go where it wants you to go? You have to compute and answer your questions first—that's your creativity. You have a conflict from impulse; and you must resolve that conflict first. If the conflict becomes a driving force, you are confused. You will take shelter under fear and phobia.*

> *"What we are trying to achieve is the meditative, creative mind and the intelligent assessment. You must have the intuitive, analytical assessment to compare and decide. That is your beauty. All I know is, if we can create this basic intelligence, which is creative, which is comparative and which is meditative in each individual, and then each individual by his grace can work in a group consciousness to effectively foresee danger and direct and correct his life to the utmost happiness, then we can live by creative intelligence not impulse. That is the force which keeps me going, motivated and talking to you. I know I was a worse nut than you. You don't do those terrible things which I did in my life. I used to shred people into tears. That's true. If that much insanity can be totally harnessed into the effectiveness that one feels civilized and humble I must share that so you can try, too. You can feel absolutely amalgamated, merged and totally flowing.*

> *"Human relationship is not like a piston and steam engine where we say, 'Well, I have made love.' Yeah, you are an idiot. It's gross. You are talking of a steam engine; you are not talking about a human being. Human being creates the pulse of the impulses at the same harmony and sophisticated field. It has the vibratory sense that it expands and it contracts. It expands and it contracts. To your radiance, miles and millions of miles do not mean a thing. A person is feeling—that is called sensitive intelligence.*

> *"There is something higher in sensitivity in the human life. That sensitivity is more precious and more corrective. It's more near, it's more clear, it's more precious than any impulse. There is only one problem; this sensitivity only comes after crystallization. When the basic crystallization is turned into many facets, then it is*

those facets which are ultimately the aim of human life. That is called the Radiant Body; it is the tenth body." [72]

In meditation we envelop our consciousness in a body of sound; this body of sound is like a sensory system that connects you to the boundless sound, the *anaahat naad*. This vibratory level of existence has two primary characteristics: radiance and boundlessness. We perceive this brilliance as intelligence in itself and a part of our being. We begin to find that radiance everywhere at once. This is another step in a profound transformation of perspective, perception and skill. We attune to the natural power and function of our Radiant Body. Instead of trying to get to things, our radiance attunes, attracts and delivers things. When we expand this radiance we are beautiful. No amount of makeup or physical alteration can compete or replace our radiance and its capacity to attract. Just one word spoken with our Radiant Body will uplift a heart and open doors. Our communication becomes sophisticated, appropriate and directly effective.

> *"You have not understood me. Projectivity is the essence of your radiance. It's a light. Your body, this physical body does not create an impression. You are foolish. The impression you make is the radiance of your body. If you take a candle, give it to somebody what he is going to do with it? Nothing. If the candle is not lit, it's just wax. The beauty of the candle is when it is lit. The beauty is when it spreads light and removes the darkness.*
>
> *"When you go somewhere for an interview and the person doesn't get up to receive you, you are not a complete human being. If your light cannot lift up the other person, you have not achieved your full radiance or potential. You can sense you have a handicap so you have to do some kind of makeup. That's why you dress up to impress. You never dress just original to express your uniqueness just as you."* [96]

In every Kundalini Yoga class we sing a final blessing song, which has deep implications for this stage of meditation:

> *"'May the longtime sunshine upon you,' what a blessing! We bless everybody and say 'all love surround you,' not of God only, but all. What an affirmation! Then [we say] 'the pure light within you,' not your light, the pure light, which is the Radiant Body and the soul. Your soul is the direct descendent of the Radiant Body, and the Radiant Body is the direct shield of the soul. We say, 'the pure light within you,' not 'follow me'. We say, 'guide your way on,' and keep going. When we sing it, it gives us a feeling of our Self. Sometime we should sing it within our Self and understand that we know all."* [74]

Stage Sixteen: Radiance Everywhere

The goal of this practice—to sense our presence as radiance everywhere—is just to be happy. It is not to go to some far away heaven or to gain some great earthly power. It is to be powerfully human, our potential fulfilled, and to be able to attract what we need to succeed, grow, and be happy. Essential to that happiness is the cultivation of our Radiant Body and the capacity to sense our radiance everywhere. All our other efforts, including religions and rituals, are for this same end: to expand our radiance and make our presence work in relationship to our soul and consciousness. The one thing that gets in the way is when we try to project from our ego, from our limitation. When we project from fear and conflict then we create either fantasy or confusion. To experience ourselves as everywhere radiant we must be whole. That is the challenge of this meditative stage.

> *"I didn't come here to eat peanuts; I have come here to make people happy. I know you are here for that. I am aware of it. Without happiness there is no purpose for life. Why do we worship God? Are we crazy? God is everywhere. Where are we going to find God? Why find Him in something when He is everywhere? It's crazy isn't it? The real purpose is to find our own Unknown, which we call God, which is truly not true. Just as we say the sun rises; but the sun never rises, we move. We find God in the shape of our Unknown.*
>
> *"We want to be happy that's true. It's a very personal selfish thing. We want relationships to rid loneliness, for sexual happiness, for partnership. Behind everything the purpose is to be happy. We do the meditations to be practical, to experience something which cannot be disputed, something which can really deliver us to happiness, and to keep on living each moment as good."* [75]
>
> *"That's why we meditate, that's why we chant, and that's why we read those Banis and all that stuff. It's a totally selfish thing; it's not to please God; God has nothing to do with it. All the religious things we do only cater to and augment our own reality so we can have a better Radiant Body. With the Radiant Body we can attract all the wealth, opportunity, comforts, blessings, goodwill, and everything else. There are two ways to live: one is to hustle and hassle and go after everything; the other is to sit down and let all come to you. Make a choice. Either let the world, the whole world, come to you or you go after everything you want. The only other choice is to hang in-between and be nothing but miserable; that is called human tragedy.*
>
> *"This is a mental game; the mind is supposed to play. Either develop the power to go after what you want to go after, or let it come to you. Achievement is always through mental vibrations. When you achieve it, you maintain it physically. You*

may enjoy, may not enjoy; to enjoy it is again mental. And if you really want to understand the taste and the subtlety of this, ask how fulfilled your spirituality is. How much spirit do you put out through the mind to achieve what you want to achieve? Mind is only a lens which projects the light and radiance of your soul. The physical body is just a cover around it. All three are equally important. It is God within you that is forever; and as much you relate to God within you that much reality of you becomes powerful; there is no other secret."

We all have to learn to see the world through our Radiant Body. We begin in stillness. We listen to the anaahat sounds, the unstruck vibrations. We listen inside the sounds. In the following meditation, we listen to the chants, and chant the sounds but we do it everywhere at once as an expression of our total radiance. We must open our sensitivity to the vibrations and light that connects us everywhere. Let go of the usual anchors of the distracted mind. Use the current of pulsating sound to travel on. It is both pleasant discipline and hard work at the same time. Much of it is accomplished by our own radiance and by the energy in the sounds themselves. The structure and meaning of the sounds seed a sample of the consciousness we are endeavoring toward. According to the scriptures, without a deeply trained meditative mind, we give way to our temperamental mind, the monkey mind, and its monkey business; it distracts us and turns us into monkeys.

In the first stages of the initial journey, there was not yet a definite sense of you; there was no crystallization of the Self. Without that you-within-you there is no nucleus through which the infinite Radiant Body can act to project the beauty of your soul. When we are touched by the grace of radiance everywhere, our presence works and is experienced everywhere. Our Third Eye can see at will whatever and wherever our intention takes it. We become simple, humble, realistic and attractive.

Technically, in this stage of meditation, we place our Self firmly in the present and release all boundaries of space and time. We correlate the sensation of our soul, through the physical body, subtle body and aura, with the universal Radiant Body, which is our connection with the whole universe. We use mantra and meditation to create a subtle tantra between our finite and universal Self. In this way we further break the bonds of the ego-sense and empower our soul to act with the flow of our Radiant Body. This seems to be an abstract concept until we experience it, which comes with the opening of the Third Eye, called *Joti Nitra*, the radiance of the soul eye. Then we can feel, intuit or see the soul, which is the Self. It is our core reality, not defined nor delimited by what we possess or what we have accomplished. In this way, we attract all that we need to express, be happy and succeed in our unique life.

Stage Sixteen: Radiance Everywhere

"At a certain moment, when your mind is clean, the last of your ten bodies, the Radiant Body, works. When your radiance starts to work, then you start living, loving and enjoying being a human. In other words, in simple words, when your Radiant Body starts doing your public relations you are in good shape, do you follow? That Radiant Body will start working very well when the mind is clean and clear. If your subconscious is clean so that your conscious and supreme conscious become one then you become a very beautiful human being. And that's the purpose of the life: to become a beautiful human being." [76]

"Your power to earn is not you, your power to live is not you, and your power to attract is not you. Not these cheeks. Okay, she had high cheek bones, therefore every man loves her. That is your philosophy. This is not what is going to attract anything for you. What attracts for you is your Arc Body, because when the Radiant Body shines in combination with the Arc Body, you get everything. I mean everything. When the candle is lit, the moths come in the thousands. In the same way, material worlds come where light is. That is a law.

"Talk in any religion, say anything, it doesn't mean a thing. Things will come to you only when you will shine. Radiate. Don't you see at night, there is a moon, there are stars, we all get into our home, switch off our lights and sleep? When there is a sun, everybody comes out. You have to have a potent biological, psychological, sociological, and personal account of your own Self, and know who you are." [77]

If we know our own light, our own presence, we know our Self. In Stage Fifteen we expanded the projection of a beam of light to our target. In this stage we dwell and immerse into the ever-present radiance and gather that in through the lens of our subtle body and aura. This changes our relationship to our efforts. We begin to live with effortless effort. We become stewards of all that is given. We passionately embrace a life of gratitude in which service is as natural as fragrance is to a flower.

Polishing the Radiant Body

June 18, 2001

This exercise sequence is done as a group. Place yourself in rows, side by side with your neighbor, before you begin.

PART ONE

Sit in Easy Pose or other meditative position, with a straight spine, and apply Neck Lock. The eyes look past the tip of the nose.

A) Raise both hands with the elbows relaxed down by the sides. Make fists of the hands. Extend the index finger straight up, and lock the thumb over the other fingers.

Chant the Ik Acharee Chand shabad from Guru Gobind Singh's *Jaap Sahib*. Chant each word distinctly and pull the Navel Point in rhythm with the words.

Ajai Alai	Invincible. Indestructible.
Abhai Abai	Fearless. Everywhere.
Abhoo Ajoo	Unborn. Forever.
Anaas Akaas	Indestructible. Within Everything.
Aganj Abhanj	Invincible. Indestructible.
Alakh Abhakh	Invisible. Free from wants.
Akaal Dayaal	Immortal. Kind.
Alaykh Abhaykh	Unimaginable. Formless.
Anaam Akaam	Unnameable. Free from desires.
Agaahaa Adhaahaa	Unfathomable. Undamageable.
Anaatay Parmaatay	Without a master. Destroyer of all.
Ajonee Amonee	Beyond birth & death. Beyond silence.
Na Raagay Na Rangay	More than love itself. Beyond all colors.
Na Roopay Na Raykhay	Formless. Beyond chakras.
Akharamang Abharamang	Beyond karma. Beyond doubt.
Aganjay Alaykhay	Beyond battles. Unimaginable.

Stage Sixteen: Radiance Everywhere

As you chant this beautiful mantra, project an attitude: You are vibrating and speaking to the real you. Wake up! Elevate your spirit. Simultaneously hear the sounds coming from everywhere. This mantra is boundless. The sound already vibrates throughout creation. It flows through you; uses your tongue; speaks your heart. Hear it as the whisper of your soul. Let it awaken your consciousness. Expand your mind and release your ego, soften the boundaries. Let each word chisel you and reveal your divinity, dignity and depth. Feel you are shining everywhere. Feel that your radiance is already everywhere. In this stage you are sensing it not projecting it. The light arises from the space of the "unstruck sound," the anaahat, which is everywhere.

Keep chanting for 50 minutes. Continue chanting as you move into the next exercise.

B) Continue chanting in the same posture but begin moving your torso in circles from the base of the spine in rhythm with the chant. As you chant move with a sense of ease like a tree swaying in a gentle breeze.

Continue for 3 minutes.

Inhale deeply, straighten the spine and suspend the breath into stillness. Grasp the hands of your neighbors on each side. Exhale and immediately switch to the next exercise.

C) Holding hands with your neighbor on each side, keep the hands at shoulder height and form a connected chain of people and move your spine in circles from the base. The spine remains straight; that is, this is not a flexing and contracting action but a simple circle. Continue to chant the mantra. After 2 minutes, begin to whisper strongly. Continue for 1 more minute.

Move directly to the next exercise.

D) In silence, continue holding hands with your partners and sit absolutely still. Close the eyes and focus at the Brow Point. Begin long, deep, steady, slow breathing through the nostrils. **Listen to the mantra.** Establish a mental attitude of the Buddha. Be in perfect balance and feel your presence everywhere like a calm perfect sea. In your radiance sit with truth, with reality, with the presence of your unlimited Being.

Continue in this deep meditation for 6 minutes. Then tighten the grip with your partners, continue breathing. Open your sensitivity to feel the flow of energy that is part of the tidal presence of your infinite Self, psyche and God. Sense the energy flowing through you and existing in all places in all directions at once. 3 minutes.

Inhale deeply, suspend the breath, and project your Self everywhere. Exhale. Repeat two more times. Then relax.

PART TWO

Sit straight in a cross-legged meditation posture, facing a partner. Relax the elbows down and bring the hands, palms facing, with your partner's hands. Do not touch; keep the palms separated by about 2-6 inches (5-15 cm). Begin chanting the Ik Acharee Chand shabad and move the hands up and down steadily in rhythm with the mantra, matching your partner's movements. You are mirroring each other and pacing

Stage Sixteen: Radiance Everywhere

the hands as you sense the energy between them. The hands move about 12 inches (31 cm.) up and down.

Fix your eyes unblinking toward your partner's eyes. Penetrate through the eyes to the light of the soul. See the unlimited space of that person. See them exactly as they are, with you, joined in this common space of energy and awareness.

Continue for 22 minutes.

Inhale deeply; suspend the breath and the hands; position the hands at the level of the Heart Center between you and your partner. Keep the eyes locked with your partner. Exhale. Repeat two more times. Then inhale with the eyes closed and bring the hands down. Exhale.

The feeling of this exercise is the presence of grace. Sit gracefully. See the grace of the other person gratefully. When we expand into these stages, the mind is insufficient. Its normal tools of classification and ego are gradually laid aside. Instead call on grace, dignity, love and neutral sensitivity.

Yogi Bhajan led this exercise with these comments: *"Don't touch the hands. Let the energy flow. Let in the name of God, heavens flow and flow. Let the winds become the breeze and touch you. Let the song of the Holy Ghost be heard. Let the spirit flow. Flow with this sound! Let the winds blow. Come in the winds, touch the heart through feeling. Feel the breath of life in every cell and everywhere."*

This partner exercise and the next one remove the tendency for isolation in your feelings and self-concept. The essence of you is immanent in your experience and transcendent of any limitation in form or thought. Together dissolve all differences into the anaahat of this mantra and into the light and radiance of your presence.

Go immediately to the next part.

PART THREE

Sit straight in Easy Pose, facing your partner. Extend your arms and bring your palms over your partner's ears. Press the Jupiter mound, the base of the index finger, against the ear. Seal the ears with a tight but not uncomfortable pressure.

According to the length of your arms you may have to lean very slightly forward to settle the lock.

Look into your partner's eyes without blinking; this is a traatik.

Chant the Ik Acharee Chand shabad loud and clear. Use the Navel Point in the sound.

Continue for 9 minutes. During the final minute keep the head up and secure the lock over the ears by increasing the pressure slightly.

Inhale deeply, suspend the breath, look straight, exhale. Repeat two more times with the eyes closed. Then relax.

This exercise is the polarity of Part Two. You are doing the chant in the nirgun mode of anaahat. You are hearing the sound inside as you block the ears. Inside the inner sound is the subtle pulse of the naad. When the body is in balance, its praanas organize into a meditative sensitivity, then these sounds polish your Radiant Body which is everywhere. The sounds created by the tenth master, Guru Gobind Singh,† capture the energy that brings stability and shine to your Radiant Body. The tongue makes the sound in the earthy language of humans and the ears hear it in the language of the angels as you rise through the heavens with joy and ecstasy.

This meditation will help us guide those who will be struck by the overwhelming levels of change in the present change of the Age. Radiance everywhere is our capacity to uplift those who are shivering and shattered and elevate them to their reality— spirited, secure, self-radiant and successful—that we may all express our destiny in every condition.

---

† Guru Gobind Singh (1666-1708) was the Tenth Sikh Guru and the Father of the Khalsa.

STAGE SEVENTEEN
Prayerful Stillness

Prayerful Stillness

Sitting at the feet of God and Guru a
new stillness comes.
You relinquish the struggle to control
your world.
In that moment the universe rushes to serve you.
Free will gives way to Divine will.
You act through the totality of consciousness beyond
time and space.
Nothing moves in your being.
You have no boundary.
Your presence communes with the vast presence
of the Creator
Together they intermingle and act seamlessly.

Your praanas, the nose, and your awareness, the uncoiling snake, meet and make every movement and thought prayerful.

This stage is filled with surprise and delight at what we are able to let go of, what simply drops away; and what we're able to receive, what comes to us. One of the four base stages of this third journey, it consolidates a seismic shift in our sense of Self and our way of operating. It changes where we get our energy from and how we go about enacting our will and intention.

Stage Seventeen: Prayerful Stillness

Think for a moment of the three journeys in terms of life's cycles. The first is to crystallize the Self, where like a child we rely on our parents and our inborn energy. The second journey, where like a young adult, we rely on our own efforts, accomplishments and intelligence to achieve our goals. In this third journey, our maturity, we begin to rely on the Radiant Body, intuitive wisdom, and the energy that comes from exploring the whole cosmos and discovering that we are an integral part of that cosmos.

To shift into this stage, we once again become still, then we become prayerful and receive what is always flowing to us from our infinite Self. We prepared for this by crystallizing our Self and developing the disciplines of consciousness. Then we gained the skills to project and enact our will. Now we must be able to effectively invite the Infinite to work through our finite. At this stage we find abundance not in what we conquer but in how we conquer our own mind. As the mind expands and refines its neutrality, it becomes a portal for every blessing and opportunity.

Prayerful stillness is part of our potential; it's a part of our human nature, along with fear and love and a sense of what is just and true. As we attune to and begin to rely on our totality, our infinite spirit, we can recognize that every part of our experience contributes to our growth and fulfillment. We have a right to exist and fulfill our soul's destiny; life is given to test our totality and provoke our growth. Our nature has many parts that interact and serve our growth, even when they appear negative on the surface. Each thing in our nature benefits us when used proportionately and in balance with the other parts. Fear, for example, can alert us not only to danger but also to what we must correct in our Self. It is basically a good thing in small doses. Fear in the extreme or too persistent and chronic, damages us and we develop phobias.

It is with a prayerful stillness that we stay attuned to our totality under the challenges and changes that life brings. It is from that still point that we stay aligned with our true self and do not take on the shape of our fears and conflicts

Prayerful stillness abates our instinct to react to others and to control others' choices. It brings our focus back to ourselves and the expression of our own authentic Self. A paramount law of life and human consciousness is that we have the right to experience our Self but we have no right to interfere or dominate the life of another. When we violate the dignity and self-integrity of another person we limit our own. When we respect others and let them live as themselves, it is no favor to them. It is a requirement for us if we are to expand and transcend our ego to become real. The power of prayerful stillness comes from the full embrace of life as it is and our Self in totality.

"One day you will be called upon to be you. That is the purpose of life. Life is a practical source of testing one's own totality. Life is given to you with all the richness. Poverty is caused by you; pain is caused by you, because you waste time on things that are not true; not true to anybody, not true to yourself.

"The Creative mind, which God has given to you, is a very prayerful mind. The policy of life, which is most basic, is 'live and let live.' Some people are touchy about one thing; some people are touchy about other things. Why put your boat into the water and hit the boulders when you can safely go through a very small, beautiful, well-laid passage?

"Some people think they love conflict. What a waste of time! You have no right given by God to interfere with any other life. There can be a mutual acceptance of each other. You try to give a gift to God. The very life of you is a gift of God. But have you taken this gift of God and given it to somebody? Can you give yourself to somebody just like a gift? You give a car to somebody, it's okay. You give somebody some special thing, it's okay. But can you give your total Self to somebody?

"God gave you your Self, can you offer this Self back to God? That is the purpose of life. If you [don't] love your neuroses, take off those covers and let yourself out. Have you seen some people who just lay a trauma on you? Have you seen those? These are the children who didn't find in their heart the love of their father. Have you seen people who pretend to be very good? But when you really rely on their goodness they just pull the rug out from under your feet. You must have met them all. These are all children who didn't find the love of their mother. Have you seen people who just go flip-flop out of the blue? These are the people in their childhood who didn't find out who they are. They couldn't find their identity.

"These things happen because of your childhood, but now you are not children any more. Why are you satisfied being in childhood as an adult? The life is now; and now just welcomes tomorrow, don't worry about it. You ruin your tomorrow by worrying about it. Welcome tomorrow and thank God for today that will become yesterday. Take this attitude wherever you are and you will be happy. The moment you are happy, you are radiant and you will be rich. The moment you will be rich you will be giving. And when you start giving you will be Godly. Be mindful that richness does not just mean money. Richness also means giving a smile. Richness is also having a sense of humor in life; richness is having creativity." [78]

Stage Seventeen: Prayerful Stillness

Progressing through the stages of meditation is like removing layers and layers of insulation. We live each day burdened by unnecessary attachments, covered in fears and false ideas, bundled in cultural and family narratives and surrounded by our necessary but finite circumstances. For the final unveiling we become an initiate before our infinite Self; and for that a coin is required. The only coin that works as legal tender in the realm of spirit is your whole Self. To deal with the realms of unity and totality we need the ability to totally commit, totally surrender, totally give, and totally receive. To that end, we practice residing in the still point of the soul, which presides over our every action. We go to the actor that lets us act, the One. In this radical openness to all that is, prayerfulness comes naturally.

> *"When you work with God, with Infinity, with soul, then everything falls in place for you. Otherwise, you will fall in every place. You know what I mean? Do you understand? . . . It is a simple answer: everybody has been created by God and God knows how to take care of the creation. The most powerful thing is the prayer. There is nothing we can do alone; all we can do is pray with our prayerful meditative mind, and then it happens."* [79]

Great power resides in the capacity to dwell in prayerful stillness. It moves the universal field of consciousness. It changes the inflow, our context and surroundings as an individual unit of existence; it transforms. When we prayerfully sit with a person who is suffering under their imagined limitations, beliefs or circumstances, we bless them to be able to sense their own reality. They begin to qualify themselves before their own higher Self. They activate their soul and are inspired to act for their own highest good. In stillness you do not force them, act for them, or become passive. Your active witnessing is a catalyst for all that is original in that person's life and destiny, which is why the blessing of a teacher and a mother are so powerful. They give us a moment of sensitivity to our Self; and life is lived in these moments of awareness and action. We take the moment or we let it pass. In prayerful stillness the moment is never lost. In each moment, we find the soul's own song and bring to life our spirit and commitment.

With prayerful stillness we hope to change our karma. We forgive our Self and recognize the next step forward. For a Christian this stage means we die in the consciousness of the infinite, Christ-consciousness, to be born again as our true Self. As a Hindu or a Buddhist this means we elevate our awareness to end illusion and out of compassion liberate our Self and all others to never be born into illusion again. As a Sikh, prayerful stillness means we merge our mind into the Infinite mind, which merges us with the living god in us all—liberation while alive—Jiwan Mukht. All of these ideas reflect one simple idea: in prayerful stillness, let my reality be me.

"The idea of religion is to be prayerful. The power is in the word not in you; the real power is not in the atom bomb. Power is in prayer. All we have to do is create a prayerful mind; that is religion. A religion is not when your body prays; it is when the mind prays, when it is prayerful and still. Try to separate these two parts of you. Soul is a reality, a part of God, and a religion; you don't have to bother about it. It is there and already yours. Your body is given to you as a gift; it's a shell. The working force in this shell is the mind. It is the mind, not you, that has to learn prayerfulness.

"This does not mean you train the mind to say, 'Oh thank you God; I am very sorry. Please help me.' Now do you think God is crazy? He's going to listen to you? Forget it; that is not what God wants and He doesn't have time for that. Your mind must tune-in to the Infinite mind; that's what prayer is; that is what naad in laya is." [80]

"I was asked to explain time and space. I gave an example. Suppose at this time right now you have one hour. I am tired, I am broken, I need help; or at this time I am hungry and I need food in this moment. Or I have this task to complete and I need assistance now. This time is the time!

"If you can put your spirit, mind, body and everything into this time, for that time, for that one hour, then I can get through that handicap. I shall be grateful; I shall become prayerful; I shall be beautiful. But if you are willing to waste this hour instead to attend and care for your neurosis, your fears, your thoughts, your complications, your preferences, then this hour will pass and never come back again. The bell shall never ring this hour again. I'll be there, you will be there, but this hour will be missing. Life, time and space, is just exactly like that hour. It is that moment. It is that time and space, and it the chance that is in that hour.

"If there is no water in the glass you may drink it topsy-turvy bottom up, you won't get a drop out of it. If there is no spirit in me, you will not get anything in that moment. You can only give what you have. If I have ego, I'll give you my ego. I'll build your ego to relate to my ego. If I have divinity, I'll build your ego and transform it into divinity. Then from divinity I'll transform that into Infinity. That can happen if I have that Infinity, that experience. That is why if someone is a messenger of that Infinity then they are the same as that Infinity. Whosoever can touch, relate, feel and receive that messenger shall become part of that Infinity because at that time they are, 'I am I am.'

Stage Seventeen: Prayerful Stillness

"This applies to every individual. This will never change. This cannot change. Because this is the quality of that Infinity, of that time, of that Self, that is in us and in our time and space. The subtlety of life, the subtlety of the flow of life and the subtlety of the spirit of life can never die. It will channel itself from infinite to finite. And whosoever shall receive, accept, relate to, touch, feel, or even think the thought to think of that channel shall receive the purity of that message.

"But for many people, their egos are so sick they cannot accept the truth. Not even the truth itself comes to explain it. It is difficult because ritual becomes a habit. To break the habit of ritual is very difficult. It is as if there is a house. To do an addition and alternation to that house it takes more time, it's more headache than to start all over again with just a piece of land. Then it's easy, it is clean, it is straight. To instead tell an egocentric idiot some truth, you have to first break his vision and take a big machine to make a hole in his brain. Even then you will have to sit there in a prayerful still mind and through that you have to change the entire cosmos to make him feel this thing, and open the sensitivity." [81]

One of the reasons we use the shabads and mantras from the Siri Guru Granth Sahib is that they came from this place, this prayerful stillness. They were heard by the clear souls of many great teachers who in prayerful stillness expressed the presence of God within them in beautiful and effective poetry. The words contain wisdom and move the mind and soul into alignment. Many wisdom traditions exist; and none can lay claim to a singular truth. But some mantras and *sutras* make the wisdom of all traditions more easily accessible. Delivered by very pure channels to all people of all traditions, they were words of the soul expressed through the heart to elevate the mind in order to see the world though prayerful stillness. These shabads and mantras are songs of truth, both universal and intimately personal, which transcend time and space.

Prayerful stillness is sometimes the only state that can open up an opportunity for time and space to prevail. When we are in this stage of meditation we become a channel for healing through our words, deeds and blessings.

Deeksha Patra for Prayerful Stillness

April 29, 1976

POSTURE: Sit in Easy Pose, with a straight spine, and apply Neck Lock.

MUDRA: Bring the hands palms up in front of the torso at the level of the solar plexus just below the Heart Center. Place the back of the right hand into the palm of the left hand. The fingers cross at an angle. The left thumb rests in the right palm and the right thumb crosses over the top of the left. It is a very contained, secure and cozy mudra.

EYES: The eyes are slightly open. Concentrate through the Brow Point.

MANTRA: Whaa-hay Guroo. Chant the Gur Mantra in a monotone; project the voice and concentrate on the sound and the energy of the mantra. The sound of Hay vibrates in the back cave of the mouth and resonates gently in the upper conch of the skull, but without a nasal sound. We listen to the sound as we make it, as if the sound is given to us and we only have to receive the vibrations deep within our consciousness. To practice this sound current correctly you must take in a deep, full breath and chant the mantra once as you let the entire breath out. The pace is about one recitation (including the inhalation) every 10-12 seconds. Do not try to extend the length of the chant by drawing the exhale out; keep the rhythm and pace at 10-12 seconds per recitation, including the breath. With each deep inhale check to be sure your spine is erect and the Neck Lock applied before you chant. Then the sound will come from the central fiber of your spine, your central channel of energy. Gradually apply the locks as you exhale.

TIME: 31 minutes.

TO END: Inhale deeply, suspend the breath and hear the mental echo of the mantra. Exhale powerfully. Repeat three times. Relax.

Hints for Practice and Mastery

The name of this meditation speaks of self-initiation; drop the blockages and acquire the skills to meditate in merger with the infinite Self. *Deeksha* is a blessing or initiation. *Patra* is a vessel, one who receives something. So the meditation is a mental, emotional and spiritual reception of the blessing and initiation of higher consciousness. In the traditional sense, this would be the merger of the mind of the student and the guru.

In Kundalini Yoga and Meditation we do not initiate. Instead, we learn how to be secure within our Self; our status is granted by our own dignity and consciousness. In this new Age each of us can tap into the energy of our infinite Self, through our Self, when we use a mantra that is anaahat and whose naad attunes us. It is in this third journey that this is most possible. We must become ready to receive, rather than gain. We must be comfortable that the Unknown in us touches the known.

Practicing this meditation almost always brings sleepiness. The mind thinks it is on vacation or offline and can go to sleep. The normal distractions and impulses that keep us awake and identified with our life stop. It is a *gutkaa* (a small stick on a water wheel) meditation, it stops the root of the thought. We don't even begin to chase a thought. We instead are a vessel. We are receptive to our own infinite now.

One of the other limitations is the ego's sense of the immediate. It must act upon its every impulse. It must be entertained and engaged. But in this stage, the infinite is the immediate. Intuition keeps company with the Self and invites the spontaneous revelation of your soul, which is why this stage is called prayerful stillness. No action is needed. A prayerful attitude and projection brings the touch of grace. It will vanquish negativity; and it will make you your own being. In the prayerful stillness of this meditation everything is being done. Relax; God is on duty; your Unknown knows the known of you.

Stage Eighteen
Preacher

Preacher

Giving becomes a spontaneous joy and duty.
Giving is not a calculation, exchange,
a deal or even a merit.
You give without limit.
You give and trust that the Infinite acts with you to
fulfill your act of giving.

Giving in innocence as part of the flow of
consciousness you become a preacher.
You witness the Creator everywhere.
Your words inspire and elevate anyone
who hears them.

Your words come from your heart and from that still,
vast presence within.
You give people merits, knowledge and values.
You respond to people's prayers and bring them the
opportunity to experience their spirit.
You point the way
And serve them on their way through all the stages.

Reach out, reach out, reach out. Touch every direction. Keep every door open. You dangle from the teachings like a fruit that is finally ripe.

This is the last stage at the base of this final journey. We drop one final layer of the Self in order to transform our Self and become comfortable with the formless Infinite within us. The final three stages complete our merger and embodiment as human beings.

Stage Eighteen: Preacher

When Yogi Bhajan named this stage "Preacher" I double-checked to be sure I understood him correctly. In many of his lectures he speaks about the consciousness of a preacher in contrast to the consciousness of a teacher: one talks, one acts; one explains, one chisels and creates change. One shows the way, the other walks the path. In this sense I thought of the preacher as negative. He laughed and reminded me that there is always a polarity. This stage of meditation represents the positive projection and function of the Preacher; in this sense, it is not a fixed object or goal but an action, a function of the meditative mind. So although the contrast between the terms "Teacher" and "Preacher" Yogi Bhajan makes is correct, it could obscure the essence of this stage, the positive function that this stage represents, which is the final removal of fear. In this stage we see through the eyes of the formless; and when this happens we become a fearless giver. It is this fearless giver that is the Preacher. It is often hard to give because we think we have a limited amount; that if we give too much we won't have enough. But as we transcend our dependence on the finite sense of Self, we tap into the resources of spirit, of God, which has no limit. Laws, structures and qualities, yes; but it cannot be exhausted. It is what comes through like a miracle to cover us when what we know of our Self relies, prayerfully, on the unknown Self.

As we master this stage our words flow with a magnetic quality. We are gifted with a golden tongue, not from cleverness but clarity, which comes not from ego but from our real Self. Our words serve each person who hears them in reaching their own formlessness. We become inspiring and encourage others to grow not by conquering their egos but by showing them the way to gratitude and its fruits.

The preacher finds the compassion in a person's heart. By embodying consciousness the preacher awakens consciousness in others. In this stage there is a deep passion to share, which comes from simple duty and love. The fire-branding emotional appeals of politicians, salesmen and religious zealots have nothing to do with the consciousness of the true preacher and the consciousness of meditation this stage represents. Rather, the skill at this stage is to rest firmly on the formless and to express that vision in words, actions and inspiration. When we master this stage of meditation we become irresistibly attractive. There is a sense of standing at the doorway to hope, success, and the relief of pain. We point the way forward. We are very tempting (and in that temptation, we too are tempted).

The error commonly made at this stage is to drop away from the sense of the formless once we approach it. Instead of staying in that vast presence, we stake a claim. We believe that we have become the answer; that the Infinite speaks only to us and through us, guiding our every step. We put everything on the Unknown and take no responsibility for our own decisions. Instead of gratitude to God and reliance on spirit, we blame the Infinite for everything. We quote scripture instead of helping others read for themselves. We become the epitome of cleverness and spiritual ego. This is the one illness that Yogi Bhajan said had no cure—spiritual ego. We suddenly stop listening to the formless, to other people and to our teacher. We fall back on our deep-seated habit of relying on what is seen rather than trusting what we cannot see.

This meditation counters that deep-seated habit and teaches us to rely upon the Unseen, to be comfortable in waiting for what may come, not just relying on what we can grasp right now. It has at its heart a profound patience with all that is; mixed with an equal portion of enthusiasm for what can be. Like a master gardener who plants a new seed, we see the future of this moment and work hard to fertilize the seed and give it all it needs to grow. In this stage of meditation, barriers are removed and we witness the Creator everywhere. Our words inspire and elevate anyone who hears them. We respond to people's prayers and bring them the opportunity to experience their spirit. We point the way and serve them on their journey through the stages.

> *"What you do not know to do with yourself you cannot do with me. If I am in higher consciousness, then you have to find a higher consciousness in you, to come at the same frequency. This is the difference between a teacher and a preacher. Preacher can arouse the compassion and the consciousness and the conscience. Teacher will confront the ego and wants you to penetrate through with your consciousness; they create a conflict. Mastery is when you conquer the ego. It is called going through and that going through is going away from the black hole. Ego is I, a limit, it's a small thing and the white light of Self is great. If you pull from there instead of ego you won't be limited here and then things become smooth and beautiful."* [82]

The consciousness of the preacher is a necessary and useful stage. It uses positive projection, understanding and persuasion to inspire. In comparison, the stage of teacher or master prepares us to measure the gap between our Self and our consciousness.

> *"You can always find a difference between a preacher and a teacher. You just hassle a teacher and he will hassle you right back. That's the first sign. He is totally non-tolerant of nonsense. He will go all the way to see from where it came from in you. A preacher will start lecturing. He won't react to your nonsense. The difference between a teacher and a preacher is a preacher becomes positive at that time when you are negative. Teacher becomes hundred times more negative than you are, then you get put onto your defense mechanisms. A preacher will guide you to understand and have you read books, which tell you about God, but do not tell you*

Stage Eighteen: Preacher

how to get it. You understand what I mean? They paint a beautiful painting of God, they paint a beautiful painting of hell, they talk about everything fantastic; you will love it, it's beautiful! But where it is? That you don't know." [83]

"What is a preacher? A bombardment of words! What is a preacher? He won't give you time to think wrong. Otherwise he is not a preacher. He lifts you up, hangs you up with your imagination and your mind and keeps hitting you. And a teacher? With his words he shreds you like mincemeat. He tears your ego apart to the extent that nothing is left. Then he laughs and says, 'Get it together. Ha, ha, ha.' That's why people hate their teachers. And it's easy to love their preachers. Do you know that? If you have a teacher you are going to, first thing, hate him. Why? Whenever you are in his presence he is going to shred you. How many times can you take it? He will take you to a point where that shredding doesn't matter at all. When that doesn't matter, nothing matters. Then you become the total matter of life yourself." [84]

Another way to grasp the positive nature of this stage and the concept of a preacher is the distinction Yogi Bhajan often drew between a Jupiter teacher and a Saturn teacher. The Jupiter teacher is positive, expansive, projects you to your ideal and is associated with knowledge, intuition, prosperity and grace. The Saturn teacher is confronting, practical and disciplined and is associated with purity, piety, knowledge and patience. So the preacher stage reflects Jupiter's capacity to expand, point the way to the One within and organize knowledge. The teacher reflects Saturn's capacity to chisel you and is known for its discipline, surrender and self-correction.

We need both, like the left and right hands, they lead us to awareness. They progress us through the stages of meditation and the realization of our most human and complete Self. Here is a specific technique which helps us to lean onto the formless and catch the light so that we may give, share and spread what we discover in our consciousness and cultivate the spirit of happiness and success in life.

Chautay Padma Nirgun Mantra

November 17, 1980

POSTURE: Sit in Easy Pose, with a straight spine, and apply Neck Lock.

MUDRA: Grasp the left thumb with the right hand. Close the left fingers around the right hand. Rotate the wrists until the hands rest comfortably in the lap.

EYES: Close the eyes 9/10ths; keeping them 1/10th open.

Stage Eighteen: Preacher

MANTRA:

Ek Ong Kaar Whaa-hay Guroo	One Creative Creation, Inexpressible Wisdom
Sat Kartaar Whaa-hay Guroo	The One is the Doer, Inexpressible Wisdom
Nirankaar Whaa-hay Guroo	Formless, Inexpressible Wisdom
Nirankaar Whaa-hay Guroo	Formless, Inexpressible Wisdom

This mantra is chanted musically. The two sutras are balanced and are done in different tones and patterns. It can be done as a group or divided into male and female voices with the males calling in the first line and the females answering with a higher pitch in the final two phrases.

TIME: 31 minutes. The time can be extended.

TO END: Inhale deeply, suspend the breath and squeeze the spine from base to top. Exhale and project from the crown in all directions, everywhere. Repeat two more times. Relax.

Hints for Practice and Mastery

The emotional posture for this meditation is one of joy and appreciation. You have reached the end of your barriers. You sit enthralled as though on a beach facing a great ocean. You sit relieved of what you do not need to carry forward. You become clear, innocent and receptive. You receive so you can give. You give because you are grateful for what you see and because to give freely is the ultimate victory.

As you attune to this jappa allow yourself to sense its energetic pulse. The first two lines are the *sirgun sutra*, with form; the second two lines are the *nirgun sutras*, formless threads, of this mantra. This is a common structure in mantras empowered with laya.

The sense of the first sutra, the first line of the mantra, is "Every part of this universe is one creative reality; infinite is the ecstasy of That. Every action is done by the doer of all, they are the hands of God and the expression of my soul; infinite is the ecstasy of That." Everything in this reality that we sense as a separate form is in fact connected to all others by the thread of Being. When we open to that there is nothing to say except Whaa-hay Guroo which is the naad of the formless One; it is a trikuti mantra that balances all the *gunas*, from which this entire universe is formed. It is the sound of neutrality, love, ecstasy and infinity. It takes you beyond the mind to mind your infinity.

The sense of the second sutra, the second line of the mantra, is "Beyond All Form, the Unity is One; infinite is the ecstasy of That." The phrase repeats twice. In the realm of the formless there is a mirror-like echo of any subtle sound. It is reflected either by a tonal inversion, as it is here, or by a syntactical turn as with the mantra Ek Ong Kaar, Sat Gurprasaad, Sat Gurprasaad, Ek Ong Kaar. The effect of this is to sense the play of the polarity of *Shakti* and *Shiva*, of stillness and action, which happens before any manifestation of form. It is similar to the way we talk about particles in modern physics. There is a virtual particle that has the potential to become a particular manifestation. This mantra is the virtual polarity before it reflects into the experienced polarity of *prakriti*, creation.

When you chant the first sutra you gather your crystallized Self. When you chant the second sutra you transcend that Self and immerse in the One. When you chant both in the laya rhythm of this meditation, you present your Self before your higher Self and become a channel. You put aside ego. You rely on Whaa-hay Guroo, not your idea of Whaa-hay Guroo. You recognize and accept the hand of Whaa-hay Guroo in the actions, the Sat Kartaar, around and through you. You become the best projection of the preacher, filled with the vision of the Infinite and your own soul. The radiance that comes through you is testimony to the current that flows through you.

You speak from the you within you and from the silence that presides at the gateway of your infinite Self.

Stage Nineteen
Teacher

Teacher

Your identity shifts. You are a teacher.
Your mind has but one calling:
to love, serve, obey and excel!

People come to you.
They find you according to their destiny.
They come with divided minds.
They suffer from the conflicts
that you have now mastered.
They long to experience the unisonness
of their spirit.

You elevate the life of each person and
deliver the touch of grace.
You chisel off the final remnants of ego.
Then you pull them toward the Infinite as you
confront the pieces of their fractured identity and ask
them to elevate themselves.

You bless all to find their innocence,
integrity and commitment.
As a tool in the hand of God, you deliver each person
back to an experience of their Infinite self.
Acting only as needed.
Through the grace of God and Guru,
deliver them to the feet of the Guru.

Beyond duality. Both sides open wide. The brilliance of the inner sun lighting every move. Each negative balanced by its positive. You go diagonal and direct to everything. There are no dark corners. Just truth.

This stage is also known as the Master. It represents a profound shift in both our sense of identity and our capacity to guide our Self and others. As a stage of meditation it requires us to begin in shuniya, which we developed in earlier stages. For in shuniya it becomes easier to drop the ego and shift our focus onto the soul, the infinite Self. The central capacity of this stage is to discern, confront and eliminate the gap between our Self and our consciousness; between our reactive thoughts and feelings and our intentions; between our clear awareness that is the soul, the infinite formless Self, and our experience of our personal identity.

Stage Nineteen: Teacher

When we practice and refine the capacity of this stage, we become a chisel for the One. We confront the divided areas of our minds, which harbor our conflicts and fractured identity. We elevate each errant thought and each inner crisis as we connect and project them to our infinite Self. We chisel our minds to experience the unisonness of our spirits. We bless ourself with direct truth and the discipline to live our innocence, integrity and commitment.

We need this final unmasking in order to continue to elevate toward the final stage of meditation—the infinite pulse. Our growing awareness strikes each thought like a chisel and knocks away anything unnecessary. We go to the essence, and beyond that to the origin of each thought. We attune to the path our soul declares and keep the mind on track. We follow the path laid before us. In this stage, our meditation corrects our missteps before they happen. We realign to our path quickly whenever we stray. It is a completely neutral process of witnessing, assessment and correction. As Yogi Bhajan said, consciousness at this stage is the ability to say no to nonsense and to uplift our Self.

The teacher, as a stage of meditation, must be applied beyond polarity. We see the negative and the positive, each balanced in relationship to the other. We begin to see the diagonal energy at play. We become completely open and accept what is, as we experience it, as the truth of our Self and our actions. There are no dark corners; no hidden agendas that escape our view. As we meditate, we sit in the full brilliance of the inner sun, which lights our way.

When we begin to put aside the burden of the ego, we start to accept our own depth and dimension as a human being. We are radiant. From the very beginning, we are given all the wisdom—in every cell—to uncoil our potential and be who we are. At this stage we lean on that reality and remove all negativity and every excuse. We meditate with the perfect balance of compassion and discipline. When we observe our own mind or investigate the condition of others we remain centered and clear; we are undeterred by discomfort or comfort, by emotional judgments of good and bad, or doubt and certainty.

The first gap between our Self and our consciousness, which we confront in this stage, is trust—self-trust. As the preacher, we could explain, direct and share our ideas and feelings. But the teacher is not a preacher. Here we must apply our consciousness to identify and drop self-belittlement, self-doubt and egotism. We must polish our Self on the touchstone of consciousness.

> *"Now this is a simple law: First you must trust your Self, and then only can you trust the teacher. Once that trust in your teacher is one hundred percent, only then*

can you trust God. If you don't want the teacher don't have it. If you don't want God, don't have it. If you don't want yourself, don't have it. Whose problem is this? It is simply your own problem. . . . You have been made that way, you don't know anything else.

"You satisfy yourself with the preachers. Preachers are not teachers and teachers are not preachers, they are two different words. The teacher does not talk about truth all the time; he makes it happen. He is a chiseler. He chisels you to carve out of you what is authentically just you. A preacher just tells you what you should be. A preacher tells you what it should be and leaves you to do it. A teacher will grab you and just do it.

"Now, the Self, what is the Self we are talking about? There is a formula. You have notion about Self. You think you have a Self or that there is a Self. You think about it. Then it is not only a notion, when you start thinking, the moment you get the thought, you have the object because thought makes you work on the object of the thought. You have the intuition that you have a Self, you have the notion that you have a Self, you have the performance that you have a Self, you have the experience that you have a Self, but you have not found it.

"Why? When everything is there why couldn't you find it? Because you have not yet trust in yourself, so whatever your Self is, you will not trust it. Everybody has the Self and everybody knows the Self and everybody finds the Self, but nobody trusts the Self, nobody.

"To trust the Self you have to trust the higher Self. And you have to have somebody higher: Jesus, Moses, Nanak, somebody, someone as an example. I don't know why God made us like that; He must have goofed. It's funny, he gave us everything in our very structure and nature, intuition, intellect, intelligence, reason, logic, thought, wisdom, pattern, actions and reaction, instinct, time; but there is a gap. Just acquire the trust . . . the total end of all spirituality is that trust." [85]

We have all the parts we need to unfold and bloom. We have an ability to meditate and act as the teacher. We can master our Self and go beyond it, into our infinite Self and live practically and fruitfully. But our minds get in the way and we create a conflict, a self-conflict, because we lack self-trust and self-acceptance. Instead we rely on our ego, our diversions, our fantasies and our impulses. This stage of meditation looks with a subtle eye past the surface into the heart of what is. Then it allows us to act and experience the flow of our transcendent Self.

Stage Nineteen: Teacher

In the meditation for this stage we present our Self before our infinite. We zero our Self in relationship to our own infinity. Only from there can we then serve our own consciousness.

> "The first principle of a teacher is, 'I am not.' If you cannot practice shuniya, you cannot be a teacher of Kundalini Yoga. Shuniya means zero. The moment you become zero, then all powers will prevail through you. The power of a teacher of Kundalini Yoga is in his zero, in his shuniya. In shuniya you become zero, you reduce everything to nothing: 'I am nothing. Everything is nothing. There's nothing to be nothing.' The moment you become that, then everything radiates from you.
>
> "Second, you are a servant. The moment you become a servant, you automatically become a master. You can never become a master if you want to be a master." [86]

Keeping to the True North of Your Consciousness

Instead of applying the state of shuniya to the task of embodying the teacher, our mind plies our consciousness with tantalizing systems to explain things: numerology, astrology, shamanism, spiritual realms, the list goes on. As a teacher, our consciousness does not take the bait and instead leans into its reliance on awareness. We take the teeth out of the ego and rely on the inner nectar, the quality of our soul. No other supports will work at this stage. The ego falls away like walls that had once blocked the sunshine. Now we must act from the light of our soul alone. In this stage, when we select and commit to an action, we support and stand for that action, guaranteeing and delivering our Self with it. Yogi Bhajan addressed this in a talk to teachers in training:

> "There's another foolishness which Kundalini Teachers do. They mix so many things—astrology, numerology, tarot cards, yum-yum, yu-yu, bananas-pananas-chatanas. They are afraid to cover their head when they teach. They want to be very popular. If you want to sell yourself, sell in the open market, but do not take the profession as a teacher. Don't insult this institution. In the end you will be sorry and regret it." [87]

There is no problem in practicing or teaching about any of these avocations. It is only when, in this stage, we apply a mental system outside ourselves, rather than the touch of awareness itself.

As the ego's attachments drop away, we need no support other than our own, the word and the infinite pulse of God in all. Life has many twists and turns. The meditative mind refines itself with the *sattvic* qualities—clarity, calm and intuition. At the teacher stage, we apply those qualities to see the essence of a situation, recognize our own reality and role, and correct the gap that comes from ego, commotion and intellectual diversions. To the teacher the path is always clear.

> "My basic concept is that life has many turns, but only one road. People do not know how to teach you spirituality. I have learned under forty great teachers and I can tell you, in writing, that many of them were nuts! You go and buy a diamond and spend all your income. When you bring it home somebody tells you you have got nothing but a glass. That happened to me time and again. They are so built up and sit so high, but when you talk to them, no matter how many students [they may have], you will end up just talking garbage.
>
> "They teach one thing wrong: there are many paths. There is actually one path with many turns. Each turn gives you a different view but there is one truth, one reality. I have traveled on that road; I can talk to you about it. The path is one, and the path is truth; isn't that one path? Truth. Simple. What else do you want? Truth. The path is truth, with many turns. To go off the road you need a permit. You go up the mountain, going round and round, until you reach the top, the end of the path. That is what it is.
>
> "Someone is on the sunny side and for him the light is warm. Another guy is on the other side where the light is dim and it is cold. Yet the path is the same. There are not many paths. That is why we say Sat Naam, 'Truth is Thy name, O Lord,' what else do you want to say?
>
> "The idea of a teacher or a Guru is one idea only: he should reach you to the top of that path; he should carry you through the warm side of the hill and the cold side of the hill and levitate you equally all the time. As you levitate along your path, you will go through the warm and cold, warm and cold, this is how you circle. That is the way life is. Every love life has a dark side with it. If you do not support the guy in the darker moments, he is not going to support you in the happy moments. Is it true or not? Every married couple has a sick period and a healthy period. If in

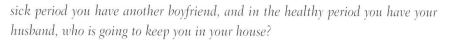

Stage Nineteen: Teacher

sick period you have another boyfriend, and in the healthy period you have your husband, who is going to keep you in your house?

"Some people are sincere in this, others are not. Look at my life; whenever I have done anything for sincerity I get garbage coming back to me. Still I keep on doing it; that's my habit of consciousness. I feel my job is to do it, and it is somebody else's job to understand it or not. As long I am doing it right, and my soul is there with it, everything is okay.

"You must remember a very powerful truth, which I am going to tell you now, in your life, if you relate to your soul, you are going to get to your higher consciousness. Your body is together with you as it is because of your soul. Your mind is also there because of your soul. If your soul is not there, neither do you have mind nor do you have body. Then you are just a dead thing. Your body and mind are there together because of soul, and soul must be present itself in you. So begin with gratitude." [88]

This stage of meditation is an applied intelligence that serves as both chisel and compass. The compass is used to keep us traveling true north. That true north is set by the axis of our soul and recognized by our neutral mind. We are all lured away by the magnetic north; by things that pull us away from our path because of fear or toward other distractions and desires. But for each of us the path of true north is one. This stage of meditation must discern the difference between true north and the false north that would draw us away from our own fulfillment. In this stage, our judgment is clear and we can instantly say no to reactions and yes to our consciousness. That is the ultimate test of this stage.

"You must have a space in this world where you know you can ask a question and the person [or consciousness] will not answer you because of your personality and ego. Without that you are an orphan in this world. Teacher does not mean to cater to your ego, remember that. A teacher does not teach you the truth. That is not a teacher. A teacher is when you ask, 'I want to do this,' and the answer comes, 'Shut up you idiot, you can't do that!'

"If you have not found that in your life you are really helplessly nothing but a stooge of time. You are an orphan, and you can never enjoy your life. Never." [89]

We must become this teacher within our own consciousness! Mastery in this stage means that we can take the perspective and consciousness of teacher and challenge our own mind. We can choose consciousness over ego. This is very difficult. The mind is insufficient without the touch and help of our infinite Self. Fortunately, we all have an inner teacher within our consciousness; and nature, too, is a teacher. When we develop this inner teacher, the Guru Dayv, we begin to recognize teachers in every part of our life: people, places and things. This stage marks the development of the teacher within us and the discipline to apply it.

It's one thing to talk about it, and another to touch it briefly; but still quite another—and the most difficult—to dwell in it as a committed custodian of our own soul. We all misjudge our success in refining this stage. We get distracted by popularity and material success. Instead stay steady and through every twist and turn walk the soul's path (and keep a few close companions nearby to reflect the higher Self back to us when we need it).

> *"Teacher is the custodian of the soul and the discipline—two things. The problem is your emotional Self and your ego Self have merged together to become temperamental. The process of purifying, which is painful, which you cannot accept, is to divide you from your temperamentalism and move toward consciousness. As long as a person is with his or her ego, that person feels secure and such a person cannot be with their consciousness. Consciousness and ego cannot work at the same time; only one will work.*
>
> *"The teacher will bring out of you the conscious discipline of yourself. If you are working with somebody who can give you the whole world but not the conscious discipline of yourself run away as fast as you can, that is a fake teacher. You need two things, consciousness and self-discipline. That will bring purity, kindness and crystallization to make you a saint and a perfect human being. The moment you become conscious and start practicing discipline, you will be separated from the flow of this earth, this world, maya.*
>
> *"To that meditative consciousness they sing the hymn, 'Guru Sikh Jogi Jaag dey maya dey vich karn udasee,' which translates, 'Guru Sikhs who are the yogis, they are awake, they are alert. The conscious person is always alert, awake and in this worldly realm they are nonattached.' It's very difficult to switch from ego to consciousness; it is the most difficult practice on the earth. Even Lord Ram, who was God, had his life put to the test, three times to five times between consciousness and ego. And He just passed it with a zero margin! And Lord Ram was a God incarnation!"* [90]

Maturing the Stage of a Teacher

This stage may seem like a type of bewitchment to some. But our dedication to seek our natural fulfillment and perfection comes above all else. We've tasted the One Reality and nothing else will satisfy our hunger. We are beyond friend, colleague or preacher; we are satisfied only in the real. We listen for the quiet whisper of the soul for that whisper is the awakening of the kundalini. We become vastly more open. As the burden of ego lightens, our capacity to listen magnifies. With that comes an equal measure of clarity and the applied discipline to walk our soul's path. Consciousness is a deft softness held steady like steel.

> *"Who is a teacher? The answer is: he who is the best student is the best teacher."* [91]

Two common errors challenge the mastery of this stage. The first is that we grasp too quickly to attain the status of teacher; instead of going steadily and incrementally, we try to leap. The second is that we become idealistic and fall into perfectionism, to the point that we block our own fulfillment. Remember, the perfect kills the good; balance is the key. We need to cultivate moderate, continuous and incremental progress. The teacher acts with a constant meditative correction of his or her path. This is the secret. Otherwise we try too hard. And in order to sustain that kind of effort, we rally emotion instead of consciousness in our meditations.

> *"When Mahatma Gandhi was shot George Bernard Shaw said one thing, 'It shows how dangerous it is to be too good.' In Canada I didn't realize the meaning of this, but in the United States, in Los Angeles, I am now an authority on this subject, that 'it is too dangerous to be too good.'*
>
> *"Draw a line in which you are reasonably good all the time. That is also one of the secrets to happiness. This was my thought in my meditation this morning. I wanted to communicate to you that a balanced life is the happiest life and the disciplined life is the most charming life ever an individual can live on this planet or in this universe. The more you will discipline yourself, the happier you shall be. Happiness is within us; it cannot be bought, it cannot be sold.*
>
> *"A teacher is a humble guide who with all his love can lead you on those lines. But to walk on those lines is always the capacity of the student. I teach you these sacred exercises and meditations which I call sacred because these exercises can enable you to have mental, muscular and nervous control at your will. Therefore they are very beautiful and can quicken the method to realize the truth. And there*

is no danger to yourself in anyway. Your muscles, your inner system, your glands which are the guardians of health, your seventy-two thousand nerves and all their centers all can be tuned up. But it is such a process that is going on in you that as you continue you will also gradually realize the differences slowly. It is not a very fast thing. It is not something that takes off and immediately shoots you up. It is a steady, slow involvement to recognize the flow of the divine power in an individual and to shed the blocks; it is opening to the inflow of the divine power and keeping away the weaknesses and fears. This is a very priceless thing, which you can buy at a very cheap rate. It has to be bought with a little effort and the involvement of your personal Self." [92]

This stage is nothing but a constant practice. We must stay open and grow. As we create this stage of the teacher within our Self, we will also find the consciousness of the teacher in every person, situation and circumstance in our life. With practice, this radical openness helps us to see the uniqueness of each moment and each person as well as the root cause of each thought. Our task is to penetrate to that root and understand the final effect of any action. The power to penetrate and see the subtle, the power to chisel our own thoughts and feelings to align with the soul's path, the practice of remaining open—that is the work of this stage of meditation.

"When we chant Sat Naam, we are not doing something new. . . . It is a truthful way of union with the Creator. It should not be misunderstood as a sect or a religion or something. You see I am very afraid of this thing. You have to make your mind bow. Be open, be vast, be clear, and be clean.

"Don't run into these religious channels. If you do, then this is a religion, then that is my religion, then this is the Yogi Bhajan religion. This is just another religion; and there can be hundreds of religions. Instead, there is one clean, truthful and simple way of life through which you can achieve the truth. . . . . Kundalini Yoga is the yoga of awareness. Whatever you have to do, you have to be aware about it and about what you are doing. You must fully understand first what you are doing and then do it consciously. It is totally wrong that I just say, Sat Naam, Sat Naam, Sat Naam, and that everything will be all right. No, first I have to explain what it is and the technology to use it." [93]

"Man walks like the kundalini. All men have a vibratory circle, it is never straight. Each individual has his own walking pattern. You people think as a human you are just born, you are out and then you are in the grave and that's it. No my dear

Stage Nineteen: Teacher

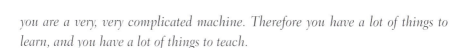

you are a very, very complicated machine. Therefore you have a lot of things to learn, and you have a lot of things to teach.

"Each one of you is a born teacher, each one of you is a born student, nobody among you is a perfect teacher, and nobody among you is a perfect student. It's a teacher-student, student-teacher relationship within each person. Sometimes the ego takes over: 'Oh, I am a teacher.' Sometimes the ego goes down, 'No, I am a student.' This is how life runs, up and down.

"When I want to understand something, I go deep, right to the very root of the cause, not just to the cause. When you are not with the root of the cause, then you are not with the effect of it. It is just learning to do this. The most effective thing, the root cause, which triggers the things in another human, is the tongue. The whole universe of you is based on two things: the sex organ and the communication organ. If you analytically understand everything, how it caused, how it finished, how it will end, you will be shocked. These two things must come into operation somehow to produce something." [94]

The expertise in this stage of meditation is to use the intuitive insight to challenge the ego, see what needs to change, and engage a discipline born of awareness and love, not forceful effort in order to make the change. This doesn't imply the discipline will not take great effort, it often does. But the effort moves from a place of stillness, shuniya, and ease, sahej. In the meditation for this stage we entrance the mind with the feeling and flow of the Infinite. We sense our innate capacity and power to love.

When this stage is fully developed, we do not need to control anyone else. We attract the resources we need naturally. If we feel we cannot make the necessary change and we still have something to learn, then we will attract an experience or a person to learn from. This stage is based on authenticity and openness by which we always recognize and follow the frequency and projection of our own soul.

Enchantment of the Infinite: Traatik to See Love Within

April 17, 1975

POSTURE: Sit in Easy Pose, with a straight spine, and apply Neck Lock.

MUDRA: Raise the right hand, palm down, just in front of the hairline. Extend the right thumb down so that the tip lines up with the Third Eye Point. If you look straight your eye focus should be just under the tip of the right thumb. Make a fist of the left hand and place it just in front of the chin; extend the left thumb upward. The left forearm will be parallel to the ground with the shoulders relaxed. The tips of both thumbs are separated by about ½ inch (1.25 cm) to a maximum of 1 inch (2.5 cm). The arms are held so the thumbs are 6 inches (15.25 cm) away from the face.

EYES: Your eyes are fixed open in a *traatik* stare. You look exactly between the thumb tips. Watch the flow of the energy as if a flame dances between them. The energy flows from the lower thumb tip to the upper one.

MANTRA: Whaa-hay Guroo. It is the *Gur Mantra;* and it is very specific. You chant aloud once, then in a whisper or very softly. You create a pulsation as you alternate from loud to very soft. The pace is steady. The sound "hay" is emphasized and distinct as it resonates in the upper back of the mouth.

TIME: 31 minutes.

TO END: Inhale deeply, suspend the breath and fix the eyes on the flow. Feel it throughout the entire body. Mentally pulse the mantra. Exhale powerfully through the mouth. Repeat the breath again. Repeat a final time with the eyes closed. Then inhale and stretch the arms up and shake, vigorously. Then sit still for a minute or two to sense the complete change of your energy.

Hints for Practice and Mastery

The distance of the thumb tips is important. This exact alignment makes sure you can tune into the energy that flows through the entire body and begin to sense and see that flow. Any wider and some auras would not be seen easily. Keeping this distance also assures the automatic pressure at the Third Eye to develop the intuition.

The best way to do this meditation is to tune into the energy that flows through the entire body; the yogi feels a flow of cosmic energy in every cell. It is subtle. Open yourself to this sensitive field of consciousness as you begin to sit for this meditation. Most of the time, you are not aware it is there at all. In the stillness of this meditation you must realize you are you plus your energy. There is the energy you always know and the energy you do not know, which is between your limited Self and the unlimited; between the finite and the infinite aspects of your being. For this meditation open your consciousness to this energy and sense its flow and vibration throughout the body's meridians, cells, spine and everywhere. Then as you sense this flow, feel it through the thumb tips. The lower thumb tip becomes like a brilliant flame. Its energy undulates and shines. It will take on different shapes and often colors. It rises like heat and passes like electricity. You focus on the flame at the space between the thumbs, and you open your sensitivity to all directions at once, around and through you. This will develop your intuitive sense.

The mind is filled with good and bad, the soul is filled with awareness, kindness and committed action. If you take any thought or potential action and focus on it, you can easily assess it and know what to do from the meditative mind of the teacher. The meditation for this stage uses a *traatik* to beam the mind and penetrate past the surface of things and see things through the eyes of the soul. The meditation that refines and strengthens this stage is a subtle practice that leads to pragmatism and humility. It establishes our royalty and dignity; the mantra entwines the simultaneous presence of the finite and the infinite in the practitioner's consciousness.

At this stage we need at minimum this ability to see the subtle, to penetrate to the essence of the cause and to observe it openly in the state of shuniya. Any movement or reactive emotion will shift what you see. Stay steady. To remain in this space you create an axis of sound, using the pulse of the mantra. The sound "Whaa" expands you to infinity. The sound "Hay" locates, centers and alerts you. The slight pressure of the sound produced in the upper back palate sends a stimulus to the pituitary and hypothalamus to adjust and to support your developing awareness. The sound "Guroo" projects and transforms you. The loud mantra is the sirgun, the world of manifestation and qualities. It is personal. The soft mantra is the *antar,* the essence, and so nirgun, beyond form and quality. It is impersonal. The pulse of the two sounds is impersonally personal and personally impersonal; it is awareness, presence and reality at once. Your projection is the seeing eye of the teacher.

Stage Twenty
Sage

Sage

Your meditation has reached to the core of your Being.
You are merged.
Discipline and duty, once burdensome,
have become a spontaneous expression of love.
Discipline has conquered the little you.
Your ego falls silent.
You no longer listen to the chatter of your mind.
You are no longer distracted by the world around you.
Instead you hear the constant pulse of God.
Love of the Being, of the inner Self,
motivates your consciousness.
Harmony exists between Creator and Creation.
You no longer experience God
you experience being God.
It is an ecstatic intimacy, a reality that has no words.

Happy. Full above and below. Heaven and earth mingle in the heart of the sage. You are balance. Fruition comes to those who encounter you. Your prayer is reality.

At this stage our Self, our infinite Self, silences the ego. The meditative practice is to discern the Self in its fundamental nature. Illusion fades away; the notion that there is a separation, a me and a you and an it, falls away.

Stage Twenty: Sage

The sage brings wisdom to his or her consciousness and shows it in every action. The sage does not have special knowledge about something out there; a sage has special knowledge about their own Self, the unlimited Being that is all that is. The sage realizes this, sees this, feels this and *is* this; it is a lived wisdom. It cannot be possessed as a concept or explained as a philosophy. This wisdom is the process by which we un-know all we know to become known to our unknown.

A sage is not a pundit. A pundit relies on intellectual knowledge, cultural discourse and social prowess. A pundit wins the debate and revels in the status it gives them. There are a million pundits for every one sage. The insight of a sage is based on a radical internal stillness, a stillness which emerges as awareness comes to dominate the mind. The sage sees aversion and desire as the same. A deep equanimity grows within the neutral mind, and the play of the intellect is seen for what it is. A sage penetrates through the fog of impulse and intellect, and a pristine clarity guides each choice, in the ever-present now, evidenced in an adaptive, flowing flexibility and effectiveness. The sage excels while fully engaging in each role and relationship in their life. But in this stage, the meditative mind knows that no real effort or action is needed. There is an underlying relaxation, a meditative stance that supports and delivers every action.

The sage embodies the quality, saibhang, which Guru Nanak named in the Mool Mantra[†]. It means self-illumined; self-effulgent; complete, content and conscious with radiant awareness of the Self. In the Mool Mantra, saibhang comes just before *gurprasaad*, the grace which takes one into complete merger. Within the stages of meditation outlined here, that grace, gurprasaad, is found in the final stage, the Infinite Pulse. So, too, the sage—codified by saibhang—first meditates and discerns the reality of the Infinite in all as the Self, within them and within everyone alike. There is nothing to attain, but much to enjoy in the accomplishments and play of the creation as an expression of the Infinite energy and consciousness we call Creator or God. But there is no longer any separation between the Self and God; that is the disciplined perception and perspective of the sage. This is not a belief. It is a quality of this stage of awareness, which arises as the meditative mind penetrates to the consciousness and source of every new experience.

In all the wisdom traditions of the East there are stories that illustrate the nature and qualities of a sage and the meditative mind's capacity to free the heart and spirit. There is a palpable spontaneity in the life of a sage; a lightness of being that seems to radiate

---

[†] Ek Ong Kaar, Sat Naam, Karta Purkh, Nirbhao, Nirvair, Akaal Moort, Ajoonee, Saibhang, Gurprasaad, Jap. Aad Sach, Jugaad Sach, Haibhee Sach, Nanak Hosee Bhee Sach.

from within. A sage's wisdom awakens knowledge in others. It is not a wisdom held in ego; but delivered with love, kindness and grace.

Yogi Bhajan gave examples of the sage in the Sikh tradition: Guru Nanak, Guru Ram Das and Guru Gobind Singh, the first, fourth and final teacher in the path that came to be known as Sikh Dharma. He emphasized the *sattvic* character of their minds, their ability to universally see God in every person and their capacity to discern right action under every condition. He also gave many examples from Christian, Sufi, Hindu, Native American and other traditions. He charged each of us to practice the technologies that would allow us to demonstrate this stage in our own lives. He rejected strongly any attempt to limit this stage of human consciousness to any particular religion, philosophy or belief. He remained true to his original mission, to deliver and make available the most effective ways to awaken this ability in each and every soul.

> *"Please don't misunderstand that we want you to be this, or we want you to be that. It's not true. Actually, Sikhism is not a religion; believe me or not. If you really understand it, it's not a religion. It became a religion; we made it a religion, because we wanted to escape persecution. That I can understand.*

> *"What is a Sikh? A Sikh is a living sage who helps another person to become a sage in every age. Sikh means student. A student is one who studies to be a student, and whosoever becomes a perfect student, becomes a perfect master. And what is a sage? The one through whom wisdom flows. A sage is not wise. A sage is one through whom wisdom flows."* [95]

He challenged each of us to test and verify the dimensions of our own consciousness. He was clear about the need to discipline the mind in order to enter this stage of meditative ability. Though the higher stages of meditation always require a touch of grace from your infinite Self, he was adamant that effective contemplative technologies were essential as well. If we did not want to be tossed hither and yon by our impulses, negative and positive minds and circumstance, we must discipline our minds. The meditative insight of the sage breaks the intrigues of the mind:

> *"Those who follow their mind end up crazy; those who make their mind to follow their consciousness end up a sage; that is the game. Please look at yourself and talk to your own mind. Assess your own mind, mentally talk to your mind and create a relationship. The biggest game player in the world is right within you. If, with your meditative mind, you start to talk to it, it will stop working; it won't be able to play a game. When you are in conscious relation to it, it cannot skip past you, it cannot trip you, and it cannot do anything to you. Once you start knowing it and you start*

to master and use it—that is the beginning of the era of happiness. Let your mind follow the path of truth, what truth? That you choose." [96]

Yogi Bhajan tells the story of the great sage, Rishi Gherenda, who is attributed with creating the basic text of Hatha Yoga, the *Gherenda Samhita*:

"The great sage in Kundalini Yoga said, and these words you should remember in your heart, 'Oh man, oh man, without technology, nothing can happen. And without practice of that technology, nothing can be achieved.' Kundalini Yoga, my friends, is not the idea of one person. Thousands and hundreds of thousands of sages have dedicated their total life to experiment and to find a system, a technology, through which a human mind, a human being, can from nothing become everything. The great sage and teacher of Hatha Yoga, Rishi Gherenda, gave a definition when he was asked about yoga. Somebody asked him, 'Gherenda, Maharaj, the greatest Rishi, I bow to you. Tell me about Kundalini Yoga.'

"He said, 'What I can tell you? Whenever a man from nothing wants to become everything, he has to do something—and that something is Kundalini Yoga.'

"What a beautiful definition. You think people never had wisdom then? They had perfect wisdom. This Sadhak, this questioner, asked another question, 'Sir, why is it so?'

"He said, 'Because it is a technology of everything. It contains everything. It contains all the twenty two systems of yoga. It is the essence; the taken over essence of everything. By virtue of this, a person in the shortest possible manner, living as a worldly [person] can totally, intelligently progress himself. And it is very fascinating.'

"He says it is very fascinating. What is the fascination and beauty to be with holy environments [with spiritual people and conscious technology]? It's a simple thing. Both yogi tea and coffee have the beauty to accelerate and help you. One makes it in the long run; the other makes it in the short run but eventually breaks it. That's all it is. One stimulates the nervous system for a short while, but in the long run damages it. The other makes it and makes it and makes it and makes it so strong that you can be fully alive." [97]

The sages left us the legacy of Kundalini Yoga and Meditation. These are techniques—technologies—that help us see what is real and choose promoting habits in our lifestyle, our livelihood and our relationships. Promoting habits call on our own inner strength and resources to build our vitality and consciousness through time instead of creating external dependencies on things we believe we lack. The sage sees that everything comes from nothing and that from nothing we can excel and become everything—for we already are! In the end this subtle perception is simple and practical.

Yogi Bhajan frequently told tales of the sage, Rishi Ashtavakra, whose name means, "A Sage Who has Eight Gnarled Parts." The name is a record of his condition as a child, crippled from birth, with many gnarled and twisted limbs. Yet these limitations did not deter him. He became a great Rishi and master of meditation, yoga and philosophy. He also became one of the two prominent teachers of the legendary ruler, Raja Janak, who was king of the known world, father of the bride of God, Sita. Many stories recount this ideal ruler. He was humble, courageous, wise and always ready to learn. He sought the deepest philosophy and training from the best teachers and sages of the time. From Janak, and others, came the lineage that passed down many of the techniques in Kundalini Yoga and Laya Yoga. Janak's lineage informed the Naths, Udasees and even Guru Ram Das, who holds the essence of compassion in this tradition. So this relationship between sage and student and the technologies they shared became a significant contribution to what is recorded here, the 21 Stages of Meditation as outlined by Yogi Bhajan.

Ashtavakra is a good source for understanding the consciousness and nature of a true sage. One of the most important classical texts for meditation and yoga is the *Ashtavakra Gita*. It is so powerful because every word is aimed at awakening the deep meditative stage of the Sage and ultimately realization. It is a sound current. It is not a how-to manual or a moral disputation of good and bad. It talks directly to the soul. On hearing the words of Ashtavakra, Janak attained his realization and acted for all future time with wisdom and munificence. Here is a sample from his Gita. You will recognize in it some of the themes that Yogi Bhajan spoke of and gave us a way to experience.

Of the four kinds of beings,
from Brahma to a blade of grass,
only the Sage can renounce aversion and desire.

Rare is he who knows himself
as One with no other—the Lord of the Universe.
He acts as he knows and is never afraid.

You are immaculate, touched by nothing.
What is there to renounce?

Stage Twenty: Sage

The mind is complex—let it go.
Know the peace of dissolution.

Indulgence creates attachment.
Aversion creates abstinence.
Like a child, the Sage is free of both
and thus lives on as a child.

Seeing everything as imagination,
knowing the Self as timelessly free,
The Sage lives as a child.
Rare is the right-minded person
who neither covets nor shuns
religion, wealth, pleasure, life or death.

The Sage neither cares for the universe
nor desires its dissolution.
He lives happily with whatever comes his way.
He is blessed.

Knowing Self, mind empty and at peace,
the Sage lives happily,
seeing, hearing, touching, smelling, eating.

The Sage is not conflicted
by states of stillness and thought
his mind is empty.
His home is the Absolute.

Though he may perform actions,
the Sage does not act.
Desires extinguished,
free of thoughts of "I" and "mine,"
he knows with absolute certainty
that nothing exists.

The actions of the Sage, free of pretense and motive,
shine like clear light.

*Not so those of the deluded seeker
who affects a peaceful demeanor
while remaining firmly attached.*

*Until self-realization, illusion prevails.
But the Sage lives without thoughts of "I" or "mine."
His tether to illusion is severed.*

*Where is illusion? Where is existence?
Where is attachment or non-attachment?
Where is a person? Where is God?
I am Awareness.*

*Where is activity or inactivity?
Where is liberation or bondage?
I am timeless, indivisible.
I am Self alone.*

*Where are principles and scriptures?
Where is the discipline or teacher?
Where is the reason for life?
I am the boundless Absolute.*

*Where is existence or non-existence?
Where is Unity or duality?
No-thing emanates from me.
No more can be said.*[†]

Here is one of the many stories Yogi Bhajan recounted with the same twinkle in his eye that Ashtavakra must have had. It illustrates how the wisdom of the sage is seen in the meditative capacity to be fully alert, without emotional distraction, and to hear what others do not, using conscious communication. The wisdom that is imparted is experienced in action and from an unexpected angle, what Yogi Bhajan called "the diagonal energy of awareness."

[†] Translation quoted from "The Perennial Way: New English Versions of Yoga Sutras, Dhammapada, Heart Sutra, Ashtavakra Gita, Faith Mind Sutra, and Tao Te Ching" by Bart Marshall, 2009. Used with Permission.

"In one of the scriptures a man came to a sage and said to him, 'Man of God, when one realizes God, how do we know that is true?'

"The sage answered, 'Son, people who realize God talk very consciously. You can talk emotionally, you can talk cleverly, you can talk diplomatically, you can talk humanly, you can talk the language of an angel, and you can talk the language of scriptures but beyond all these there is a way to talk and that is to talk consciously.'

"The man asked, 'How do you speak that way?'

"The sage replied, 'It's very simple. Whatever you have to say, just feel you are saying it through the Third Eye, between the eyebrows and the root of the nose. Don't speak from here, where your mouth is, speak here.'

"If you remember to speak from here then you remember to speak at the consciousness where destiny is written. Whatever you say, either it is writing the destiny, re-writing the destiny or erasing what is written in the destiny. That is why it is better to say practically nothing than to create ugliness with your words. You can quote me on this, it is the greatest sin to take any sinful tendency you have and speak it to another human being to show how ugly you are! Words create worlds.

"Consider the story of Janak and Rishi Ashtavakra:

"Ashtavakra was one person born like a blob and slob together. In each joint of his body there were misshapen twists. Ashtavakra means eight curls, eight twists, so between each joint of his body there were eight twists. He was so ugly that his parents first looked at him and called him Ashtavakra.

When he became a young boy, he asked his father, 'Do you know of Emperor Janak?'

His father said, Yes. Almost everyone knew of this great ruler.

The boy said, 'Emperor Janak has spread the declaration that whosoever will give me the knowledge of God before I can mount and ride my horse with a complete saddle, I will give him whatever he wants.'

The father said, 'Ashtavakra, you are crazy to even think this.'

He replied, 'No. I am not. I am not crazy. My name is not crazy; my name is Ashtavakra!'

The father warned him. Though Ashtavakra was recognized to be very wise for his young years, he said, 'Do you know how many wise men and saints and sages have *gone to be tested and give this knowledge to Janak? Janak is a Brahm Giani, he is a Raj Yogi.'*

He said, 'Father that's okay. But you know the watery jail is full of those that failed, that's why I am going.'

His father disturbed at certain fate said, 'Well, I can't take the responsibility to take you to Raja Janak.'

His son said simply, 'Do me one thing; take me to where the palace road splits from the main road and drop me on that crossing.' His many twists made it very difficult to travel unaided.

So they took him in a cart and dropped him there. After a while some of the king's horsemen came on the road. They saw some very mind-numbing type of a thing sitting in the middle of the road. It was disturbing so they wanted it to move from the King's roadway. They thought perhaps this fleshy bundle is some animal. They approached it and just wanted to poke it with spear. On close inspection they were surprised to find it's a human being because its head was normal.

They said, 'What are you doing here?'

So Ashtavakra said, 'I want to go and give knowledge to the emperor.'

The horsemen were under orders of the King as all state officials. The orders were whosoever says that he wants to give knowledge must respectfully be brought before the King. That was the law; it was not for them to judge.

They got off their mounts and sent for some more horsemen and a cart. He could not be transported well on a horse since he was so upside twisted, sideways and things. Just think of a person with that kind of a situation. So he was brought before the king and everybody laughed. Ashtavakra himself laughed!

King Janak said, 'Why did you laugh in my court?'

Ashtavakra said, 'Why did your people laugh?'

He said, 'They laughed because they've never seen a man who can look like you.'

Ashtavakra replied, 'Well, they only know the meat on my bones and my malformed, twisted features. They do not know my wisdom and consciousness. I have come to teach you. That's why you have to learn; because you are surrounded by butchers who only know meat!'

Stage Twenty: Sage

The great King became totally alert and astonished. He said, 'Okay, but you know my condition?'

He said, 'What is your condition? Your condition is I have to give you knowledge, right? Before you mount the horse!'

He said, 'Right!'

Ashtavakra said, 'Okay, are you ready to get knowledge?'

He said, 'Yes.'

He replied, 'Start!'

Now, there is a spiritual and cultural law that when you seek knowledge from a man of God you must take an offering or you will leave empty handed. You must take something to give so something can be taken and all is balanced.

So Janak said, 'I want to present you an offering.'

Ashtavakra said, 'Oh, Emperor, the offering should be deserved according to the value of the knowledge you want to receive.'

Raja Janak said, 'All right. Then I offer everything which I possess. Everything I have.'

Ashtavakra said, 'Everything includes you. You belong to me.'

The King open eyed said, 'Yes.'

The test began. Janak issued his order, 'Bring my horse.'

Ashtavakra immediately spoke and countermanded the King! 'Stop!'

The king said, 'Why?'

He said, 'All these horses belong to me! You gave them to me for receiving the knowledge.'

The King said, 'But I have not received the knowledge.'

Ashtavakra said calmly, 'But you have already given something. You have given the word, your word. That was your offering. It includes you. So you cannot order anything. The horse cannot be brought to you. You cannot go on your own.'

The King just realized what he said and what had happened. Then Ashtavakra laughed again. He said, 'Janak, don't you see? A minute before can you see what greed can do? This was all the result just of greed. It was greed for the knowledge of God. You wanted it and thought you could just get it. But see what greed, what one word can do. Just a moment before you were an emperor and everything was at your command. Everything was there. Now, in this moment later, you are my slave. You can't even order your own horse to come. This is God.'

Ashtavakra quoted a sutra, 'In the spell of a moment He makes the king the beggar, and He makes the beggar the king.' He makes the ordinary person a Yogi. He makes the Yogi an ordinary person.

Janak realized what he just learned and bowed. He said, 'Master, it's all yours.'

And that became the third time Ashtavakra laughed.

He said, 'King, oh Janak, I don't want anything, I have everything. I have wisdom and consciousness.'

"That is the difference in those who are sages and godly people, divine people, people of faith, people who want to walk on their path of destiny. They do not want to be just butchers, people of meat, only sexual and sensual. Instead they rise up; they sublime themselves; elevate. You know that word? Sublimation is a process; there are certain materials which are heated into their purest form. When they are cooled they are distilled, crystallized into purity. Sublimation is transformation; and spirituality is just the same. A human being is transformed from the first chakra, second chakra, third chakra to fourth, fifth, sixth, seventh, eighth. Whenever a person talks sublimely, sophisticatedly, decently, delicately it will bring love otherwise it will bring hatred. Love or hate are not things. There's no such thing as a relationship or no relationship. These are the result of your expression and it boils down to which center of consciousness you talk from." [98]

The Sage is a meditative stage where the reality that already exists is seen. Each word is consciously experienced and expressed through the highest centers of consciousness. We meditate in the simplest way to see that there are no separate things, only the One, which reveals itself in all things.

It may seem that such a meditative state is so rare that it should not be attempted. But no, it is a normal, natural capacity we all share. It simply requires a shift of mind and an application of discipline. Yogi Bhajan felt that we should each develop this stage to the best of our ability before the age of 54. By that time our life is well on its path; we have made many choices, learned many lessons and life itself expects us to regulate our own direction and energy. The protective hand of our mother is long gone. We must rely on seeing with wisdom and acting from our authentic Self if we want to be happy.

> *"If you are twenty-seven years old, then you have another twenty-seven years in which to develop your caliber. It doesn't matter who you are, if your caliber is not standardized with grace, dignity, and it doesn't have the character of a sage, then even with all the money and all the other privileges, for the rest of your life you shall be empty and in pain."* [99]

The meditation that we practice for this stage is very simple. It places your hands before the Heart Chakra in a double Gyan Mudra. It is a posture of attentive humility and openness. It calls on all knowledge; it calls on the refinement of knowledge within you, which is wisdom. The mind dwells in the constant relationship between Ek Ong Kaar and Sat Gurprasaad. The first is the sirgun, the experience of all finite forms, their indivisibility and their connection. The second part of the mantra is the nirgun, the experience of the formless, the grace and blessing of the Infinite Creator, which flows to you and all of creation. The phrases of the mantra are symmetric and reverse themselves like a mirror image; sirgun to nirgun then nirgun to sirgun. As sages, we are neither and both. Sirgun and nirgun, the known and the unknown, are replaced with awareness—the Self abiding in the Absolute Self, selflessly.

Sarab Gyan Kriya

April 2, 2001

POSTURE: Sit in Easy Pose, with a straight spine, and apply Neck Lock.

MUDRA: Gyan Mudra, the tip of the thumb touches the tip of the index finger, is applied in each hand. With the elbows relaxed at the sides of the body, bring both hands up in front of the Heart Center. The right hand rests in the left; palms up and the fingers cross. The four tips of the fingers in Gyan Mudra (index fingers and thumbs) all touch in the center. It should feel very contained and cozy.

EYES: The eyes are closed. Be aware through the Brow Point.

MANTRA: Ek Ong Kaar, Sat Gurprasaad, Sat Gurprasaad, Ek Ong Kaar

God and Creation are One, So I know the Grace of the Embodied Wisdom,
Graced by Embodied Wisdom, I realize God and all Creation are One.

This is a perfectly balanced mantra. It is called the Siri Mantra. It is a mantra of mantras that opens you to the creative power of the Self merged with the Infinite. To chant this properly, it is done slowly, consciously, in a monotone, without being drawn out. It takes about 15 seconds for two rounds of the mantra. A small breath sneaks in-between the cycles of the mantra; but there is no break in the rhythm; that is, there is no rhythmic pause for the breath. The sound "Ong" vibrates in the conch at the Brow Point.

TIME: 31 minutes.

Stage Twenty: Sage

TO END: Inhale deeply as you extend the arms straight up and bring the palms together in a gesture of neutrality. Press the palms and tighten the body for the length of the held breath. Then exhale powerfully. Do this a total of three times. This will equalize and distribute the energies you generated and released in this meditation.

Hints for Practice and Mastery

Commenting on this meditation Yogi Bhajan said, *"The entire Siri Guru Granth Sahib is born in this mantra, including Japji Sahib. It is the summary in one line. In the old days it was the custom to worship Ganesh for the knowledge to cut through the cycles of life, beyond ignorance and arrogance. That was shown in the swastika cross—opposite to the recent German one—as the flow and cycle of life. Then there was a mantra to open and celebrate that knowledge: the mangala charan mantra. That is this mantra. It is known in the Sikhs. What is not properly recorded in the scripture is the seal of the mudra that creates the flow of that mantra in the body. With the seal the mantra and breath start to change the energy to change your consciousness. That is what I share with you in this meditation."* [100]

This mantra is a *gutkaa*[†] *shabad*—one that stops and reverses the tendency of the mind. It is the essence of the Siri Guru Granth Sahib. Yogi Bhajan explained: *"If the mantra is chanted even five times, it will stop the mind and put it into reverse gear. The Siri Guru will sit in your heart. It can stop anything negative. It is so strong that it elevates the Self beyond duality and establishes the flow of spirit. This mantra makes the mind so powerful that it removes all obstacles. Its positive effects happen quickly and last a long time. It needs to be chanted with reverence, in a place of reverence. This mantra brings great intuition to the practitioner. After chanting this mantra, anything you say will be amplified and created with great force. So have a positive projection and do not say anything negative for a while."*

The first practitioner and master of this mantra was Baba Siri Chand who was given it directly by his father, Guru Nanak. As in the stories of the sage, each word must be conscious. Each word has an effect. As a sage you are responsible for your word; you can see the long-term effects as well as the short-term. Practice coming from a place of innocence and consciousness; create a sacred space. Ultimately you will attune and your ego will get out of the way. Make a point to chant and speak from that sacred space of zero ego.

[†] Referring to the small stick that regulates the speed of a water wheel.

This mantra and mudra are to command the creativity of nature—your own nature and the nature of all things. It invokes the diagonal energy of the kundalini, beyond the polarities that split our attention and awareness. It is a *mithana*, an intercourse of the finite and infinite, the masculine and feminine. Joyous, simple and profound, it can only be done with humility.

Stage Twenty One
Infinite Pulse

Infinite Pulse

One last step. A step that is bestowed.
A spiritual crown given only by Thee which
can never be earned, never taken.
It is a final quantum leap.
A small step beyond the sage that changes everything.
It is unlimited. It is beyond the limits of
language and mind.
To be a sage is a state called "Aane Manee".
The mind serves and you are silent before the Infinite.
This final state is "Sun Aane Manee Dhian".
A perfect one-pointed meditation that feels the Infinite
pulse of God everywhere.
There is nothing to do.
You rest in the bosom of the great
Mother of the universe.
Your stillness radiates limitless actions.
Your absolute containment knows no bounds.
Every project is done by Grace.
Every thought honored throughout time.
The three forces of the universe dance.
A perfect balance lets you dwell in the heart
centered, graceful, joy
filled with excellence, gratitude and Truth.
The Self is home.
Your home is the Self within the self.

Three gunas play in harmony. The opposites intertwine and support you without effort. Your heart center is open, your mind still. You sit in the heart of the great Mother, the Adi Shakti, that maintains the universe. Everything is done. You watch and in stillness feel the Infinite pulse of God.

Yogi Bhajan called the final stage of meditation the Infinite Pulse. This is the stage in which the Self is merged; the finite and Infinite selves are one. The formless, which gives rise to the forms, becomes a comfortable cozy home for our consciousness. This stage establishes an equilibrium that knows no bounds, effort becomes effortless and peace and bliss abide. It is difficult to describe; and all practitioners say that it has to be experienced, for only our life can be an explanation of its dimensions. This is a stage whose very name suggests that we open to a radically new perception that can hear, see and feel the interconnection of all things as well as the consciousness within all. The universal play of the *gunas* balances out; and the pervasive polarities in our experience become obvious to us. We see how they dance and each movement of the dance makes sense.

Stage Twenty One: Infinite Pulse

Unlike the previous stages we have now dropped all sense of ego. The Self within the self is home. The burden of ego and the effort to maintain a persona or a position in the great dance of life is replaced by the playful embrace and love of all that is. This is basically a step beyond mind, and it cannot be accomplished by any effort. Woven through it is a patient surrender to all you are, then only is the crown of spirituality bestowed. It is beyond words, and this vacuum fills otherwise meaningless, empty words with life and creative potential, giving birth to worlds.

This stage is not about ego at all: not egomania, not ego inflation, not ego depletion and not ego perfection. The ego question has ceased altogether. The Self has become its own reality, in itself; it is finally given a place in the heart of everything. When we grasp at this stage our efforts only echo back to us from silence. Any words to describe it resound in poetic tropes that serve to misdirect our minds as much as they entrance our hearts. This stage is, in some profound manner, only given to us. And with that gift, we experience the joy of receiving rather than the satisfaction of having found something. The gift of consciousness is nowhere if we cling to ego and everywhere if we can let go of the ego and allow the Infinite in.

Not bound by the sequence of previous stages because it has no sequence, the realization of the infinite pulse can happen in the beginning, in the middle or at the end of our journey. By its nature it gifts itself to us without an appointment—and certainly not on our schedule. Occasionally we hear a whisper that it is near, that birth is imminent. But it slips in by its own will between the inhale and the exhale; between seeing and perceiving; between effort and surrender.

The change is not in something one sees but in the nature of seeing itself. That is why it is so profound, ubiquitous and often sudden. It is like recognizing something for the first time that was directly in front of our eyes all along; we looked but did not see. This sensation is a perennial topic in the practice of Zazen; it is called Kensho. It is the transformation that strikes when we see our true nature, non-duality, and experience shuniya, the nothingness or nonexistence that gives rise to all that exists. This capacity comes concurrently with what we call the infinite pulse, the "unstruck sound." It precedes duality, form or instrument; it is not abstract or far away. Instead, it is intimate, at the very heart and center of everything that exists. It is the shared DNA of existence. In this stage we perceive mind and beyond mind. It is not that we know everything, but that we are wise in everything we know.

It is fortunate that realization takes no time, for we are all so busy with the "busyness" of life. To plant a seed, sprout it, grow it, and bring it to bloom and harvest takes not only time but also timing. But our infinite, spiritual Being is always here; it is timeless, which is why this stage seems surprisingly familiar. Everything in life is suddenly known to us, like discovering your own hand. And this sudden familiarity brings with it a grace and an ease, an elegance even, to everything we do. This stage opens the way for a touch of grace in everything. We see the play of God in each pebble and our discipline is gratitude in action. Love, patience, humility, peace, stillness and wonder often accompany this stage. As it solidifies in our experience we are kind and compassionate in every circumstance and completely at home in the world and in ourselves.

The effects of this meditation are many: First it clears our subconscious so that we get out of our own way. Second it uses a sample of the formless infinity in the mantra, Whaa-hay Guroo, which is a seed that balances the *gunas*, the qualities that give birth to form and experience. This mantra is a conscious pulsation of the Infinite in finite form. It brings us to a neutral stillness, the state of shuniya, where there is total balance and nothing baits us into reaction. In this state we begin to see the subtle, the creativity of the creation, in all things. Third, by pulsing the mantra 16 times as we keep the *mahabandh* engaged, we energize all the chakras. If we are balanced in one chakra but unable to flow appropriately in all the chakras, we can experience power and openness, but never become truly elevated. This meditation guides the seed of shuniya through every chakra. Fourth, we flow with the sound current into yoga, into merger. Throughout the meditation there are moments when we sense, hear, feel and merge into the pulse of Being itself—the infinite pulse. It is in everything that exists. It is the heartbeat, the pulse of God. It is the core of creation. As we sit in stillness with this pulse everything happens; all is done. We sit in the lap of the Divine Mother, the Adi Shakti. There seems to be nothing to do for everything is enacted before even thought has taken form. Fifth, we become intuitive.

The benefits of this stage are many. Yogi Bhajan said this gives us the essence of meditation and the experience of yoga.

> *"This is one kriya where they didn't give any explanation except one line: whosoever knows and perfects Sodarshan Chakra Kriya shall be complete. They shall realize themselves as God and a human, and human and God. They recorded that line about this experience. The symbol for this kriya is simply Infinity.*
>
> *"Yoga means nothing but union with your own vital energy inside. It is when you can understand and you are united with the Infinite spirit of creative God. That's*

Stage Twenty One: Infinite Pulse

all yoga is. A simple science though now we have got so many different brands and games we manufacture about it. But fact is, it is what it is." [101]

"Of all the twenty two types of yoga, including Kundalini Yoga, this is the highest kriya. This meditation cuts through all darkness. The name, Sodarshan Chakra Kriya, means the Kriya for Perfect Purification of the Chakras. It will give you a new start. It is the simplest kriya, but at the same time it is the hardest."

"It cuts through all barriers of the neurotic or psychotic inside nature. When a person is in a very bad state, techniques imposed from the outside will not work. The pressure has to be stimulated from within. The tragedy of life is when the subconscious releases garbage into the conscious mind. This kriya invokes the kundalini energy to give you the necessary vitality and intuition to combat the negative effects of the unchanneled subconscious mind."

In essence it retrains the mind to give room for the Infinite within the Self. The tantra writings, known as the *Shastras*, speak in terms of purification, mental refinement and spiritual distillation. When we are flowing, unblocked and transcend our own mental play, then a new depth and dimension arises. We realize our co-creativity with the universe, within and without.

When we hear the infinite pulse everywhere, within and without, we sample a taste of reality beyond form; we take a sip of the divine beyond mind and the senses. When this sip flows into our senses, body and mind, it is ecstasy:

"Everything else is just candy in the mind. If you can transcend the mind forget it! Nothing compares. Once that sweetness of the divine starts then all these tastes you sought and fought for, they look shallow. Once you get to that taste you realize that divine is within us. These meditations help charge you for your own experience."

Prepare to go on this final step of the journey. Prepare to sit, meditate and allow the sacred space to prevail in our consciousness. There is nothing to do. There is everything to be: the doer, witness, receiver and servant all at once, with each pulse.

Sodarshan Chakra Kriya

December 12, 1990

POSTURE: Sit in Easy Pose or Lotus Pose, with a straight spine, and apply Neck Lock.

EYES: Focus at the tip of the nose.

BREATH: Block the right nostril with the right thumb. The other fingers point straight up with the palm facing to the left. Consciously inhale through the left nostril, taking a slow deep breath. Suspend the breath as you mentally pulse the mantra at the navel. To exhale, unblock the right nostril and place the right index finger or pinkie finger on the left nostril to block it, exhaling through the right nostril. Let the breath go in a steady full exhale as you draw back the navel. The breath repeats in this way throughout the entire practice. **Inhale only through the left nostril and exhale only through the right nostril.**

MANTRA: Whaa-Hay Guroo.

Repeat the mantra mentally as a three beat sound: Whaa is one; Hay is two; Guroo is three. On each mental vibration of the three parts of the mantra you pull the Navel Point in; that is, 3 pulses of the Navel Point for each Whaa-hay Guroo.

TO PRACTICE: Inhale deeply, suspend the breath and repeat the mantra a total of 16 times. The total number of Navel Point pulses is 48. Then you exhale completely.

Stage Twenty One: Infinite Pulse

Mentally focus on the pulse of the mantra, and be consciously conscious of the subtle energetic changes that accompany merger with the sound.

TIME: 2 ½ hours maximum. This practice can also be done for 3, 11, 31 or 62 minutes.

TO END: Inhale deeply, suspend the breath 10-15 seconds, and then exhale. Repeat. Then inhale and stretch the arms, shake every part of your body. Relax the breath and keep shaking and moving your body. Then deeply relax.

Hints for Practice and Mastery

Yogi Bhajan said the practice of this mediation has an effect even in 3 minutes. It is unlimited by time, space or situation; it is effective as soon as you bring yourself fully present, become mindful, and begin to merge into the sound created by the pulse of this mantra. You can decide for yourself how fast or slow you want to go through this cleansing of the subconscious and opening of your formless reality and intuition. The most common practice is 31 minutes.

For a powerful and immediate effect in your life, practice it one hour before the rise of the sun. Then ideally do 31 minutes at noon, when the sun is at its peak (though you can do it at any point in the day if needed). Then do a final hour after sunset.

Build your practice time up to match how well you can be physically solid, mentally present and consciously conscious. It is more important to be fully engaged with your awareness than to do a long session if you are unfocused, asleep or inattentive. Doing this practice means you merge into the infinite sound of your soul and the cosmos. It is simple and profound yet requires you to transcend your presence.

While doing this for an extended time, such at 2 ½ hours, you can regulate the breath with the right hand held near the face, or you can let the hand relax down during the breath suspension. Simply move the hand smoothly in and out of the position as needed.

To maximize the effectiveness of this practice you must pay attention to the basic body locks or *bandhas*. These capture, direct and intensify the flow of energy in your nervous system and praanic body generated in the meditation. The Neck Lock, *Jalandhar Bandh*, is held throughout and is essential to suspending the breath properly. The position is maintained by lifting the chest and keeping the chin pulled back slightly. As you pulse the mantra at the navel, the Root Lock, *Mool Bandh* is activated simultaneously. Gradually the *Uddhiyana Bandh*—the diaphragm lock—becomes stronger and more sustainable. So you are applying *Mahabandh* in this meditation.

The steady pull of the navel and the pulse of thwwwe mantra vibrate the string of the central channel of the spine—the *sushmana*—which is held taut by the locks. With regular practice Yogi Bhajan said,

> *"Your body will start changing after forty days. Your looks will change, your body will change, and your energy will change. It will start to give you intuition. In ninety days you will feel comfortable. In a hundred twenty days you will start feeling lighter and higher. In about six to nine months, an ordinary person can master it. Once you master it, it will master you. It'll give you command on twenty-seven facets of the universe. It is true. We have the experience and we are speaking from the fact. Not that we read it in a book and it's true. It is true because we know it. It is our experience and it is perfect."* [102]

Realization[†]

If happiness is the sap for the tree of life, then realization is its fruit. We are often told that realization or enlightenment is the goal of all our practices. Yet realization is not something we can grasp or possess; realization possesses us! People's expectations and definitions of realization vary widely; but it's essentially a maturity of consciousness. We all recognize that the state of consciousness we call realization is hard to capture in words and may never be something that can be explained by intellect alone. Instead, realization is best understood in the life of someone who demonstrates it.

[†] Realization is the third level of training in The Aquarian Teacher ™: The International Teacher Training Program in Kundalini Yoga as Taught by Yogi Bhajan®.

Yogi Bhajan often spoke of self-realization and God-realization as one and the same. In the state of realization, our concept of Self and God shifts and resolves into the fulfillment of the true identity of the human being—to be fully awakened and aware. When a student asked Yogi Bhajan about God-realization he answered,

> *"A student wanted to know why he could not realize God in six or seven days. Actually what is God-realization? I want to give you the definite, the short-cut definition, of this: God-realization is not the craziness you might sometimes feel when you are all locked within yourself; this is absolutely wrong. Don't have any such funny idea about it. God-realization is when you are so well self-controlled that the pair of opposites do not disturb you. That is God-realization.*
>
> *"When fame and shame do not bother you, when you are mentally so satiated and feel you are one with Him so that all the pairs of opposites do not affect you, then you have realization. It is not that you can control them or not. No, it is that they do not affect you at all. If somebody says, 'Yogi Bhajan you are wonderful' or 'you are just nonsense,' both projections have the same value for me. I do not say, 'Right, thank you very much,' for the first and then say, 'Hey, what do you mean?' for the negative judgment. A person who is in tune with God, with the cosmos, he experiences, 'Tera Pana Mitha Lagey,' which means, 'THY WILL IS MY WILL.'*
>
> *"When you can realize this, you are in tune with God. We earn a degree and reach some level in the scope of the material world. Or we try with higher training or even drugs to get the astral experiences and travel out of the body to higher planets and places. But these are not permanent nor are they realization. Then, even with little practice and not being able to sit with a straight spinal cord, you want the shortest path without your effort? God bless you and protect you from damaging yourself with extreme efforts or drugs."* [103]

Realization is a natural potential within each of us. We have a unique opportunity in this human body, through the breath of life, to experience the Self. So the body is something to be refined, directed and treated with respect and gratitude.

> *"Your body is your best friend. Without coming into a body you cannot exist and God-realization cannot be done, even by God Itself. If the Kundalini Shastras are correct, then the sutra in it is absolutely correct: Those who are not friendly to the best friend of the being, the body, they are not friends at all. You must love your body first; the best friend who serves you, who is the caretaker of your soul, the consciousness; and that is what we have to do with meditation. What we are*

doing is cleaning and making our body beautiful, trying to improve our nerves, and bringing in us awareness. We are using the awareness 'nerve'. Some people call it kundalini; some people call it awareness nerve; some people call it a stage of bliss or realization.

"The difference is we talk less. We are trying to do it technically and mechanically. It is possible to get this feeling or experience for a few minutes with certain powerful drugs or extreme efforts. But such techniques and drugs do not develop you to reach your Self and to come back to your Self. In Kundalini Yoga and Meditation, you reach your Self, and you come back. You have a gradual, beautiful, balanced and correct systematic approach." [104]

Meditation is not just sitting still or becoming calm. There are many techniques and skills to develop your awareness, and the body is a part of that, not separate from it. In fact, several of the meditations he gave us throughout the stages require us to regulate the breath, chant sounds and hold specific postures and mudras. It is through the body that we process realization so that our body and the body of the cosmos may unite.

"The stage of mind where realization comes in the man is when he is nothing, and all is He. He is nothing, all is He. Man realizes that he is nothing, all is Thee! That is the realization which will pull you up. It will take you to infinity. In realization you have no fall and there is a spring all around you. Out of that spring whosoever shall drink shall be blessed.

Anter ka soma kholo, diyo gyan natar aab kaisa avana javana aabkee kysee baar.

When the spring inside opens up, it opens all that is inside. Then, O Lord, what is there to come and what is there to go?

The comings and goings all belong to the man, but the Lord wants him to learn to become the Lord. Practice makes perfect and that is why we practice, so we may do it and become the doing. In this life you have got to make it; the time is now and now is the time." [105]

In many ways, the division between the Self and God is false. The ego, which identifies with emotions and commotions, is the only barrier. When we realize our true Self we automatically realize kindness and compassion, and find that God is not something separate to be attained, understood or found. Instead, we are asked us to test our own experience and come to our own conclusions. Realization, according to Yogi Bhajan, is our capacity for attunement with God and all things, and our capacity for communication with our Self, which he often called "intunement." The test and the catalyst of realization is to act godly yet remain fully human, beyond all judgment and reaction to what is.

> "This is the shore, and that is the other shore. You have to travel from this shore to that shore. There are two ways to proceed. You can sit in the boat and let Thee, the Creator, row your boat and take you. That is the passage of the person who believes in God, who gives his free will to God; he sails with that help in consciousness.

> "The other way is you take a dive, swim across, and try to reach the other shore and think, 'In this ocean, there are crocodiles; there are sharks; there is everything.' If you can fight with all those things you imagine and can reach the other shore, well, please try. There is a way to pass over, just thinking constantly with many thoughts and not thinking of anything or projection. But this is not a solution.

> "God, God, God, God. Computer, computer, whatever you call Him, I don't worry. People are so allergic to the word 'God,' they say 'Don't talk about God.' All right, call Him something else; Bhai, Creator, Supreme, Energy, whatever you want to call it; it doesn't matter. It doesn't bother me because I experience and I know that there is some superior thing which controls you and your destiny. I talk about this because I know that Supreme; you do not care because you have not yet realized That Supreme. You think eating, sleeping, living, and hugging and bugging is all that life is; but there is something beyond this.

> "Talking phony things about yourself and God does not make you God. God is the realization within the Self; projecting that realization into practical actions makes a man God. The greatest power in a person is when he has realized that he is God and then he acts like a God. Saying it does not make you realize your Self or God. I am a holy man. But if I overdrink and lie down in that drain so the police take me up early in the morning and say, 'Yogi Bhajan overdrank and was found in the drain,' what type of holy man am I then? Just tell me.

> "If my actions are beautiful, then I am a holy man. Now, you are all God, G-O-D, I am declaring it! I want to be challenged by any of you. After all, you have all read books; you are the wisest people, while all the time searching in others' pockets without knowing the diamond is in your pocket. You are all Gods provided you act like God! God is not to be imported from Canada and no duty is to be paid on that. There is no aircraft that can bring it. There is nobody who can receive it. You all are Gods, living Gods. Until you stop breathing you are a living God.'

"Do you see with what power, with what authority, with what confidence I am talking? I know it. I have realized it. I have acted with it. So I don't care, you can hang me with a rope, I will still say every man who breathes is a God, provided he realizes this truth and acts like the God. That is the entire secret. Be happy, live well. Don't worry, don't be bothered. He will look after you. I can guarantee you one thing: that Supreme is going to act for you if you link with Him; if you feel each breath is the power of the God.

"Everybody forgets the first lesson I gave everybody. When you are negative, when you are weak, when you cannot think, when you are going to make a decision, when you are going to talk to someone who matters to you, first breathe five or six times. Feel that God prevails and sits in you and then talk to him. Bring softness in your tone. Bring tolerance and love in yourself. Discipline yourself. Don't show off like a child. By crying the gate of the house will not be moved to the other side. Nothing is going to happen. In the vastness of the seven oceans, you are one little bubble who has a very limited time. Therefore, grace will come to you, glory will come to you, and happiness will come to you, everything will come to you when you act like God. God gives, God never takes anything. God loves everyone. He sends his tender charge every second. He lives in you. He guards you. You do not remember Him, He remembers you. And that is so great, that whenever you call on Him, He answers you. Whenever! Whosoever, with an honest mind, has called on God, God has remarked and come to him faster than when he has called on Him. God does not live anywhere. The strong God, the true God, lives in each one of us." [106]

This sense of realization, qualified within the human experience, owes nothing to any group or religion. It comes as the relationship between the finite sense of self (the ego) and the infinite Self matures. Meditation is the royal way, the path to clear the mind and test our own potential. By locating realization, our sense of the Infinite, the Unknown, the God within our Self, Yogi Bhajan looked to the awakening he envisioned in this New Age. Each person must qualify themselves based on actual experience. He called on each of us to authenticate the Self within the self, to recognize the All within the small. In this way we bring our own integrity and radiance to those relationships or groups we participate in, rather than getting lost in membership norms and pressures, tradition or groupthink. In such realization there is courage, innocence and kindness in equal measure. In such realization we act directly, in complete acceptance of our soul's unique destiny. Purpose becomes a sensitivity, not simply an idea; in realization, purpose becomes a sixth sense, supported by intuition, applied intelligence and vitality—and happiness runs after us.

To experience realization through the 21 Stages of Meditation, we must begin with the Self. Each of the three journeys that guide you through the stages focuses on different tasks and skills that refine, expand and awaken the Self. In Yogi Bhajan's terminology there is the ego, the little or finite Self, and the infinite or real Self. Awareness comes from that real Self; so our task is to bring that awareness into each level of our existence and through all facets of our mind.

"If you do not know who you are you cannot know who somebody else is. If you do not love yourself you cannot love anybody. It's a fundamental truth. Until you know yourself everything else you know is totally a useless trip. It is useless because without knowing yourself, you are going to fall apart anyway. If you go in an airplane and you sit in the captain's cockpit, right, and you do not know which switch is which, what you are going to do? By luck you may go twenty miles and be all right; on the thirtieth mile you may go berserk.

"Self is the greatest thing, it's a gift. If something teaches you to promote yourself, expand yourself, elaborate yourself, correspond with yourself, correlate with yourself, build yourself, that is fine; but if anything teaches you to mess yourself up, if anything tells you to destroy yourself, then get out of there and run—don't stop there for a second!

"Self is very precious, because you have to find it to give it, and when you can give the Self then you become selfless, right? And that's the highest state. But you can never become selfless if you cannot find what Self is to begin with. As long as you do not find the Self, just stick to it; and once you find it give it away. Give it away to the One who gave it to you. You will become a legend as a human being; it's a simple secret to immortal living. Those who found them Self and gave it back to the One who gave them the Self are still worshipped, remembered and respected on this Earth, in spite of the fact that they were nobody.

"Meditation is nothing but a living human phenomenon. It's a phenomenon of those who want to live. It is not a phenomenon of those who want to die. You need not meditate when you are boxed up for death. Those who do not have a meditative mind have two boxes for death: one is a coffin, the other is a free coffin called the body. Without a meditative mind, you live in this coffin for free; but you are dead. You can't decide for yourself, you can't speak for yourself, you can't

control yourself, you can't move yourself forward. You are in a car which has all doors closed, no brakes, no gears and you cannot start or stop. Communication of life at your frequency, that's number one. Receiving communication, with an understanding at your own frequency, is the secret of happiness." [107]

Through the 21 Stages of Meditation we change and refine our sense of Self; we shift our perspective and open up to new perceptions, new choices and new capacities. We change the things we identify our Self with; and each new quality of Self has its own particular tools and potentials. The use of meditation, Laya Yoga and the *Shabad Guru*, passed on by yogis and the Gurus in the Sikh tradition, are powerful tools to develop the Self and its depth. Authentic realization is a life well-lived and a destiny fulfilled.

Appendices

The Nature of Meditation

"What kind of life do you want to live? How can you develop it? What approach and formula can we use so we can grow and not suffer? Make meditation the art of life. Make meditation the science of life. Because only with that, and with that only, can you can develop intuition." [108]

We need to hone our meditative skills in order to clear our minds. For when we clear the mind, we open our intuition and expand our sensitivity and with it our capacity to create, prosper and heal. Through the 21 Stages of Meditation, realization becomes a reality. But before we explore the stages themselves, let's touch on the basic nature of meditation as taught by Yogi Bhajan.

The mind is the mediator of our happiness. We can suffer or we can experience our own happiness and bliss; simply refine the relationship to the mind. When we confront and master the mind, we recognize our real Self and tune in to our spirits with each inhalation and exhalation. In this way, the steps to happiness become easy to climb.

The royal science for refining and mastering the mind is meditation. Yogi Bhajan didn't view meditation as something we could choose to do or not do. No, meditation is not a choice; it is a necessity. Meditation is as essential to a happy life as breathing is to living itself. We meditate naturally. We all find ways to go into stillness, self-hypnosis, states of awe and blessing. Meditation refines, expands, stabilizes and strengthens our capacity to apply our minds effectively, so that we can act consciously and intuitively, from our real Self.

> *"With intuition you shall know the initial position, and with intuition you shall know the final position so that at your initial position you shall have no doubt. Once you are sure, you are good and you are happy, then you are behind it, and then you will get it. That is enough; you have nothing else to do."* [109]

Meditation helps us develop our intuition. Intuition is a natural capacity within each of us that empowers us to relax, flow and be happy in our lives. With intuition our core anxieties decrease, and our minds can then become still. We see things through a neutral lens, a subjective-objective stance, which is what Yogi Bhajan referred to as innocence. In our innocence, we relax and rely on our own resources, our own awareness, our own being; we dwell in our infinite Self. Filled with the courage that comes from self-trust and clear perception, we are fully engaged and alert in every moment as we let the Unknown serve us. The opposite of this meditative capacity is the frantic emotional and intellectual grasping for control that most of us live in from day to day. We don't trust our connection to our self and the infinite Self, which is part of all things. Instead of co-creating with the Infinite from our own consciousness we manipulate, creating dramas and false personas. In the short term this works just fine. But in winning the battle, we've lost the war. In grasping for the coin, we've lost the treasure.

Despite all their many varieties and procedures, all meditations begin with the same basic function and process:

> *"Meditation is the cleansing process of the mind just as bathing is one of the cleansing processes of the body. If you massage your body, and then you take a bath, and use soap, and then a take a towel and clean yourself, you feel very fresh, very new, very good. This process of yours, when it is applied to your mental life, cleans*

the mind. This is meditation. Have no misunderstanding that this is what happens in meditation.

"When you meditate you try to recite one word, whatever the mantra is, and you concentrate on one point, whichever that point is, then your subconscious releases all the garbage and dirty thoughts. It fills you up with garbage. Then, as you use the soap—the mantra—all the dirt comes out. When you meditate, every negative thought should, will and must come out. But when those thoughts come out and the subconscious releases those thoughts, you keep on chanting the mantra. You concentrate on the positive rhythm and projection of your mind while the subconscious releases the negative rhythm. Ultimately the negativity is balanced out and you are left new, fresh, and mentally strong for the day.

"It's a mind-cleansing and mind-rejuvenating process; it is called meditation. It has been commercialized, but it's a very, very, very scientifically well-elaborated science. You understand? Meditate so that you may not have any mental weakness. Meditate so that you will be clear and you will always know the pro of the con; you will always know the sequence and the consequences. Meditate and you all will always know what is needed and what is important for you. Meditate and know the best of you. Meditate and you will enjoy the very rhythm of life, the happiness and the greatness of it.

"Your personality has a radiance, a shine; it has a projection that is effective and very penetrating. But if your mind is not neutral and meditative, you can't retain your positive attitude all the time—that's the loss. And it's much more of a loss than any person can sustain. When you meditate you are very beautiful, mentally you are very beautiful, very effective, very cozy, you understand? People have made meditation into a commercial thing, a special thing, a personal thing, a secret thing; but in reality it is just like sunshine. Whosoever shall meditate shall benefit—whosoever shall meditate. And however he meditates he will benefit. In any way, shape or form that you meditate, you will benefit.

"I met a person who used to meditate like this: he chanted nothing, he did nothing, he closed his eyes and played with the tip of his nose. He liked it, he perfected it, and he went into a deep trance. He found his very neutral mind. His arc line and aura were so bright I couldn't say anything. It looks ridiculous, but for him it works. He asked me, 'Should I change it?' I said, 'You would be a fool. Why change it? Don't change it, keep going.'

> *"Meditation will give you constant and consistent happiness in your own personality. If something takes away your happiness from your mind or life, it brings mental confusion. 'Should I, should I not; may I, may I not; is it, is it not?' There are lots of questions, but when you meditate you have all the answers and no question. It is very essential that you should enjoy your body and your mind and have control over them. Meditation is a science and it's an art for any individual to enjoy the fullness and virtues of his life. Understand? Is the definition of meditation clear?"* [110]

As meditation clears the mind and releases the subconscious thoughts, impulses and fantasies, the brain changes. We can now create and project our intention more freely and with greater clarity. But the nature of meditation goes beyond clearing the mind and focusing our intentions. Yogi Bhajan gave hundreds of different meditations with specific effects that went beyond the universal cleansing process common to all meditation. Those powerful effects come from a sophisticated use of the brain's complex and systemic natural functions; the flow of the meridians; and the mobilization of the nerves and glands in our bodies.

> *"Open yourself up and try to work through the art of meditation. How does it work? Meditation is brainwork; it's not just body work though the body supports it. The brain has two hemispheres: initial and projective. Eastern hemisphere and western hemisphere are the two parts of the brain. They work in sympathy and harmony with each other so both can pick up each other's work. But if we can combine them properly then we develop a meditative mind; it's the function of the brain. . . . The meditative mind doesn't see what you see. If you tell a meditative mind, 'I love you,' it will immediately know what you have said, why you have said it, and what that means in the future. There is no need of ifs, ands, or buts."* [111]

Yogi Bhajan taught these myriad forms of meditation openly so that anyone could use and master them for their own benefit. He rejected the idea that meditation should be taught only in secret. Instead he encouraged us to focus on acquiring the skills that come from proper technique and mastering our Self within that experience. What secrets remain are only those that lie in the depth of our personal experience.

Recognizing the great range of differences and individuality in each of us; not every meditation satisfies the needs of all people nor do all people experience the same thing in every meditation.

> *"With meditation, you can develop your life for whatever situation you want to pursue, it doesn't matter. Meditation is only for widening the horizon and developing*

the capacity of the individual to serve their purpose. Every meditation is personal, and every meditation is secret, even though the technology may be a known, public thing. Even if you all learn it at the same time, from the same person, in the same way, your individual understanding will be individually different. The individual experience of the same technique will be individually different. The gain from that personal experience will be so different and varied that even if you wanted to explain it, it would be impossible.

"Therefore learn meditation as a basic science to develop your life and not as a security, folks. Don't follow the man, follow the technique. After all, the first man followed the technique. In the West we love to follow a Guru but nobody follows the consciousness and the frequency. When the individual reaches the frequency of the meditation, individually, then one's consciousness works. You can feel good about it and then fall apart later because psychologically you satisfy yourself but technically you may not reach the skill of it. It is that technical gap which we are trying to fulfill.

"We would like research to reach a point that we can give a person a brochure filled with certain questions and computerize it. That person will know exactly which type of meditation he should do to compensate for which mental deficiency and which glandular system or which particular gland is not speeding enough to help his mental level. We want to do this not to mess up the art of meditation but to clean the mess out of meditation. It should be left to individuals to purify themselves without subjecting their personal freedom. Yoga is a yoke between individual consciousness and the infinite consciousness; it has got nothing to do with group loyalties or fads." [112]

To open up this vision of meditation for every person to practice and develop themselves in the Aquarian Age, he verified these ancient techniques within himself and taught them with authenticity, accuracy and precision. He specified the proper use of each kriya and meditation. He avoided techniques that relied on the power of a single chakra or didn't have the grounding of a root sound or *naad* as the nucleus of the practice. Instead, he chose practices that balanced all the chakras and used ashtang mantras, which have a rhythm of eight and a balance of qualities, to insure a steady, safe, and incremental progress on the path to realization and personal development. In this way he was both traditional and revolutionary. He put the focus on the technology of meditation and personal effort—self-initiation—not lineages. Although he respected other systems, more traditional paths, he taught a system that firmly rests on individual dignity, effort and potential.

"The wrong way of meditation can bring weird thoughts to your brain and can open your negative channels more than your positive channels. So you are supposed to be more careful practicing meditation than practicing anything else. Nobody will give you this warning because it's a very sellable thing, now, to close your eyes and any thought that comes, bring the thought out and even magnify those emotions. I am fed up with that kind of gimmick and its effects. Those are not my practices.

"I am not teaching you what I know about; I am teaching you what I have learned; I am teaching you what I have practiced myself. The results I have found are wonderful. Normally, you sit down calmly and quietly and saintly. Sometimes, in some meditations, you will weep, you will cry; don't stop and hassle with that, just let it happen. It's a normal outcome. Some people may even start yelling, crying, shouting, many things happen. So everybody should understand that a meditation saadhana is a natural therapy as well. One's experience will be as the mind's state is, as the energy one gets involved in is. Sometimes one overcomes the thought, sometimes one does not overcome it, that doesn't make any difference. Be very natural, be very kind, and be very exclusive as you sit still and continue your meditation.

"Do your job, you have to do your job; that is what meditation is. Concentrate on your own Self, grow your own thing, pull your own boat, drive your own ship. This is the first law of meditation: once you set yourself in the surroundings, you have to forget the surrounding, first, then you will proceed with the meditation instructions; then you will grow and grow and grow and grow. These body pains are not actually body pains; they are just a nerve adjustment. The nerves resist, muscles resist, body resists, thought resists, intellect resists, all these guys whom you feel are your friends become the opponents the moment you want to join with your Supreme Consciousness. It only takes one minute and they turn their backs on you. Every garbage and distracting thought will come when you are meditating. Every pain will come. You will remember every part of your worldly work only when you are meditating. All these things will happen to you during your meditation time. In this way, you can understand who is a friend and who is an enemy of your consciousness among all the thoughts, impulses and emotions." [113]

"Now it is a very subtle knowledge which you are listening to, so tune yourself in. Normally, I never understood it the first time, and I know you will not understand it, but just try to concentrate and listen to what I am teaching you. It's a very great secret and sacred talk. I will just explain to you these ancient words.

'The individual proportional self-involvement shall be equal to the nearness of the joy (bliss) which is ultimate that he can perceive and feel. And thus if one can charm himself into an imaginary good Self one can actually get into that in a practical way. Thus by cheating yourself and using the Maya to overcome and cut down or pierce through the veil of Maya it is a rightful action to reach the truth.'

"Now I have explained to you and it has been tape recorded also, a word for word statement of Manu.† Now I'll explain to you what it means: Manu feels that we cannot perceive God; but in order to perceive God we may create a Maya in us that we are the God. We are not God, he said; well, we can't even perceive that, so let us believe that for a moment, but let us use this Maya to pierce through the veil of Maya. How? To perceive in us that we are the God. He says, 'If we can honestly even perceive that in us, surely we'll reach God.' How? Feel the proportionate nearness: God is in me. He is divine. I am beautiful. I am not a slave to any man. I am not going to tell a lie, I am not going to speak a truth. I shall speak what He wants me to speak. My God! Bring in you that much giving and see what happens around you!

"I am not joking. I have passed through this channel myself as a human being. I have been made to suffer through many erroneous methods. Those errors were the necessary acts without which I would never have been a complete man. I must explain further.

"These ashtang mantras will get you ashtang powers—earlier than the God realization. Well, I have to speak truth to you, and if you will get hung up in those ashtang powers, you are never going to reach realization and God. I know how difficult it is to get out of that ashtang power. I am not joking! I am simply sharing with you an experience; these mantras do give you power. I can't hide that truth from you. I took a vow before my teacher that I will teach nothing but the scriptures as truthfully as I have experienced them. I shall not take the responsibility of mixing and mingling anything into the truth. I don't want to run into a personality cult at all. If you worship me, and rub your entire nose at my feet, it is immaterial as long as what I teach you honestly do. I love you. If you don't do it, God bless you, I don't hate you. The method of teaching is dependent on a basic scripture, therefore, I can't juggle around with you. I can't tell you that the powers will come to you because of God-realization. I am making it clear that

---

† Editor's Note: From the Laws of Manu; An historical-mythological person, the giver of the first known recorded law and progenitor of the Indo-Aryan civilization.

these ashtang siddhis, according to the scripture, come at an earlier stage than the God-realization. If you can escape from that then God-realization you will have.

"I have been advised not to tell American people that this gives powers, because they are very power crazy and they will just go on that number. In my teaching I have not given you the mantram siddhi for each chakra. As a teacher I have the right to withhold it. The ashtang mantra† I was teaching will open up all the chakras, but it will never open you up chakra by chakra. Therefore, with Kundalini Yoga you are very safe. It will be a wholesale clearance, and you will never be stuck. Because if the kundalini gets raised by one chakra, or one at a time, and if it doesn't come back and doesn't go up, you are through with your life. And this happens in many samaadhis. It happens in Hatha Yoga, Raj Yoga, Gyan Yoga and even in sound current yoga. It happens because you are sucked into a very powerful process, and you are not instructed and prepared technically.

"My simple idea is that everyone has the right to learn, and everyone has the right to make it this lifetime. But I am a little revolutionary. I don't want to establish a Guru–Chela relationship in a physical form. I love it in a spiritual form. You treat me as my teachings, and my teachings are not mine, so I'll be individually free. All the time they tell me that Western people are not capable of learning the higher spiritual teachings. I am a revolutionary. I teach the exact scriptures, and I focus my entire intention on one thing because I have earned it: I took a vow that if I will be given a chance, I will create such beautiful, standard teachers that India will have to learn from them." [114]

Yogi Bhajan took great care to be open and to provide safe teachings that anyone can practice. Instead of seeking personal power, he shared techniques that guided us toward reliance upon our own consciousness, our Self, as the ultimate power. When our ego is in check, we become infinite, and all powers serve us when we are innocent before our higher Self and soul. We have no need for other powers; they are a side track, a misdirection of the play of Maya, a diversion by misguided spiritual ego. Whether we float above the ground physically or float above others because of status and fame, the real questions is, can we float above our own ego and emotions to clearly realize our consciousness?

---

† The Kundalini Mantra, also called the Adi Shakti Mantra: Ek Ong Kaar Sat Naam Siree Whaa-hay Guroo.

Laya Yoga Mantras

The technical use of *praanayam* for expansion of consciousness and energy, *dhyan* to contract and direct the mind, *aasana* to seal and guide the quality of energy, and *laya* to open and refine the chakras are signatures of Kundalini Yoga and Meditation. Laya Yoga mantras are an essential component because they guide the internal flows of energy and guarantee a steady unencumbered growth within the individual practitioner.

Laya Yoga mantras and the techniques associated with them are integrated throughout the kriyas and meditations taught by Yogi Bhajan; in fact, they are one of the distinguishing features of Kundalini Yoga. Laya Yoga takes us smoothly from the gross to the subtle within us.

> *"The difference between Kundalini Yoga and every other yoga is that you will never find a Kundalini Yoga Kriya without a mantra, and every mantra is a form of Laya Yoga. It means it has the perpetual perfect power of the word; therefore it must transfer the destiny from the indignity to the dignity. It elevates you from the reactionary action of karma, cause and effect, to Divinity. What is Divinity? When vanity is divided between you and God, and God is found."* [115]

> *"Laya Yoga is the most powerful and accurate yoga; Laya Yoga is when you get lost into the mantra, into the Divine. It is true! It is really a powerful thing. But technically speaking, this develops from the Jappa Yoga. Jap is when we sing or when we chant out loud; that is Jap. Laya is when you get lost into it, then it prevails through you, and that is Laya Yoga. Jappa and laya, they are two interconnected things. The sadhana we must practice with this is to be humble and to do service, Nishkaam Seva, to serve without asking for a reward. There are three ways of doing service: one is to do physical service; another is to give an offering, it can be any type of offering; and third is to create tapas, inner heat, from doing a disciplined practice. Jappa Yoga and Laya Yoga come under that third type of service—tapa. For that we ought to have a clean body and clean thoughts so these vibrations will prevail through us and it will stand."* [116]

This extraordinary Laya Yoga Kundalini Mantra brings the soul and destiny present. It suspends you above conflicts attracted by success and the activity of the positive mind. It focuses and guides your actions to serve your real identity and purpose. It clarifies your priorities and raises your mental energy through the chakras so that you can be creative. It builds your strength from the subtle body so that you can sacrifice what you must in order to accomplish your destiny and express your identity.

> ### The Laya Yoga Kundalini Mantra: Ek Ong Kaar Sat Naam Siree Whaa-hay Guroo
>
> *"These eight vibrations, this holy sound, are sufficient to tune in the unit consciousness into the supreme consciousness. Now let us be one with Him who is Ek Ong Kaar Sat Naam Siree Whaa-hay Guroo.*
>
> *"We have given an illustration of the ashtang mantra which has eight notes in it. Those who know Laya Yoga can really understand how powerful this chant will become. It will take us across the infinite shores of the cosmic world. Once we create these vibrations through our mental tune up, the mind goes into it, the body goes into it, and ultimately the spirit, the soul, takes over everything; then one who is a physical, mental and spiritual being becomes one Divine Being. In this natural way one crosses the infinite boundaries and, for a moment, that great power of the cosmos prevails through him."* [117]

The word *laya* refers to suspension from the ordinary world. Laya Yoga fixes your attention and energy on the essence of you higher consciousness, removing the power that normal distractions and attachments might have over you. It brightens the light of your consciousness and steadies your way through life; you no longer fall prey to your reactive mind pushing you into endless diversions and dead ends.

This mantra opens the secret book of Laya Yoga; it enables you to consciously remember and experience the link between you and the Infinite Creator within you. If you practice the mantra for 40-120 days, it will etch the experience and memory of your true identity into your awareness and your subconscious, where it will always serve you. This mantra was once secret and guarded like a gem. It is the key to the inner doors of naad, the realm of creative sound. If you listen to the sound of the mantra and then concentrate on its subtle sounds, you will become absorbed into the boundless domain of your higher Self.

The mantra uses an energetic structure of 3-1/2 cycles along its spin. Each lift of the diaphragm commutes the energy of *praana* and *apaana* across the heart center and up through the rest of the chakras. This 3-1/2 cycle is attuned to the pulse of the kundalini itself, which is often symbolized as a rejuvenating serpent, coiled 3-1/2 times, which generates the pulse and spin of it. Each coil unwinds the virtues and consciousness from three zones of the chakras: the lower, middle and upper triangles. Its full uncoiling marks the mature flourishing of our potential as a human being.

Yogi Bhajan shared his attitude and approach to this practice in his fifth class on Laya Yoga in 1970. The insight he describes about who we are as humans, the nature of our impulse toward the unseen and the potential we all have to mature are consistent themes across his 35 years of teaching:

> *"God bless you all. Today we have the fifth lesson on Laya Yoga. I am relating to you the secret of how to reach God. First four lessons, I related to you as you and you as a God-consciousness. You had a relationship between you and God-consciousness because you are not only you; you are a part of God-consciousness. Now I will relate directly to the higher consciousness. This is when the me and the you die, then the other part of you lives, which is the real One, the pure One, the Unseen.*
>
> *"The reality is that you are true to start with. You are by nature complete. You are both seen and unseen. Ninety percent you are an unseen being; ten percent you are seen. That is the tragedy, that is the Maya, that is the mirage, that is the illusion; whatever you call it is immaterial. We only need names and words to express and communicate between two individuals.*
>
> *"The totality of your way is unseen. Your design, your place of birth, your growth is unseen. Yet you relate to the seen only. You have never thought for a moment that all that is seen in this world has been made so beautifully by whosoever—an Unseen; you have no time for that. You have never cared to consciously relate to that Unseen who built this scene around you. That is your fundamental problem as humanity. As humans we all share this problem and suffer under this tendency. It is not my problem, your problem or a problem of a Hindu and not of a Buddhist and not of a Sikh. It is a problem with every human being.*

"Yogis do not divide humanity on the basis of religion, color, caste, creed and all that. Reality has not been allotted to certain organizations or religions in this world. If any of you can relate for a little time during the day and in the evening to that unseen in you, you can cross the barrier. You can look forward to happiness.

"The principle is very simple: because you are the product of the Unseen, the moment you consciously relate to the Unseen you will be energized. You will be very strong and energetic. It only takes a moment for the inflow of energy into you because there is already the Unseen in us.

"What is God? Did you ever see it? No. It is that unseen hand. It is a directive force. It is a creative force! The egocentric person always says, 'I did it,' but the one who has seen the Unseen and through experience has realized this [knows the true doer]. This gap in consciousness is a very little barrier, a very little difference in the consciousness. Your seen is so conflicted, unclear and impure because it is constantly changing to be alive. Within seventy two hours every physical body changes, your surroundings change, your way and thought changes, your health and sickness changes, you love someone then you hate them. Motion is the principle of life and you are alive, therefore, you must change. You are never stationary and you cannot stop. You are a living vibration. The only thing which does not change in you is the unseen part of you. It will never change; it has never changed. Call it God, Creator, Creative Force, the Unseen; it doesn't bother me.

"It is so easy to focus yourself on that Unseen for a while and practice will make you perfect. If you know the art to relate to that Unseen, then you do not have to telephone anybody; just sit down and communicate with that Unseen. You think a friend will answer the call and that the Unseen which is right in you is going to be lazy? That Unseen is not going to appear in some way or the other? What are you talking about? It is not a matter of faith or unfaith. It is a factual fact; it is a reality and we don't want to relate to that reality. Instead, shops have been opened as religions. They all promise, 'I'll take you to the kingdom of God,' as if they have got special engines which I don't have so you can fly into the kingdom of God! These religions have come because in each of us there is an urge to relate to the Unseen which is already in us and to fulfill that urge, we run left and right seeking.

"In Indian mythology, they made a human being to look like the grand demon of demons, Ravana. They make him to have ten heads and in the center they put the head of an ass. In spite of the wisdom of the ten people in him, and all his cleverness, he was fool enough to kidnap and take away the wife of another man. So he ends with a donkey's head as a result. We do not want to believe in and communicate with the Unseen. We want to communicate at a very donkey level. You slap me, I also slap you. It is an animal level. It has got nothing to do with a human because human is the highest level of consciousness in the evolution of the seen-level (sirgun) of consciousness.

"Laya Yoga says to do pranam (bow and be humble) at the feet of anyone who can show you the way to see the Unseen. Learn from someone who can give you the map and consciousness of how to relate to that Unseen (nirgun) which is the reality of you. This world is a mirage itself. It is a ten percent part of you. It is your ignorance and foolishness that you have made it ninety percent and you have forgotten your unseen Self.

"You think you know everything. These two eyes serve you at a level of consciousness so that you do not accidentally collide into somebody. You should not break your head into the wall! That is all the two eyes can see; nothing beyond that. There is another eye, a third eye, which is an unseen eye to see the Unseen for you. When the layers of the mind and all its dirt of conflict, egocentricity and commotion that cover each layer of your union with the Unseen is washed clear by experience and the blessings of the guru, then it is a clear crystal. The light of consciousness passes through the crystal at that time. The energy of the higher mind creates another eye which is known as the unseen eye. People call it the Third Eye. It can continuously see the unseen. Then you can see all the seen and you see the unseen. You do not need to go anywhere or belong to anything to be seen. The unseen is here and that is your destination.

"My loves, it is a very fortunate moment, if even just for a moment you can meditate on who you are and where you came from. You came from the Unseen and you have to go to this Unseen. In between, your journey has the mind and body as vehicles and energy. The body as a vehicle was granted to you to relate through the seen and always live with the Unseen. That stage of consciousness is called Jivan Mukht. It means you are liberated while alive and have no need to wait for death and promises beyond.

"Children of the Age of Aquarius, Age of Awareness, will follow this way of living. They will relate in this manner. I am not talking about America or any other country. I am relating to a period, an era, a time in which man will relate to truth that will be the age of truth. What is a truth in you? Who are you? You are the seen product of the Unseen; that Unseen wanted to create a seen here. So I must be able to relate to all that is.

"How can one relate? Anytime you will relate to the Unseen you will be liberated. There is no condition that you should be a Sikh, a Hindu, a Jain, Burmese, Japanese, nothing doing. There was no such condition laid down for any human being. There was only one condition that was laid down. The condition is that at any stage of your development and consciousness, if you for a moment consciously relate to that Unseen then like a mother you will be picked up into the lap and disconnected from anything which bothers you.

"To have the experience now, very constantly and very convincingly tell yourself that 'I am going to relate through this vibration, this laya, to that Unseen. I am going to do it with personal determination.' Do not do this as a favor for me or to please me. I am just giving you the technical know-how. We are going to relate to that Unseen right now through the vibrations of this Ashtang Mantra. It is a mantra that never ends and goes directly into Infinity. Tell yourself, 'I am going to relate to it, through it, with my total consciousness.'

"You all know it. This time you will pull the rectum, pull it and keep it pulled. It pulls a little bit of the sex organ and other organs will automatically get pulled with it, don't worry. Rectum is one of the gates out of the nine gates of the body where we pass our stool. It has a ring of seventy two thousand pranic nerves. We will only concentrate on the base of the spine and that is the rectum area. After fully concentrating on that we will start very slowly and go higher and higher; higher and higher just as a group and as one unit to vibrate with this laya mantra:

Ek Ong Kaar-(ah) Saa Taa Naa Maa-(ah) Siree Whaa-(ah) Hay Guroo.

"The scripture says in this realm for the search of the unseen, man cannot stop as you chant even as you sweat. When you sincerely practice this, whether it is cold or it is hot, after a while you will start sweating. This lock underneath, at the base, the gate of our instinctual, animal nature will become steady. Then, as the energy flows upward, sweat, like rain, sweat will come out of each pore of the body. It is sufficient to take out many poisons from your body. After a while you will start to get a cold sweat. First you get a hot sweat, then a cold sweat, then you will be free from cold and hot alike.

"My idea to teach you my dear ones is that you may not have to go to Tibet to find a Lama to learn it. My entire intention is that some fortunate ones who are seeking the God-consciousness and realization as a human being should all be provided this technical know-how. It is not difficult to reach that consciousness

and be creative while living in this seen world and relating to the Unseen. There is nothing very special which you have to relate to. The techniques you need are all very simple processes and are in this body and mind. All we have to do is condition this lock and unlock the system for your energy and consciousness. We can simply relate to ten percent in the seen and ninety percent in the unseen.

"We have read books and books. A student asked me, 'Yogi is there anything so that I can be a human being again?' I said, 'Yes. There is a possibility. Promise that you will get up at that time when the truck drivers do not run, in the early morning when there is no worldly noise and few vibrations in the atmosphere. Sit down to meditate and make your nerves strong. Pull your consciousness up from the first center. If you are successful to bring it to the second center of consciousness, relating to the sex organs, you will be a normal active human being. Now second is to pull it from that to the third center of consciousness which is greedy and makes us grab and possess everything. He carries too much load on himself and doesn't know it. After that, comes a stage when you uplift the energy to the heart center. Then you feel cool; it is all right, there is no problem. Up to that time you are caught in problems. In this body, if consciousness is stuck in the lower triangle of chakras, you are bound in the realm of time. You simply act and react; caught in cycles of cause and effect; birth and rebirth. That is the normal case. It is nothing special or wrong. Moment you pull your energy to here, one thing is over. You may not serve others, love others, but one thing you are going to do is start to break the time cycle of cause and effect. You will not have to go to a wise man or to a Yogi to know certain things. Your inner Self will answer you right there as the Heart Chakra opens.'

"If you clean the mirror of your mind with this meditation and relate to the Unseen in you, you will find exactly how the God is living in us. That Unseen is living in us but it has been coated with karma all the time. We can't relate to it, to our own Infinity, consciousness and reality. But somehow by mercy, by actions of the previous life that get awakened, one finds a chance and a workshop or garage where one can repair himself. You can bring yourself together; see yourself in your own mirror. When that is possible you are on the right path. You will make it no matter what. Other than this, what is spirituality? Nothing. That is all it is.

"May that Unseen Infinite Cosmos relate to all of us. May it bring us health, happiness and awareness. May all be what they ought to be and what they should be, from the stage of consciousness where they are. May That who causes a cause

take a cause in hand and deliver us all to the Supreme Consciousness which is oneness with that Infinite Oneness that has no end and no beginning. May the will prevail and for the sake of all may all be raised to express the highest consciousness. Sat Naam." [118]

As with all other genuine mantras, the depths of this Laya Yoga Kundalini Mantra, its vibration and technique, is discovered only by the seer who travels in the subtle realms of consciousness. It has been confirmed by countless practitioners who disciplined themselves to master the naad and experience the inner intensity of this meditation. When you are consciously conscious, present, and a witness to your Self witnessing your experience in this meditation, you can hear the inner sounds at many levels of your consciousness.

The vibrations of naad have many different octaves with many types of creative impact. This mantra takes you to the most subtle realm of creativity. It makes you attractive, creative, prosperous and conscious as you express your true Self in your activities, relationships, communication and professions. It awakens the kundalini force that energizes the whole creation. It awakens and empowers your aura. Raise your energy, clear your chakras and express yourself freely as you embody your uniqueness, joy and creativity in both your finite and infinite aspects.

The technology of Laya Yoga was never written; it was a rare oral tradition. Used before religions came into being, its sounds are the seed of all religions. We still honor this tradition by opening our summer solstice celebration with a walking prayer that intones the root laya sounds from all traditions: ya, ha, la, ra, sa. Each elementary sound is a seed that attunes to the frequency and chakras of one of the wisdom traditions. Many Laya Yoga techniques were given only on the condition that they be taught to someone in a respected family, a family that had proven itself worthy through several generations. Yogi Bhajan believed that in this New Age we had to drop the past and end the attachment and entanglement of ritual, lineage and spiritual materialism. He wanted realization and prosperity for all. Still, he respected the tradition by creating 3HO—a family of like-minded practitioners who verified their own worth through self-initiation and the healthy, happy, holy lifestyle.

"Today we are talking about a very simple thing, which is in naad, in laya. First of all you must understand that Laya Yoga is not a yoga of books; neither is there any scripture about it. It goes from person to person, and it cannot be taught other than through a family. It took me six years to make a family of 3HO, everywhere. I can call it a family in spite of the fact that sometimes you become negative to me

and what I am doing. I am making a very simple and honest effort. I am trying to provide a filter so that whatever we have suffered should stop here, and it should not pass on to our future generations. It has to stop here. It must not be allowed to pass on to our generations, and there are only three generations we can clean. It doesn't take hold in the first generation; first generation just suffers as pioneers. Second generation finds it easy because they have already experimented with things and gotten the benefits. The third generation can know the value and then pass it on. To make a family with a good reputation and supportive environments takes you about a hundred years." [119]

"The next theory will be Laya Yoga. I am going to teach it on one condition: that you should realize what God is. I am willing to teach you Laya Yoga on a second condition: that you may do good to humanity in general. Laya Mantra is a powerful way through which each person can heal, serve and save mankind.

"You have to be in a sitting position, then meditate and chant. Without Laya Yoga, there is no use belonging to any kind of religion or spiritual path. That is why in the very beginning we taught everybody Laya Yoga. That is why all the mantras are rhythmic, and based on a coordinated breath cycle. Every mantra has a technical know-how to it. . . . You have got to develop and my job is to deliver you as developed. I cannot buy anything less than that and neither you should rest for anything less." [120]

The Laya Yoga Kundalini Mantra

The Adi Shakti mantra, Ek Ong Kaar Sat Naam Siree Whaa-hay Guroo, is the foundation, the DNA of Kundalini Yoga. We practice this ashtang—eight beat—mantra every day in the Aquarian Sadhana and we use it during each of the three journeys outlined in this book. This practice is the Laya Yoga form of the Adi Shakti mantra, which takes us into a powerful mental suspension of our normal attachments and attentions so that we can dwell with the unseen within us.

The unseen is the source of the seen; the non-existent is the source of existence. The experience of Laya Yoga places you at the gateway between these two profound aspects of our Self. It connects your creativity to your actions. It keeps you in touch with your subtle body under every condition. It is energetic, joyful and a once profound secret is secret no more. Now it is up to us to discover its inner gifts.

MANTRA:

Ek Ong Kaar-(Ah)	One Creative Consciousness in All Creation
Saa Taa Naa Maa(Ah)	That Identity is Truth
Siree Whaa-(Ah) Hay Guroo	Great Indescribable Wisdom

CHANT: On Ek pull in the navel and retain a slight pull of the Root Lock, releasing it on Hay Guroo. On each [Ah] lift the diaphragm up firmly; this sound is a result of the powerful movement of the diaphragm rather than another spoken syllable in the mantra. It marks the pull of the diaphragm with each of the three cycles of sound When you say, Hay Guroo, the navel and abdomen relax.

VISUALIZATION: As you chant the mantra, visualize the sound spinning up the spine. Mentally guide the energy of the chant in a 3-1/2 turn spiral, from the base of the spine to the top of the spine. As you chant, imagine energy and sound spiraling up and around the spinal cord in a helix formation. Start at the base of the spine as you initiate the energy from the navel; move the energy in a counterclockwise direction around the spine and up the chakras with each cycle of the mantra; end with Hay Guroo, as the last ½ spiral takes the sound up and out the Crown Chakra to infinity. Mool Bandh is applied as you say Ek and kept slightly applied throughout the chant.

Hints for Practice and Mastery

The sound becomes a flow. It gradually and naturally builds up a tremendous amount of energy. As you listen to the sounds you chant, suspend yourself within the rhythm. Laya means the suspension of the ego as your consciousness dwells in the Infinite. The pace is about one cycle every 5 seconds. In some classes the energy builds and the speed of the chant and the pitch of the sounds rise together, without any effort. Typically the pace and sound elevate after 11 to 15 minutes to about 4 seconds per repetition, then again during the final 5-7 minutes to about 3.3 to 3.5 seconds per repetition. You immerse and become lost in the energy, flow and bliss of the sound and the experience of the inner light.

Do not simply say the sounds. Keep your mind focused on it. Sense the shifts of energy and let the rhythmic pulse of the chant vibrate every cell of your body. The sound is a pulse of the infinite creation. It is everywhere. You are equally saying and receiving; speaking and being spoken. Be aware of the sounds. Become aware that you are aware of the sounds. Sense the impact of the sound and the expanded movement of your mind as negative thoughts and habits dissolve. As barriers drop, sense your still presence amid the circumfluent sensations and feelings.

Skill Enhancement Meditations

The Adi Shakti Mantra

The entire process of Realization depends on one thing: awareness. According to schools of wisdom and yogis through the ages, awareness is the fundamental characteristic of our real, infinite Self. Yogi Bhajan translated Kundalini Yoga as the Yoga of Awareness because so many of its technologies are keys to arousing the potential that is awareness, transformation and realization within each of us.

We are fortunate to have the Adi Shakti Mantra; it is a kind of master code. The first technique that Yogi Bhajan shared when he arrived in the United States, this mantra is the DNA of the kundalini energy, and the fastest way to initiate the awakening of the inner resources needed to master meditation and understand the nature of our true Self.

Yogi Bhajan approached each practice respectfully, seriously and lightly at the same time. He knew that accurate technology and consistent practice were the only things that would make a difference in the end—not enthusiasm, or belief or initiation or even zealotry would yield the needed result, which for him was always the same. Be human and be happy. Being human is the prerequisite to being happy; and being happy is the result of the crystallization of the Self. We develop the insight and character to transcend the small self and realize our infinite Self.

One of the secrets of doing this mantra correctly is to apply the locks and redirect the energy through your nervous system and chakras so that we don't simply repeat the mantra but empower it. Yogi Bhajan spoke to this process from the very beginning of his teaching:

> *"Now listen it's a very simple theory and listen to it very carefully. The words are Ek Ong Kaar Sat Naam Siree Whaa-hay Guroo, these are eight words, and it is an Ashtang Mantra.*
>
> *"Sit down in any easy perfect pose. Within twenty-six chants there should be a fiery feeling in your spine if you are doing it right, otherwise you are doing it wrong. There is no duality in this. It is not that you are doing it and tomorrow you will have the effect of it. Nothing doing. You are doing it today and you are feeling the effects side by side—no problem and no duality.*
>
> *"Sit down in any posture. It should be any easy, complete pose in which you can sit. Any posture; it is not written in those scriptures which posture to take and I am not adding a word. I don't want to take the responsibility; whatever the scripture says let us follow it, because that has a greater tested wisdom than mine and yours.*
>
> *"Now, do you know how to apply Mool Bandh or Root Lock? Apply it. Root Lock is this entire lower area is pulled in to the Navel Point. That will happen when the rectum and the sex organ are pulled up and in at the Navel Point. It is not possible that it should not happen.*
>
> *"The first thing that happens is that when you chant, between your vocal cord and your sex organ you will feel a strain, one straight line connecting them. You may*

not feel it today, but you are going to feel it, because I felt it the third day. When I chanted and even now when I chant, immediately my forehead starts perspiring. It takes two minutes. Well, practice makes a man perfect. When you will practice you will learn it too, but I am just telling you how it is. Now you have to chant this mantra and keep pressure at that waistline point. Higher! This can touch the spinal column inside; the better the Root Lock is. Let us do it.

"Apply perfect Mool Bandh. Pull it so hard, up to your neck, that you can clearly feel the vocal cord and your Navel Point vibrate together. Take that much pressure so that both sides near these hernia points through which those nerves come out may be pulled in to your maximum. Spine straight and elbows straight.

"On that Guroo is a pull. That will keep your Root Lock in a very steady form. Don't be a fanatic about it; it is going to work. Just try decently without being cruel to yourself. Not that bringing everything up here is such that only then you are very divine, nothing doing. Keep every organ at its place! You know people go crazy for certain things, 'O yogi said this, and we are going to do.' No, no; if today it is not going to happen, tomorrow it shall.

"On Guroo adjust your Root Lock. I mean to say let us do it scientifically; there is nothing to hurry like fanatics or just muttering. Muttering won't do anything in the mantra.

"As much Root Lock on Guroo as you have, maintain that in Ek Ong Kaar Sat Naam Siree Whaa-hay Guroo. On the next Guroo you will pull a little more. It may be pulled only one thousandth of a millimeter. Maintain that and your Mool Bandh will become perfect; then even your power over death becomes perfect. This is according to the scripture, I do not know about it. But it is a truth. A person who has a siddhi of Mool Bandh dies at his own will. And when you have power over the fear of death you are almost divine, almost. So pull more and shout less.

"You keep Mool Bandh applied as you chant. Suppose I have now applied the Root Lock. I lock it so it will not be released. But I can talk, walk, I can speak with you for another hour and it will never be released. That is the kind of practice we require here.

"It is a very powerful Mantra Yoga, it's the **highest** yoga. How many of you were in a position to maintain the lock these twenty-six times, please raise your hands? Good, we are learning. How many had the heat and sensations in their spine? Very *good result. Those who haven't got it have either not meditated on their base or the Root Lock must have gone loose once.*

"It is the same creative action in a sinner and a divine. Energy, which is God, cleans the sinner and loves the divine. So there is no duality. Everyone has the energy, it is simply our own mistakes.

"Breathing becomes automatic. When you are keeping this Root Lock it will create a deep breathing in the solar plexus. On third or second chance you will find it. When you will pull the Mool Bandh and maintain it, more and more with each chant, the breath will not go directly into the lungs; it will go deep into the solar plexus because that refined energy has to be spread into the whole body. Now this is a natural law. Because you are creating the highest vibrations at that time, your breath shall serve you, you don't have to meditate on the breath.

"All the kriyas in Mantra Yoga, they only concentrate on the mantra not on anything else, everything else becomes subject to channeling that.

"We have chanted nine minutes. Two and a half hour chant is what you want to do. Your faces and forehead started to shine so I had to stop because this is the first day. Sometimes the face shines like a mirror as you put a Sun and its reflection comes of that. A man who has done it can shine even in the darkness. This is known as Mahadev Siddhi; he gets enlightened and shows the light to everyone. Whichever side he moves, sees, blesses or wherever his sight goes, then that place, person, or thing becomes purer. That is Mahadev Siddhi. This comes to a person who as a daily routine chants this mantra in this method. For siddhi they said two hours fifty-five minutes and six seconds. You chanted it for nine minutes. So there is nothing, which is not clear to you now." [121]

As Yogi Bhajan outlined, we want to charge the solar centers as we chant, so we must apply Mool Bandh, the lock of the lower pelvis. You begin to apply Mool Bandh when you first pull in the Navel Point on Ek. As you hold the navel gradually tighten the lock at Sat. And finally you give a last squeeze and lift at Guroo. If you master applying these locks as you chant, the breath is redirected to create a pressure through the solar plexus, which sends the flow of praana and energy through nerve channels along the spine. Sometimes this is experienced as heat; or a moving sensation along the spine to the Brow Point. This is a normal adjustment and change; just stay still and follow the waves of the mantra. Be still and let the energy move itself. There is a natural rhythm to the sound and energy pulses. Like the waves on a great ocean it washes through your nerves and glands. It clears and awakens you to a new level of radiance and projection.

To do this requires a precise physical coordination and takes practice. It also takes practice to synchronize your Self to the mantra. The heat and change from the mantra will stimulate many thoughts as the subconscious clears. Impressions will come from other people's thoughts, and energies will be felt from the whole universe. As you stay steady eventually you will see beyond your limits and intuition will develop. Then your decisions in life will be successful and you will have the caliber to be happy in every condition. When the kundalini awakens the sense of the divine is tangible and practical. We find the creative energy we call God, both inside and outside ourselves. We are present to our daily tasks and relationships but we are also present as a spiritual and formless Self. We walk the path to our higher Self.

There are two pathways to awaken the kundalini, the coiled potential, and experience the divine. One method starts with the nervous system and glands and the other method works by awakening the inner sounds. The first builds the energy, and, when praana and apaana are balanced and still, opens up the flow of that energy to the highest solar center, at the crown of the head. This awakened energy then connects you directly to the experience of the Infinite. The second method awakens the inner sounds, the anaahat, which are subtle, primal and unlimited. This is where we learn to listen to the infinite pulse that is always and everywhere; this is where we experience shabad, the sound that cuts the ego. When we deeply absorb into these sounds and guide them to resound both in the higher and lower solar centers, then the divine inner light shines. Your Radiant Body illuminates and passes through all the chakra centers and throughout the entire body. You experience absorption and the grace of the Light beyond you and within you.

Chanting the Adi Shakti Mantra in this manner incorporates and integrates *both* methods simultaneously. The solar centers are charged and the inner light shines from the flow of the perfect sound current of the mantra. It awakens the kundalini, the manifesting power of your mind and soul. It is an ashtang mantra—eight beats—which are the foundation of many kundalini kriyas and techniques. These eight beats attune us to the kundalini's rhythm and flow. The nervous system and glands function optimally. The entire brain, the *sahasrara* chakra, works as an integrated and effective whole. We expand our sensitivity and restore and heal from the losses caused by stress and trauma.

Yogi Bhajan said of this mantra practice:

> "This mantra is known as the Ashtang Mantra for the Aquarian Age. It has eight vibrations, and describes the glory of God. Thus said the Master, 'In the time period two-and-a-half hours before the rising of the Sun, when the channels are

most clear, if the mantra is sung in sweet harmony, you will be one with the Lord.' A practitioner will get connected with the Cosmic Energy, and thus will be liberated from the cycle of time and karma. Those who meditate on this mantra in silence will charge their solar centers and be one with the divine. All mantras are good and are for the awakening of the divine. But this mantra is effective; it is the mantra for this time. So my lovely student, at the will of my Master I teach you the greatest divine key. It has eight levers, and can open the lock of the time, which is also of the vibration of eight. Therefore, when this mantra is sung with the Neck Lock, at the point where praana and apaana meet sushmuna, this vibration opens the lock, and thus one becomes one with the divine." [122]

Chanting this mantra cultivates nonattachment and gives you a refined mind and emotional maturity. It blunts the hold of impulse and expands your insight and intuition. It gives you the experience of merger with the frequency of the Infinite which is beyond any person and beyond any finite conception. This mantra and its projection bring union—yoga—with the ultimate cosmic energy. Yogi Bhajan said,

"It is equal to millions and billions of suns. When you will recite this mantra, the day shall come when you shall have the light within you. You will find it equal to you cannot say what. There is no vocabulary and there is no tongue which can say just how bright that light is. But remember, that light you shall see, that is the only light through which you can overcome the cycle of karma. Then nothing disturbs you. Then you live normally, and you are beyond the power of the cycles of time and space."

Even 3 minutes of this practice gives you a taste of its effect; 11 minutes clears the mind; 37 1/2 minutes links you to the cosmos and makes your best thoughts projective and active. Yogi Bhajan said that with 37 ½ minutes you would get a "reflection," an extra boost and initiation of awareness from your total psyche. When practiced on its own, 37 ½ minutes is the minimum time to completely lock in your aura and Radiant Body for this projection. You can increase the time to 62 minutes which will give you endurance and grace under pressure; and the best of all practices is 2 1/2 hours, which will give you intuition, directly awaken the kundalini, clean out the subconscious neuroses and blocks, and open your solar centers to the experience of the inner light and sound of the subtle worlds.

The solar centers refer to the crown chakra on top of the head and the solar plexus, at the diaphragm. These are crucial for energy transformation and making the connection between our finite sources of energy and the unlimited universal energy of the Self.

Every serious student of Kundalini Yoga will at some point do a 40-day saadhana of this chant for 2 1/2 hours before the rise of the sun. During that time we eat lightly, exercise each day and speak only positive universal truth from our heart. The awareness that comes gives us mastery of our full human potential.

In general, this mantra has impact however you practice it: silently, listening to a recording, meditating with friends, or chanting out loud. Ideally you have a balanced practice that includes exercise, nutrition, meditation and service as part of a fulfilled, prosperous human experience and a rich spiritual life. But even if chanting is your only practice, when it is done very regularly and technically, this mantra will open up your entire potential.

This mantra is a gift. It is very rare to discover a mantra that directly awakens the kundalini. As you master this meditation practice, share its fruits with all. Chant in groups. Inscribe its consciousness in every fiber of your being. It is a key to the unseen cosmos. When you meditate on this mantra you are affected and shaped by the inner topology of its sounds; that is, the repetition of the mantra impacts various reflex and meridian points in the upper palate that provoke adaptation in the glands and the brain that increase sensitivity and perception.

Though ultimately the mantra itself does the work, it is useful to connect to the meaning coded in the mantra. Its simple message expresses the essence of Kundalini Yoga's philosophy of awareness. Simply read the mantra forward and then backward. Mantras are discovered whole, like seeds that contain the knowledge of the entire plant, these simple bij sounds hold the entire cosmos.

Reading it in one direction, Ek Ong Kaar awakens the Self by connecting to the whole universe to all the forms of experience and roles we play. We end the isolation that ego and intellect wrap us in. We examine all the ways we un-see what is real; the ways we reject what we do not want to see; the places in our Self we have contracted from because of fear. These three simple words remove those blocks and open our hearts, helping us realize our intimate connection with all of creation. If the creator and the creation are indeed one, then there has never been a separation: that is the first illusion. Then we chant Sat Naam, we can now realize our own identity, which is part of the reality of all that is. Our ego is one thing; it is our limitations and the way we function within those limitations. Our real Self is another thing altogether; it is the identity that lets us become a witness, consciously conscious and part of all. As Sat Naam, we are located in the center of everything, wherever we are. When we live from our true identity, we free ourselves from roles, and instead, we live spontaneously, a freely flowing unique expression of the divine. We are the divine embodied. Then we reach the final part of the chant, Siree Whaa-hay Guroo, life as an ecstatic experience of divine intelligence. Once we are connected to all that is, and know our Self as part of that all, we can let go in the same way we merge into a lover. By dissolving what we were we become even stronger; letting go of all limitations and embracing trust, grace and intuition. There are no words for this lived reality, which is why so many traditions say you cannot say the name of God.

Now read it in the other direction. Whaa-hay Guroo: We begin in formless ecstasy and merger with the creator. There is no separation from the formlessness of all existence. The will of God and ours are the same. Our existence is a gift and part of the formless reality that is. We act out of joy and bliss. Every movement of life speaks to us. Our heart is open so every movement of life is a divine dance. It is great, Siree, beyond any thought. Then we read Sat Naam and out of this unbounded joy in the formless we create an identity—a crystallized form; a specific shape for our self in time and space. We let a drop of our joy bring life into existence. We come into the finite world and experience love. We enter the finite game of life as an unbounded soul in an infinite game. Winning is the bliss of expressing that identity in every act, relationship and accomplishment. And finally we read the first part of the mantra, Ek Ong Kaar; once we bring the crystallized clarity of our being into an identity in time and space to experience things, we can see. We start to connect with all other identities and forms and create new worlds. Each word creates a world and adds new forms to our experience and to life itself.

So it goes around. There is no beginning or end. The inner essence of the mantra is a creative pulse that connects our most subtle Self with our most gross and practical self. The final result is realization of our Self as a human being in all its richness, awareness and creative potential.

Long Ek Ong Kaar

POSTURE: Sit in Easy Pose or Lotus Pose, with a straight spine, and apply Neck Lock.

MUDRA: Gyan Mudra, first finger and thumb together, at the knees.

EYES: Eyes are 1/10th open. Focus through the Brow Point.

MANTRA: Ek Ong Kaar Sat Naam Siree Whaa-hay Guroo.

Listen to the sounds and feel the energetic flow.

The Adi Shakti Mantra

Ek Ong Kaar   One Creator created this Creation;
One Creative Energy in All Things.

Sat Naam   Truth is the Name; Existence is the Identity

Siree Whaa-Hay Guroo   Great beyond description is that infinite wisdom

Chant the mantra in a 2-1/2 breath cycle. Inhale deeply. Then pull in the navel sharply as you chant a short powerful Ek. Continue the sound with a drawn out Ong Kaar, giving equal time to Ong and Kaar.

Inhale deeply again. Then pull in the navel sharply as you chant Sat. Continue the sound with Naam drawn out. Naam should last as long as Ong and Kaar together. Just as you get to the end of your breath, pull up the diaphragm with a quick Siree made with the last bit of breath. Quickly take in a half breath. Pull in the navel sharply as you chant a short emphatic Whaa, then continue with Hay Guroo. Hay is short and Guroo is longer, but not drawn out.

Ong Kaar and Naam Siree are equal in length. The final phrase, Whaa-hay Guroo, is equal in length to one half of the other two phrases. Keep the pitch steady as you chant.

TIME: 37 ½ minutes. The practice can be for as little as 7 minutes or extended up to 62 minutes or 2 ½ hours.

TO END: Take a deep inhalation and suspend the breath. Stay absolutely still. Hear the echo of the chant. Sense the space and energy you have created. Exhale. Repeat two more times. Then sit still for another few minutes and let the awareness and healing be in every cell, in every thought. Sense your presence and your connection with the entire universe, known and unknown.

Hints for Practice and Mastery

This is the foundation of the kundalini experience. There is no need for secret mantras when this mantra is open to all without initiation. Sincere, precise and regular practice awakens and regulates the kundalini energy—the basic evolutionary force of the human psyche and soul.

The sound Ek is very short and it is chanted all at once as a single sound. The sound Ong vibrates the entire skull and upper palate. It is important to do this sound correctly. The throat is relaxed, the jaw is open and the back of the tongue is pressed up against the palate even as the tip is lowered down. The air pressure is through the nose. It feels like being in a cavern that has no bounds. The sound Kaar resonates from the back of the mouth, the throat and the upper chest. Sat is short and powerful like Ek. The sound Naam resonates from the chest and throat and is very open. The sound Siree just escapes off your tongue at the front of the teeth with the last bit of breath as you squeeze the Navel Point in and lift the diaphragm. The sound Whaa is short and flows off the lips, which move distinctly, as you keep the chest lifted. The sound Hay is short and repeated immediately after Whaa as part of that same word; tighten and hold the Navel Point inward for the rest of the chant. Guroo is of medium length with the emphasis on Roo; it vibrates from the throat and mouth.

Witness Your Consciousness from within Yourself

Practice between Stage 8 and Stage 9

An essential meditative skill for this journey is to be a witness of our own consciousness from within our Self. When this inner witness is stablized we stay aligned with our authentic Self in any and all activities. We can also use this neutral position of the Self to direct the projection and energy of the mind in order to create. The mind is vast creative potential. To express it effectively we need to be able to beam the mind along with a single pattern of thought or a goal. When we can put our whole Self into that beam, without interference or too much conscious effort, we create a seed. That seed, which we call a *bija*, primes the mind to opportunities, just as a farmer prepares the field. That bija magnetizes and attracts resources to it, and synchronizes with the Unknown to complete the intention.

The first step is to develop the witness, the crystallized Self, whole and transparent like a window. You can locate your Self. You can sift through all the sensations that flow through you and bring each of them to equilibrium. When all the waves of thought and feeling are relaxed and calm, then you can beam your mind. You can be a witness to and sense whatever you focus on. You can pour yourself into another and create resonance and affiliation; it is an intuitive mode of knowing. It is the polarity of analysis and comparison, which is based on the differences between things. Meditative beaming is based on the similarity and unity we have with all things. We must develop both skills: intuition and analytic discernment. In either mode we need to be able to witness our consciousness and beam our mind and our energy into the field of awareness.

Yogi Bhajan shared this short exercise to develop the beaming faculty after a class in 1972. It provides a bridge from Stage Eight where we stimulate the upper endocrine glands and rasas to Stage Nine where our ability to witness our Self opens us up to delight. This core skill, to be a conscious witness under every condition, takes practice. This meditation has two challenges in it. The first is simply holding the physical position without distraction, which will open up your sensitivity in the somatic space. The second is the shift in mental focus. We all have a habitual position of observation. Often it is a first person observer from the eyes, ears or touch. This meditation removes that normal location and creates a polarity in the mind. You will be somewhere and nowhere at once. The mind has an ability to sense all directions simultaneously but a habit of focusing on a very narrow corridor, usually associated with sight. In order to mature a thought we need the combination of a consciously conscious wide open witness and a flow of the mind beamed from a relaxed and naturally held attention.

Developing the Beaming Faculty and the Self as a Witness†

POSTURE: Sit in Easy Pose or other meditative posture, with a straight spine, and apply Neck Lock.

MUDRA: The left hand is in front of the face with the palm facing you. The palm is held 6 to 8 inches (15-20 cm.) away from the face. Bring the right hand behind the skull, a few inches (5- 7 cm.) away from the head, palm facing you. Keep the shoulders relaxed and hold the hands in a natural fixed position. Both wrists are straight.

EYES: Fix the eyes open and look at the palm of the hand. See the lines and fix your gaze as if you could see the process of your life behind the lines. Remain alert to the flow of your life, your thoughts and your feelings.

BREATH: Slow, complete and meditative.

After a minute or two, once you become fully present and consciously aware of your front hand, shift your mental point of observation to the back hand. See your front hand and the flow of your life as if you were witnessing it from your back palm, through the transparent skull, through the physical eyes, into the palm and beyond. You are witnessing your Self witnessing the flow. You are still and beaming your awareness. You are sensing everything through a wide open mind and a non-reactive Self. You will sense the back, the front and in between. As you succeed at sensing both simultaneously you will shift automatically to sense your entire space of energy and aura. Note the flow of thoughts from your mind and from all sources in the universe.

Stay absolutely steady, and with a subtle joy, watch and know. The slightest intention will influence what you observe. Simply dwell in the witness and in that growing potential to beam and influence.

TIME: 11 minutes.

† Please Note: This is a skill development exercise given by Yogi Bhajan; he did not teach it as "kriya".

TO END: Inhale deeply; suspend the breath with eyes open. Exhale. Repeat but close your eyes as you hold the breath. Finally inhale deeply and stretch the hands and arms up in the air. Exhale. Move the arms and shoulders to relax them.

After this go on to the meditation for Stage Nine: Delight. Now you are primed to go swiftly and deeply into that jappa meditation.

Healing, Mental Beaming and Delight

Practice between Stage 9 and Stage 10

Yogi Bhajan said that in order to heal, we have to practice these stages of meditation and purify our minds. This discipline matures the personality and increases the control of the frontal brain and intuition. Then we can balance the five tattvas, the rasas and beam our praanic energy, its frequency, into another person and heal.

"An empty glass doesn't contain water and it doesn't quench the thirst. Healers have a very different personality. It is a personality of reality to put five tattvas together and out of that balance flow the praanic energy into another person. It can be beamed through the words, it can be through the sight, it can be through the touch and it can be through thought alone." [123]

"When we develop the physical purity of our body to elevate our consciousness and our passion and our energy in our body and our psyche, then we can beam that energy into the body of another person to elevate, to levitate and make things happen right. It is just like a jump start. We take a car which is running well with a good battery. We take the wires and we connect the other car until its engine starts. Then it starts to produce its own energy and handle its situation. It's no different than that; there's no big mystery. It is a simple human mental practice. Mental beam is the most powerful. It can manifest things which cannot be manifested any other way." [124]

When we engage our energy and beam it through our cells or into another being, we are healing through the kundalini. Yogi Bhajan shared many forms of healing with us: massage and direct physical manipulation; the use of diet, foods and herbs to cleanse and balance; the ability to transfer praanic energy; healing through sound and shabad; healing by self-hypnosis. And healing through awareness itself, this he called Sat Naam Rasayan because it relies on a neutral expanded identity in the Self.

"What is Sat Naam Rasayan? Sat means truth, Naam means identity, Rasayan means something which cures. So, it is where you learn truth, you speak truth and you be truth. It is when you think all is God and God is all. It is where you eliminate ego and tension." [125]

"What is Sat Naam Rasayan? To meditate on yourself first, and to project yourself for the uplifting healing of the other person; it's a pure exchange of energy. You learn it. You practice hours and hours and hours. Some need twenty hours, some need ten hours, and some need only one hour to practice." [126]

Healing in this most subtle form is not a matter of time and space but of attunement and consciousness. The more we do it the more we establish a constant state in which we can heal and share the energy of life and delight. Kundalini healing—balance of the rasas, elevation of the mind and attunement with another—is simple. Let the ego and conflicts dissolve. Go into stillness and shuniya. Then connect and sense everything at once. Feel the delight of life and relax in the Infinite that heals through you. These techniques are common practices of healers through the ages.

"It's as simple as that. The spine will become automatically straight because without that the nervous system will otherwise crimp the energy. So you have to sit very straight and hold your shoulders tight and see that you gain the experience. You know the oldest healing is the Shaman. Sha means rich, Sha means wealthy. Man is mind. Shaman means someone who is a rich in their mind. What does that mean?

"Sometimes those people who are healers won't even touch a person. They change the entire psyche. I mean there are very sophisticated things in this body. If you hold yourself steady and let your body go through the changes, it's priceless. Don't move. The body wants to move. You don't have to move. Let this energy of healing move inside. All the energy is there.

"Let in this peace and tranquility so the spirit, mind and body create a relationship for everlasting bondage as it is the will of God. So be it. Come on. You are the Temple of God; simply you recharge yourself to face the transmission against the obstacles and height of the time and space. You have two challenges. Time and space. You and your spirit are two dominant forces within you and when the spirit dominatingly helps your mind and helps your body you are successful." [127]

Healing, Mental Beaming and Delight

June 24, 1999

This exercise (which is not a kriya) can be done with any two people to heal and rejuvenate each other. You can also practice on your own. In this exercise we will do it as a group with partners.

Create a small group of eight people. Two pairs of partners sit next to each other in the center while the other four people are seated at the four corners around them. The people on the outside sit individually in a meditative posture with the eyes closed facing toward the center. They meditate on their Self and their spine.

The two pairs of partners sit facing one another, in a meditative pose, with the spine straight. Interlace your fingers with your partner's, palm to palm. The elbows are relaxed so the hands are held at the level between the solar plexus and the heart.

Fix your eyes into the eyes of your partner without blinking. Beam your attention and gaze into the center of the eyes of your partner. Feel the center line of energy in the body. Look into the eyes and sense the straight line of your own spine. Stabilize your energy to neutral.

Consciously create one thought—"Heal me"—and beam it. Imagine your spine is a light, a rod of light, the light of the infinite light. Feel the spine stretched as if you were reaching for the heavens. Expand the light. Sense that light and project the thought "Heal me". Let the Infinite heal you. Let the light bring energy into every cell.

Healing, Mental Beaming and Delight

Feel the spine become open, light, healed, and whole. Experience delight in the flow of your consciousness. Become humble and open. For a moment be devoted to the Infinite in you and beyond you. Surrender the efforts to heal and ask to be healed. Let healing flow through your spine as you mentally relax. Keep breathing slowly and deeply. Keep the eyes fixed if you are with a partner and closed if you are on the perimeter. Consciously purify yourself with each breath. Concentrate on the spinal fluid moving and energizing. Allow the infinite energy of life and spirit to flow in you. It is available to every person. Take it in now.

Let your neutral mind dwell on positive thoughts: delight, healing and light. The One that dwells in all and creates all has no limit. Become completely balanced and open to your inner light as you look at your partner or meditate. Continue to tap the flow of your subtle body and your praanic body in this way.

TIME: 11 minutes.

TO END: Now the partners close their eyes and take a deep inhalation. As the people in partners close the eyes, those on the perimeter open them and follow the guided meditation. Suspend the breath and tighten the spine. Feel it stretch. Feel as though you are rising upward as you sit. Sense the energy flowing from the spine to every cell in your body. Exhale powerfully through the mouth. Inhale again. Keep the hands locked with your partner. Feel the energy flow in and radiate out freely, smoothly, and without limit. Then exhale through the mouth like a cannon. One last time inhale, eyes remain closed, tighten the spine and let the energy flow from the spine to the cells, from the cells to the spine, and from the spine to the infinite light, and from the infinite light to the spine. Be one flow of light equal in all directions and without limit. Feel your center, still, bright, full of delight and life! Exhale and relax.

Switch roles; those on the perimeter sit in partners and those in partners take their position on the perimeter. Repeat the exercise for 11 minutes.

After the second round of the exercise take a few minutes to share your experiences of this simple practice of kundalini healing and light.

Hints for Practice and Mastery

Yogi Bhajan was an advocate of the individual. He believed that each person had within them the entire legacy of being human as well as being part of a vast universe. He taught that God was in everyone; he saw each person as a personified God. He delivered experiences that allowed each person to test their own connection and sensibility of the Infinite. He said the energy of awareness, the kundalini, was embodied in each of us.

In this simple exercise, he wants us to trust our own connection to the Infinite. Each person is a natural healer, mystic and creator. Each person can use the mind to influence another. We can create powerful experiences in another person because we are sensitive to each other and because our mind has the ability to project itself in thought, feeling and energy.

In this exercise we call on the infinite light and purity that is God. Healing is impersonally personal. We consciously let your own ego stuff go. We need a clear lens to see accurately. We need clear energy to help another see themselves accurately. When we find delight we do not need to seek satisfaction from something or someone else. We can open our sensitivity and sensibility to the reality of others and use the power of our mind and soul with innocence and clarity. When we can do that, "An ordinary man who has the strength of a rat can become as strong as an elephant."

The same creative process that created the universe began with meditation, a state of zero. "In the beginning there was nothing, just void and darkness." It was formless and pure. That is why so many creation stories start with God in meditation, sleep or withdrawal. First is meditation then manifestation. So, too, in this healing exercise, we make ourself zero and clear. We go to our beginning. Then we extend the Self into vastness. We stimulate and refine the rasas. We enter into the delight and flow of consciousness consciously. Then we pour that into every cell and into our partner.

The individual and the group are part of a single field of energy. The change in one induces a change in the other. That is a potency that we all have. When the partners penetrate into the central channel of their bodies, they are like a broadcast tower that uplifts themselves and all those around them. And yet all that is being done is through the touch of the Infinite. They do not manipulate anyone. They center, elevate, radiate and induce a natural equilibrium. Then each person naturally adjusts and heals. It seems sometimes miraculous but it is a normal mechanism we all share. It's nothing special, just the coiled potential of awareness within each of us.

The process of energizing yourself can be done with any friend, spouse, student—or even a tree! You can link to any organic living thing that is responsive and can attune and interconnect to your energy. Zero, connect, elevate, flow and glow. Believe in the Infinite of you. Test it through experience.

Breath of Fire

Practice between Stage 12 and Stage 13

This praanayam prepares our body and mind for meditation. A foundation practice in Kundalini Yoga, it is excellent for conquering stress, balancing the autonomic nervous system and for cleansing. We often do it for 3 minutes in kriyas and it is used with many exercises. It can be done by itself for much longer times if done properly.

Yogi Bhajan taught several ways to do Breath of Fire for a full 31 minutes. This series is designed to cleanse the body and elevate the body's cellular energy. We want to be in a space of flexibility and vitality to master the meditations within these 21 Stages of Meditation. Doing Breath of Fire in this manner assures that the lungs and ribcage will be clear and expansive in preparation for the meditations that follow.

Here is how Yogi Bhajan described this praanayam:

> *"Let me tell you something very simple. There is no need to take any outside energy. Sit in any posture where you are very convenient and comfortable. Now use constant breathing from the nostrils and combine it from the Navel Center and solar plexus, which is called Breath of Fire. I will tell you the simplest thing which you can do.*
>
> *"You just do a Breath of Fire for seven minutes in Gyan Mudra, then change it after seven minutes to this second finger, Shuni Mudra, then seven minutes more on the third finger, Surya Mudra, and seven minutes on the fourth finger tip, Buddhi Mudra. You do Breath of Fire for twenty-eight minutes. Then for the last three minutes meditate and project. For one minute fold your hands together in Prayer Pose and inhale deep. Hold the breath and mentally chant, Ong Namo Guru Dev Namo. Breathe as needed but try to hold for the entire minute. Then for one more minute inhale and hold the breath and pray for peace and tranquility of yourself. Finally inhale and hold the breath for one minute and give a prayer, for peace, for prosperity, for health, for anything you want. It will take thirty-one minutes.*
>
> *"If you do it for forty days your life will change for the better, that's all it is. Seven minutes by time clock on each finger. In the beginning the breath of life is what you live for and it has the capacity to change your life for better. The science of Kundalini Yoga has the capacity to change the life of any person for the better. It's a yoga for the householder. It's a yoga for every person where the strength of life is put together to be useful in life. To be useful in life is when I can use my potentials fully and take care of all that I need to care for and I can take care of others, too. My obligations, my duties, my requirements are all fulfilled plus I can do additional service to others. That requires strength; practice and you can say, 'I put my body, mind and soul together and I trained it through the breath of life and I am perfect.'"* [128]

Breath of Fire

August 27, 1986

Sit straight and begin a steady Breath of Fire.

Breathe for 7 minutes in each of the four finger locks. End with three one minute breaths and the following mental projection and blessing: Inhale and be still. Exhale. Inhale, hold, and pray for your own peace and tranquility. Exhale. Inhale, hold, and offer a prayer for prosperity, health, or anything you truly want. Exhale.

Hints for Practice and Mastery

Pay attention to the basics of doing Breath of Fire. When you do it for this extended time, even a small deviance from good form can create unwanted tension, dryness or fatigue. Done correctly, you feel it is easy, energizing and calming all at once. It seems to sustain itself by its own momentum and with little effort.

Check that you are breathing through both nostrils. The nostrils are open, not squeezed by the pressure of the inhale. The breath is powered from the diaphragm. The chest is lifted and stays so throughout. The spine is straight and does not dip or bob with the breath. The breath comes from the diaphragm movement across the solar plexus area and pulls the Navel Point in with the exhales. It is not a belly pump, which uses muscles much lower in the abdomen and will gradually tire your lower back muscles. Do it right and it will make you right and bright!

End Notes

1. © The Teachings of Yogi Bhajan, October 19, 1976
2. © The Teachings of Yogi Bhajan, June 24, 1972
3. © The Teachings of Yogi Bhajan, June 21, 1972
4. © The Teachings of Yogi Bhajan, November 27, 1973
5. © The Teachings of Yogi Bhajan, October 19, 1976
6. © The Teachings of Yogi Bhajan, December 12, 1970
7. © The Teachings of Yogi Bhajan, July 23, 1987
8. A familiar quote from Yogi Bhajan
9. © The Teachings of Yogi Bhajan, January 28, 1977
10. From the personal notes of the Author
11. © The Teachings of Yogi Bhajan, Circa 1972
12. © The Teachings of Yogi Bhajan, August 10, 1971
13. © The Teachings of Yogi Bhajan, March 30, 1972
14. © The Teachings of Yogi Bhajan, March 30, 1972
15. © The Teachings of Yogi Bhajan, April 22, 1987
16. © The Teachings of Yogi Bhajan, January 22, 1987
17. From the personal notes of the author.
18. © The Teachings of Yogi Bhajan, October 13, 1979
19. © The Teachings of Yogi Bhajan, October 27, 1974
20. © The Teachings of Yogi Bhajan, February 17, 1984
21. © The Teachings of Yogi Bhajan, January 31, 1988
22. © The Teachings of Yogi Bhajan, October 28, 1972
23. © The Teachings of Yogi Bhajan, July 5, 1979
24. © The Teachings of Yogi Bhajan, November 26, 1985
25. © The Teachings of Yogi Bhajan, May 4, 1971
26. © The Teachings of Yogi Bhajan, November 21, 1982
27. © The Teachings of Yogi Bhajan, January 19, 1988
28. © The Teachings of Yogi Bhajan, April 9, 1969
29. © The Teachings of Yogi Bhajan, October 30, 1972
30. © The Teachings of Yogi Bhajan, July 1, 1983
31. © The Teachings of Yogi Bhajan, April 22, 1977
32. © The Teachings of Yogi Bhajan, April 23, 1973
33. © The Teachings of Yogi Bhajan, January 16, 1986
34. © The Teachings of Yogi Bhajan, November 20, 1973
35. © The Teachings of Yogi Bhajan, January 2, 1970
36. © The Teachings of Yogi Bhajan, April 7, 1993
37. © The Teachings of Yogi Bhajan, July 17, 1988
38. © The Teachings of Yogi Bhajan, February 12, 1991
39. Asa Di Vaar, Siri Guru Granth Sahib, p. 466, Guru Angad Dev Ji
40. Siri Guru Granth Sahib, p. 325
41. © The Teachings of Yogi Bhajan, December 14, 1988
42. © The Teachings of Yogi Bhajan, July 19, 1991
43. © The Teachings of Yogi Bhajan, July 17, 1992
44. © The Teachings of Yogi Bhajan, May 31, 1985
45. © The Teachings of Yogi Bhajan, May 13, 1987
46. © The Teachings of Yogi Bhajan, July 5, 1993
47. © The Teachings of Yogi Bhajan, July 12, 1984
48. © The Teachings of Yogi Bhajan, August 22, 1979
49. © The Teachings of Yogi Bhajan, September 16, 1969
50. The Teachings of Yogi Bhajan, March 2, 1973
51. © The Teachings of Yogi Bhajan, March 29, 1983
52. © The Teachings of Yogi Bhajan, November 12, 1971
53. © The Teachings of Yogi Bhajan, September 17, 1992
54. © The Teachings of Yogi Bhajan, October 23, 1979

55. © The Teachings of Yogi Bhajan, April 8, 1990
56. © The Teachings of Yogi Bhajan, April 13, 1983
57. © The Teachings of Yogi Bhajan, July 17, 1984
58. © The Teachings of Yogi Bhajan, July 27, 1982
59. © The Teachings of Yogi Bhajan, November 9, 1984
60. © The Teachings of Yogi Bhajan, February 27, 1983
61. © The Teachings of Yogi Bhajan, August 27, 1975
62. 80. © The Teachings of Yogi Bhajan, October 29, 1976
63. © The Teachings of Yogi Bhajan, June 23, 1977
64. © The Teachings of Yogi Bhajan, October 25, 1988
65. © The Teachings of Yogi Bhajan, June 13, 1971
66. © The Teachings of Yogi Bhajan, March 31, 1971
67. © The Teachings of Yogi Bhajan, September 2, 1982
68. © The Teachings of Yogi Bhajan, April 8, 1982
69. © The Teachings of Yogi Bhajan, July 1, 1993
70. © The Teachings of Yogi Bhajan, August 2, 1992
71. © The Teachings of Yogi Bhajan, September 30, 1985
72. © The Teachings of Yogi Bhajan, November 2, 1979
73. © The Teachings of Yogi Bhajan, March 26, 1985
74. © The Teachings of Yogi Bhajan, January 28, 1985
75. © The Teachings of Yogi Bhajan, September 2, 1982
76. © The Teachings of Yogi Bhajan, March 19, 1983
77. © The Teachings of Yogi Bhajan, December 4, 1984
78. © The Teachings of Yogi Bhajan, August 21, 1985
79. © The Teachings of Yogi Bhajan, November 25, 1978
80. © The Teachings of Yogi Bhajan, July 7, 1985
81. © The Teachings of Yogi Bhajan, April 14, 1977
82. © The Teachings of Yogi Bhajan, November 26, 1978
83. © The Teachings of Yogi Bhajan, March 20, 1975
84. © The Teachings of Yogi Bhajan, February 13, 1992
85. © The Teachings of Yogi Bhajan, April 26, 1975
86. © The Teachings of Yogi Bhajan, July 23, 1996
87. Bhajan, Yogi. (1996). Master's Touch. Kundalini Research Institute: Santa Cruz, NM, p. 35.
88. © The Teachings of Yogi Bhajan, August 4, 1971
89. © The Teachings of Yogi Bhajan, May 4, 1974
90. © The Teachings of Yogi Bhajan, March 6, 1983
91. Bhajan, Yogi. (1977). The Teachings of Yogi Bhajan. Kundalini Research Institute: Santa Cruz, NM, pg 135.
92. © The Teachings of Yogi Bhajan, April 9, 1969
93. © The Teachings of Yogi Bhajan, September 28, 1969
94. © The Teachings of Yogi Bhajan, April 26, 1975
95. ©The Teachings of Yogi Bhajan, July 23, 1996
96. © The Teachings of Yogi Bhajan, April 5, 1983
97. © The Teachings of Yogi Bhajan, January 13, 1977
98. © The Teachings of Yogi Bhajan, November 25, 1980
99. © The Teachings of Yogi Bhajan, July 31, 1996
100. © The Teachings of Yogi Bhajan, April 2, 2001
101. © The Teachings of Yogi Bhajan, November 5, 1991
102. © The Teachings of Yogi Bhajan, December 12, 1990
103. © The Teachings of Yogi Bhajan, April 22, 1969
104. © The Teachings of Yogi Bhajan, April 10, 1969
105. © The Teachings of Yogi Bhajan, November 23, 1971
106. © The Teachings of Yogi Bhajan, July 9, 1969
107. © The Teachings of Yogi Bhajan, October 10, 1976
108. © The Teachings of Yogi Bhajan, July 20, 1978
109. Ibid.
110. © The Teachings of Yogi Bhajan, February 9, 1983
111. © The Teachings of Yogi Bhajan, February 9, 1979
112. ©The Teachings of Yogi Bhajan, April 8, 1976
113. © The Teachings of Yogi Bhajan, December 15, 1970
114. © The Teachings of Yogi Bhajan, February 16, 1973
115. © The Teachings of Yogi Bhajan, February 5, 1976
116. © The Teachings of Yogi Bhajan, March 30, 1971
117. © 1970 The Teachings of Yogi Bhajan
118. © The Teachings of Yogi Bhajan, June 1, 1970
119. © The Teachings of Yogi Bhajan, July 11, 1975
120. © The Teachings of Yogi Bhajan, November 26, 1971
121. © The Teachings of Yogi Bhajan, February 16, 1973
122. From The Aquarian Teacher
123. © The Teachings of Yogi Bhajan, August 25, 1997
124. © The Teachings of Yogi Bhajan, May 3, 2000
125. © The Teachings of Yogi Bhajan, July 16, 1998
126. © The Teachings of Yogi Bhajan, May 2, 2000
127. © The Teachings of Yogi Bhajan, April 2, 1997
128. © The Teachings of Yogi Bhajan, August 27, 1986

Glossary

Aquarian Age: The next in a succession of astrological ages each lasting roughly 2,000 years. Fully inaugurated in AD 2012, the Aquarian Age will witness a radical change in consciousness, human sensitivity, and technology. The central change of this new age emphasizes an increased sensitivity and evolution of our power of awareness and a new relationship to our mind.

Amrit: The inner nectar that accompanies an awakened consciousness. Also, the hormonal secretions from the higher glands of the brain that enhance awareness.

Antar, Bantar, Jantar, Mantar, Tantar, Patantar, and Sotantar: These describe the sequence of creative expression from inner essence to full manifestation. Antar is the inner essence and being. It is before form. Each essence has an associated structure in time and space, a dimension to it, bantar. This structure is fulfilled by an appropriate matching set of qualities, jantar, which has a unique sound resonance, mantar, and a distinct visual form, yantar. This form and energy interrelate to the universe, tantar, creating a projection and track as it threads through time and space, patantar, until finally achieving its liberated form, beyond time and space, sotantar. This form creates a neutral point that ties together many of the polarities inherent in Prakirti to embed and express the essence of the antar in creation.

Applied Mind: A cultivated capacity of the mind which allows you to focus and respond effectively with intuition, intelligence, and comprehensive comparative consciousness to any demand in the environment or toward your goal. It is creative, stress-free, and can act or not act as needed.

Arcline: Part of the aura that encodes our destiny and potential. One of 10 bodies or containing vehicles of a human being. It is a shiny thin arc that goes from ear to ear over the forehead near the normal hairline. It reflects the interaction of the soul of the person with its vital energy resources, and in it are written the potential, destiny, and health of the person.

Atma: The soul or finite form of the Infinite in consciousness. It is transcendental in nature, not a product of the mind but a part of pure awareness. It is a witness of everything and can only be revealed through itself.

Aura: The radiant field of energy and consciousness that surrounds the physical body and which holds and organizes the seven centers of energy called chakras. Its strength, measured by brightness and radius, determines the vitality, mental concerns, and psychophysical integrity of a person.

Awareness: The pure nature of existence; the power to be consciously conscious without an object or need. A fundamental property of the soul and true self; it is Kundalini as it folds and unfolds itself in existence.

Bana: A specified clothing that projects a consciousness.

Breath of Fire: Also called agni praan. It is a rapid, rhythmical breath pattern, generated from the navel point and diaphragm with an equal inhale and exhale and usually done through the nose. It is both stimulating and relaxing. It heals, strengthens the nerves, and clears out old patterns and toxins.

Buddhi: This is the first, most etheric manifestation of the Universal Mind from which all other areas of mind are derived. Its quality or function is to give the clarity, discernment, and wisdom that recognize the real from the imaginary. It forms the deepest core of the human psyche but is impersonal, existing independent of the individual sense of self.

Chakra: The word connotes a wheel in action. It usually refers to the seven primary energy centers in the aura that align along the spine from its base to the top of the skull. Each chakra is a center of consciousness with a set of values, concerns, and powers of action associated with it.

Consciousness: The nature of the self and being. In the realm of nature, awareness becomes consciousness. It is from the being itself. Being is expressed in consciousness through contrasts and sensations, in awareness through merger, clarity, and reality.

Dharma: A path of righteous living. It is both an ideal of virtue and a path of action that is infused with clear awareness and comprised of actions that are the soul in total synchrony with the universe. It is action without reaction or karma.

Dhyan: See Meditation.

Facet: An automatic subconscious predisposition of the mind to act or to prepare to act in a particular way. There are 81 Facets that result from the 27 Projections of the mind interacting with the three Functional Minds. These habits of action can either support your intention and awareness or cloak your consciousness.

Functional Minds: The three minds (Negative, Positive, and Neutral) that act as guides for the personal sense of self.

Golden Chain of Teachers or Golden Link: Historically it is the long line of spiritual masters who have preceded us. Practically it is the subtle link between the consciousness of a student and the master, which has the power to guide and protect the energy of a teaching and its techniques. This link requires the student to put aside the ego and limitations and act in complete synchrony or devotion to the highest consciousness of the master and teachings.

Gunas: The three qualities or threads that make up the fundamental forces in nature and the mind. Their interactions give motion to the world, stir the larger Greater Mind, and make up the realm of our experience. They are considered inseparable and occur in unlimited combinations. They are abstract; you can only see their effects. They are the sattva guna for clarity and purity; the rajasic guna for action and transformation, and the tamasic guna for heaviness, solidity, and ignorance.

Guru: That which takes us from ignorance to knowledge; from darkness, gu, to light, ru. It can be a person, a teaching, or in its most subtle form—the Word.

Gyan Mudra: A common hand position used in exercise and meditation, is formed by touching the tip of the index finger to the tip of the thumb. Its effect is receptivity, balance, and gentle expansion.

Ida: One of the three major channels (nadis) for subtle energy in the body. It is associated with the flow of breath through the left nostril and represents the qualities of the moon—calmness, receptivity, coolness, and imagination. It is associated with the functions of the parasympathetic nervous system but is not identical to it nor derived from it.

Impersonal Minds: The three major functions of the Universal Mind that create qualities of experience, cognition, and judgment. They are buddhi, ahangkar, and manas. They are impersonal since they exist independent of or before the individual sense of self.

Intellect: The function of the Universal Mind that releases thoughts, like the churning of the waves on the ocean. It is not the analytical acts of reason. Instead it is the source of the constant stream of thought formation from all levels of the Universal Mind. In this sense, someone who is intellectual is immersed in and often attached to thoughts and the act of making categories.

Intelligence: The use of the mind to create actions that manifest your purpose and the projection of your soul.

Jantar: See antar.

Japji Sahib: A mantra, poem, and inspired religious scripture composed by Guru Nanak. Japji Sahib gives a view of the cosmos, the soul, the mind, the challenge of life, and the impact of our actions. Its 40 stanzas are a source of many mantras and can be used as a whole or in part to guide both your mind and your heart.

Jappa: Literally "to repeat." It is the conscious, alert, and precise repetition of a mantra.

Karma: The law of cause and effect applied to mental, moral, and physical actions. Ego attaches us to and identifies us with objects, feelings, and thoughts. These attachments create a bias toward certain lines of action. Instead of acting you begin reacting. Karmas are the conditions required in order to balance or complete these tendencies. Though necessary, karma is not dictatorial or fatalistic. It is the mechanism that allows the finite experience of existence to maintain and stabilize itself. We all have free will and can take actions to re-direct the momentum of a karma. We can transform it or neutralize it using meditation, jappa, good deeds, or intuition that remove your sense of ego and the identification with that past line of action.

Karta Purkh: See maya and Purkha.

Kriya: Literal meaning is "completed action." A Kundalini Yoga Kriya is a sequence of postures and yoga techniques used to produce a particular impact on the psyche, body, or self. The structure of each kriya has been designed to generate, organize, and deliver a particular state or change of state, thereby completing a cycle of effect. These effects have been codified and elaborated by Yogi Bhajan and form the basic tools used in yoga and its therapeutic applications.

Kundalini Yoga: It is a Raaj Yoga that creates vitality in the body, balance in the mind, and openness to the spirit. It is used by the householder, busy in the world, to create immediate clarity. The fourth Guru in the Sikh tradition, Guru Ram Das, was acknowledged as the greatest Raaj Yogi. (See Raaj Yogi.) He opened this long secret tradition to all.

Mantar: See mantra and antar.

Mantra: Sounds or words that tune or control the mind. Man means mind. Tra-ng is the wave or movement of the mind. Mantra is a wave, a repetition of sound and rhythm that directs or controls the mind. When you recite a mantra you have impact: through the meridian points in the mouth, through its meaning, through its pattern of energy, through its rhythm, and through its naad—energetic shape in time. Recited correctly a mantra will activate areas of the nervous system and brain and allow you to shift your state and the perceptual vision or energetic ability associated with it.

Maya: The creative power of the Creator that restricts and limits. It creates the sense of limitation that leads us to identify with experience, the ego, and things. Because of this it is often thought of as the illusion that blocks us from the spirit. But, as Guru Nanak (see Sikh Gurus) reminds us, you need not be attached to the productions of maya. Instead they can be used to serve and express the higher consciousness and spirit. Maya is simply Karta Purkh, the doing of the Great Being. Maya takes the ineffable into the realm of the measurable.

Meditation: Dhyan. It is a process of deep concentration or merger into an object or a state of consciousness. Meditation releases reactions and unconscious habits and build the spontaneous and intuitive link to awareness itself.

Mudra: Mudra means "seal." It usually refers to hand positions used in meditation and exercise practices. These hand positions are used to seal the body's energy flow in a particular pattern. More generally it can refer to other locks, bandhas (see Mul Bandh), and meditation practices that seal the flow of energy by concentration.

Mul Bandh: This literally means "root lock." It is a body lock used to balance prana and apana (see prana) at the navel point. This releases reserve energy which is used to arouse the Kundalini. It is a contraction of the lower pelvis—the navel point, the sex organs, and the rectum.

Naad: The inner sound that is subtle and all-present. It is the direct expression of the Absolute. Meditated upon, it leads into a sound current that pulls the consciousness into expansion.

Naam: The manifested identity of the essence. The word derives from Naa-ay-ma, which means "that which is not, now is born." A Naam gives identity, form, and expression to that which was only essence or subtle before. It is also referred to as the Word.

Naadi: Channels or pathways of subtle energy. It is said that there are over 72,000 primary ones throughout the body.

Navel Point: The sensitive area of the body near the umbilicus that accumulates and stores life force. It is the reserve energy from this area that initiates the flow of the Kundalini energy from the base of the spine. If the navel area is strong, your vital force and health are also strong.

Negative Mind: One of the three Functional Minds. It is the fastest and acts to defend you. It asks, "How can this harm me? How can this limit or stop me?" It is also the power to just say no, stop something, or reject a direction of action.

Neutral Mind: The most refined and often the least developed of the three Functional Minds. It judges and assesses. It witnesses and gives you clarity. It holds the power of intuition and the ability to see your purpose and destiny. It is the gateway for awareness.

Patantar: See Antar.

Pingala: One of the three major channels (nadis) for subtle energy in the body. It is associated with the flow of breath through the right nostril and represented the qualities of the sun—energy, heat, action, and projective power. It is associated with the functions of the sympathetic nervous system but is not identical to it or derived from it.

Positive Mind: One of the three Functional Minds. It elaborates, magnifies, extends, and assists. It asks, "How can this help me? How can I use this? What is the positive side of this?"

Praana: The universal life force that gives motion. It is the breath in air. It is the subtle breath of the purusha as it vibrates with a psychophysical energy or presence. Prana regulates the modes and moods of the mind.

Praanayam: Regulated breathing patterns or exercises.

Prakriti: Transcendental Nature. It is creation as we can experience it. It includes mind and matter. It is formed from the motion and interaction of the gunas. It is multi-leveled and evolved from the original consciousness of the Absolute.

Pratyahaar: One of the eight limbs of yoga, it is the synchronization of the thoughts with the Infinite. To quote Yogi Bhajan; "Pratyahaar is the control of the mind through withdrawal of the senses. The joy in your life, which you really want to enjoy, is within you. There is nothing more precise than you within you. The day you find the you within you, your mind will be yours. In pratyahaar we bring everything to zero (shuniaa), as pranayam brings everything to Infinity."

Raaj Yogi: A yogi who follows the royal or highest path. One who excels and exalts the self in the midst of life without monastic withdrawal. One who places the self on the throne and presides with consciousness over all domains of manifestation, internal and external. (See Kundalini Yoga, Yogi.)

Sadhana: A spiritual discipline; the early morning practice of yoga, meditation, and other spiritual exercises.

Saa-Taa-Naa-Maa: This is referred to as the Punj Shabd Mantra (panj means five). It is the "atomic" or naad form of the mantra Sat

Naam. It is used to increase intuition, balance the hemispheres of the brain, and to create a destiny for someone when there was none.

Sat: Existence; what is; the subtle essence of Infinity itself.

Sat Naam: The essence or seed embodied in form; the identity of truth. When used as a greeting it means "I greet and salute that reality and truth which is your soul." It is called the Bij Mantra— the seed for all that comes.

Sattvic: One of the three basic qualities of nature (gunas). It represents purity, clarity, and light.

Shabad: Sound, especially subtle sound or sound imbued with consciousness. It is a property or emanation of consciousness itself. If you meditate on shabd it awakens your awareness.

Shabad Guru: These are sounds spoken by the Gurus; the vibration of the Infinite Being which transforms your consciousness; the sounds and words captured by the Gurus in the writings which comprise the Siri Guru Granth Sahib.

Shakti: The creative power and principle of existence itself. Without it nothing can manifest or bloom. It is feminine in nature.

Shuniya: A state of the mind and consciousness where the ego is brought to zero or complete stillness. There a power exists. It is the fundamental power of a Kundalini Yoga teacher. When you become shuniya then the One will carry you. You do not grasp or act. With folded hands you "are not." It is then that Nature acts for you.

Shushmanaa: One of the three major channels (nadis) for subtle energy in the body. It is associated with the central channel of the spine and is the place of neutrality through which the Kundalini travels when awakened. When mantra is vibrated from this place it has the power of soul and consciousness.

Sikh Gurus: In the Sikh tradition there were 10 living Gurus and one Guru, the Shabd Guru— the Word that guided and flowed through each of them. This succession of 10 Gurus revealed the Sikh path over a 200-year period. They were:

1st Sikh Guru: Guru Nanak
2nd Sikh Guru: Guru Angad
3rd Sikh Guru: Guru Amar Das
4th Sikh Guru: Guru Ram Das
5th Sikh Guru: Guru Arjan
6th Sikh Guru: Guru Hargobind
7th Sikh Guru: Guru Har Rai
8th Sikh Guru: Guru Har Krishan
9th Sikh Guru: Guru Teg Bahadur
10th Sikh Guru: Guru Gobind Singh

The 10th Sikh Guru, Guru Gobind Singh, passed the Guruship to the Siri Guru Granth Sahib, which embodies the writings, teachings, and sound current of the Gurus.

Simran: A deep meditative process in which the naam of the Infinite is remembered and dwelled in without conscious effort.

Siri Guru Granth Sahib: Sacred compilation of the words of the Sikh Gurus as well as of Hindu, Muslim, Sufi, and other saints. It captures the expression of consciousness and truth derived when in a state of divine union with God. It is written in naad and embodies the transformative power and structure of consciousness in its most spiritual and powerful clarity. It is a source of many mantras.

Subtle Body: See Ten Bodies.

Tamas: One of the three basic qualities of nature (gunas). It represents heaviness, slowness, and dullness. It is inertia and confusion.

Tattvas: A category of cosmic existence; a stage of reality or being; a "thatness" of differentiated qualities. In total there are 36 tattvas. Each wave of differentiation has its own rules and structure. The final five tattvas are called the gross elements and have the phasic qualities and relationships of ether, air, fire, water, and earth.

Ten Bodies: We are all spiritual beings having a human experience. In order to have this experience the spirit takes on 10 bodies or vehicles. They are the Soul Body, the three Mental Bodies (Negative, Positive, and Neutral Minds), the Physical Body, Pranic Body, Arcline Body, Auric Body, Subtle Body, and Radiant Body. Each body has its own quality, function, and realm of action.

Third Eye Point: The sixth chakra or center of consciousness. It is located at a point on the forehead between the eyebrows. Associated with the functioning of the pituitary gland, it is the command center and integrates the parts of the personality. It gives you insight, intuition, and the understanding of meanings and impacts beyond the surface of things. For this reason it is the focal point in many meditations.

Wahe Guru: A mantra of ecstasy and dwelling in God. It is the Infinite teacher of the soul. Also called the gur mantra.

Yogi: One who has attained a state of yoga (union) where polarities are mastered and transcended. One who practices the disciplines of yoga and has attained self-mastery.

Resources

The Kundalini Research Institute
Your Source for Kundalini Yoga as Taught by Yogi Bhajan®
Teacher Training, Online Resources, Publishing, and Research
www.kundaliniresearchinstitute.org

The Yogi Bhajan Library of Teachings
Keeping the Legacy Alive!
www.yogibhajan.org

For information regarding international events:
www.3HO.org

To find a teacher in your area or for more information
about becoming a Kundalini Yoga teacher:
www.kundaliniyoga.com

For more information about mantras and music used with these meditations:
www.kundaliniresearchinstitute.org
www.spiritvoyage.com
iTunes or CDBaby.com

About the Author

Gurucharan Singh Khalsa Ph.D. is a teacher, consultant, author and therapist who is a pioneer and expert in the applications of meditation and psychology. Inspired by the constant miracle and genius that is in each human heart, he is dedicated to sharing techniques that bring that potential and destiny into full expression.

He leads a conversation between psychology, spirit and the sciences, and holds college and graduate degrees in mathematics, followed by a master's degree in counseling and a doctorate in psychology. A leading expert in meditation and Kundalini Yoga as taught by Yogi Bhajan®, Gurucharan helped found the Kundalini Research Institute and has served as its director of training since 1972. The primary interpreter of these techniques, he co-authored two primary texts with Yogi Bhajan, *The Mind: Its Projections and Facets* and *Breathwalk: Breathing Your Way to a Revitalized Body, Mind and Spirit*. His many yoga training manuals and music for meditation can be found at the Kundalini Research Institute or his own website: **www.khalsaconsultants.com**.

Gurucharan loves anything that brings out the spirit, creativity, success and uniqueness in each of us. His signature blend of wisdom, humor, insight and poetry of the heart creates a warm presence whether presenting, instructing in universities, training meditators or coaching individuals.

He lives and works with his wife in the green paradise of Portland, Oregon on an ever-flowing river. To contact him or learn about workshops, programs, consulting or coaching visit his website.